THE JEWISH LAW ANNUAL

VOLUME TWENTY TWO

The Institute for Research in Jewish Law
Faculty of Law, The Hebrew University of Jerusalem

THE JEWISH LAW ANNUAL

VOLUME TWENTY TWO

THE INSTITUTE FOR RESEARCH IN JEWISH LAW
FACULTY OF LAW
THE HEBREW UNIVERSITY OF JERUSALEM

Routledge
Taylor & Francis Group
LONDON AND NEW YORK

First published 2024 by Routledge
4 Park Square, Milton Park, Abingdon, Oxon OX14 4RN

and by Routledge
605 Third Avenue, New York, NY 10158

Routledge is an imprint of the Taylor & Francis Group, an informa business

British Library Cataloguing in Publication Data
A catalogue record for this book is available from the British Library

ISSN 0169-8354
HB ISBN: 978-1-138-67474-5
PB ISBN: 978-1-032-61088-7
EB ISBN: 978-1-315-56113-4

DOI: 10.4324/9781315561134

Typeset in Palatino
by Nechama Rosenstein, typesetting & graphic design

The *Jewish Law Annual* is published under the auspices of
The Institute for Research in Jewish Law
Faculty of Law, The Hebrew University of Jerusalem

Editorial communications should be addressed to Prof. Benjamin Porat, Institute for Research in Jewish Law, Faculty of Law, Hebrew University of Jerusalem, at jewishlaw@savion.huji.ac.il. Contributors should consult the style sheet that appears at the end of the volume; it is also available from the editors upon request. Submissions are welcome from all. Neither the editors nor members of the Board of Editors are to be associated with the views expressed by contributors.

This book is part of a series. The publisher will accept continuation orders, which may be cancelled at any time, and which provide for automatic billing and shipping of each title in the series upon publication. Please contact jewishlaw@savion.huji.ac.il for details.

CONTENTS

FROM THE EDITORS

Volume 22 of the *Jewish Law Annual* features articles on rabbinic criminal law, tort law, jurisprudence, and judicial practice. A couple of articles relate to aspects of criminal law. Jacob Adler offers a novel interpretation of the enigmatic rabbinic punishment of a criminal recidivist who is placed in a *kipa* and fed "until his belly bursts." Adler argues that this latter expression should be understood as a temporal rather than a causal marker, and that the underlying punishment constitutes Divine retribution for a grievous sin. Yishai Kiel evaluates the essential and non-essential forms of criminal complicity in the Talmud, and the related doctrine of aiding and abetting. He argues that the Talmudic doctrine reflects a causation-based approach to accomplice liability that can significantly illuminate the statutory distinction between an accomplice and an accessory in contemporary legal systems, and point to potential grounds for reform of modern law. A third article relates to the field of torts. Amy Birkan presents an original perspective on rabbinic tort law by arguing that the primary benchmark for determining liability is the plaintiff's ability to avoid the injury, while the defendant's liability is an outgrowth of this consideration. She further proposes that rabbinic tort law is anchored in a theory of individualism, which requires the plaintiff to continually be on guard so as to avoid incurring injury from the outset. Another couple of articles explore different aspects of jurisprudence, one rooted in Western and rabbinic discourse, and the other in a historical inquiry relevant to modern Israel. Hanina Ben Menahem focuses on the notion of error, which is central to Ronald Dworkin's general theory of law. By contrast, the Talmudic notion of error and its significance differs substantially, according to Ben Menahem, presenting a formidable challenge to scholars of Jewish law who lean heavily on Dworkin's jurisprudence. Asaf Yedidya returns to the decade before the establishment of the State of Israel to recover the respective theories regarding the place of halakha in a modern, autonomous Jewish state formulated by two Orthodox German Jewish jurists: Abraham Chaim Freimann and Isaac Breuer. As each of these jurists represents a different school of German Jewish Orthodoxy, their approaches to halakha and the challenges of sovereignty overlap, but also have significant differences. Another article proposes adopting a new instrument for judicial practice in modern rabbinic courts. In their joint article, Yitshak Cohen and Shai Farber argue that *Amicus Curiae* have the potential to assist in resolving different issues in rabbinic courts in a professional and objective manner. Moreover, they claim that this method would be preferable to the contemporary practice of rabbinic courts receiving non-regulated input from external sources. In addition to these articles, two book reviews round out the volume.

While several years have passed between volumes due to Covid and other reasons, we are pleased to present the current volume to our readership and look forward to upcoming volumes that are scheduled to appear at regular intervals.

Benjamin Porat and David C. Flatto
Institute for Research in Jewish Law
Faculty of Law
The Hebrew University of Jerusalem

The Jewish Law Annual, Vol. XXII

The Mystery of the Bursting Belly: Divine Punishment in mSanhedrin 9:5

Jacob Adler*

We read in mSanhedrin 9:5:

> If a man was scourged [and committed again the same transgression] and was scourged a second time, [if he transgressed a third time] the court must put him in a prison cell [*kipa*] and feed him with barley [or barley-bread][1] until his belly bursts [*kereiso mitbakaat*].

This passage has long puzzled commentators. How can barley-bread, or barley in any form, cause a stomach to burst? Furthermore, even if it can, how can the rabbis propose such a torturous, painful death?

* Jacob Adler teaches philosophy and Jewish Studies at the University of Arkansas.

The author would like to thank the editors and referees of the *Jewish Law Annual* for their helpful comments. He is also grateful to Natalie Polzer, Roger McKnight, Ada Fredelius, Jens Liljestrand, and especially Jenny Fornell Hjelm for their assistance with the Swedish sources; and to Michael Schein for an insightful critique.

1 The Hebrew text says only *seorin* (barley), but unprocessed barley cannot be eaten by humans. Some translators render the word *seorin* into English as "barley," and others as "barley bread." Either way, bread was the most likely form in which the barley was served, since it was a staple of the diet, constituting about 50% of the caloric intake in Roman Palestine: see J. Rosenblum, *Food and Identity in Early Rabbinic Judaism* (Cambridge: 2010), 17. Bread was made in various forms, and besides bread, grains could be roasted or made into porridge or gruel, to say nothing of delicacies: see Rosenblum, *Food and Identity*; S. Krauss, *Talmudische Archäologie*, 3 vols. (Frankfurt am Main: 2010), 1:102-8; and G. Hamel, *Poverty and Charity in Roman Palestine, First Three Centuries C.E.* (Berkeley: 1990), §1.1-1.2. Still, one cannot eliminate barley porridge as a possibility, since it could have been prepared without the extra step of grinding.

It seems, moreover, that such a punishment was never administered. What, then, is the point of describing this purely hypothetical treatment of wrongdoers?

I propose the following theses:

(1) The barley or barley-bread does not cause the convict's death. The word *until* is to be understood temporally, not causally. The sentence is therefore one of life imprisonment, rather than a death penalty.[2]
(2) Being forced to eat a diet of barley is itself an element of the punishment, as opposed to being a means of killing the prisoner.
(3) Death by the bursting of the belly is to be understood as a manifestation of Divine retribution for a grievous sin.
(4) The procedure described in this Mishnah is not actually meant to be put into effect, but rather lays out the ideal provisions of law by portraying a hypothetical, but not implausible, response to a common type of situation.

The net effect is this: a person who repeatedly commits grievous sins, and is not corrected by lashes, suffers life imprisonment under harsh and degrading conditions until his life comes to an end in a way that is clearly the result of Divine judgment.

The first thesis requires some qualification. I have claimed that the procedure is not a death penalty, and from the human point of view, it is not; it protects society from a recidivist who cannot be restrained by the prescribed penalty of lashes. From God's point of view, however, it is a death penalty: the person dies in a manner that makes it clear that God has acted.

This paper will support this by focusing on the Mishnah itself, putting aside the interpretations put forward in bSanhedrin 81b. In particular, I put aside Rav Sheshet's combination of the two parts of mSanhedrin 9:5 and assume that the Mishnaic statement about *kipa* and barley should be interpreted on its own. As I suggest below, the

2 I am not the first to suggest that the punishment of the recidivist in a *kipa* is, in fact, life imprisonment. See S. Lieberman, "Perushim baMishnayot" ['Interpretations in Mishna'], *Tarbiẓ* 40.1 (1970), 12-3. His reasoning, which will be discussed below, differs from that proposed here. Similarly, Gedaliah Alon, writing in a footnote, suggests that the Mishnah is merely using a figure of speech when it says that the prisoner is to be fed barley until his belly bursts. See G. Alon, "LeHeker haHalakha shel Filon" ['On Philo's Halakha'], Part 3, *Tarbiẓ* 6 (1934), 32 n. 11.

juxtaposition of the two parts of the Mishnah is likely mnemonic.

The provisions of mSanhedrin 9:5 are paralleled in the Tosefta (12:4), though the order of the two provisions is reversed in this case. The Tosefta reads as follows:

> Those who are liable for flogging *who were flogged [and did the same deed] and were flogged again* and this happened once, twice, and yet a third time they put him into prison [*kipa*]. Abba Saul says, "Also on the third occasion they flog him. But if he repeats it a fourth time, *they put him into prison and feed him barley until his belly explodes* [*kereiso nivkaat*]."[3]

The Mishnaic Context. The Mishnaic statement under examination here is one of several that occur together in chapter 9, which all propose punishments that seem to have no basis in the Torah:

> 5. If a man was scourged [and committed again the same transgression] and was scourged a second time, [if he transgressed a third time] the court must put him in a prison cell and feed him with barley until his belly bursts. If a man committed murder but there were no witnesses, they must put him in prison and feed him with *the bread of adversity and the water of affliction.*
>
> 6. If a man stole a sacred vessel or cursed by a *Kosem* [magician] or made an Aramean woman his paramour, the zealots may fall upon him. If a priest served [at the Altar] in a state of uncleanness his brethren the priests did not bring him to the court, but the young men among the priests took him outside the Temple Court and split open his brain with clubs. If one that was not a priest served in the Temple, R. Akiba says: [He must be put to death] by strangling. But the Sages say: [He shall suffer death] at the hands of Heaven.

With the possible exception of the last one, these are all disturbing cases, where the usual rabbinic concern for due process of law seems to be waved away. These are all cases that impose punishments not specified in the Torah. These cases presumably sprung from situations that seemed to call for extraordinary measures, where the usual legal processes were insufficient.[4]

3 J. Neusner, *The Tosefta*, trans. J. Neusner (Peabody, Mass.: 2002), 2:1187.

4 Y. Reiner, "Oneshin Shelo min haDin?! Iyun beSugyat 'Kohen sheShimesh beTum'a' beMasekhet Sanhedrin" ['Punishment Contrary to Law?! A Study of the Issue of "a Cohen who Served while Impure""], *Maagalim* 5 (2007), 89-115.

Regarding our case, the recidivist seems to be beyond control by means of conventional legal measures. It is dangerous to project twenty-first-century consciousness onto the minds of our predecessors of nearly two millennia ago. However, we can note a similar concern today, when repeat offenders are often given extremely severe sentences, such as the 'three strikes and you're out' laws that can impose life sentences on those who commit three felonies.[5] In our contemporary world, such laws can be created by legislative enactment. The rabbis did not have that option. The legal basis for punishment in the *kipa* has been debated, and this paper will enter only marginally into the debate.[6]

I have suggested that the connection between these provisions is mnemonic. After discussing the penalties prescribed in the Torah, the Mishnah then proceeds to list five cases of irregular punishment. There appears to be no logical or conceptual connection among them. This being the case, we have a reason for rejecting Rav Sheshet's juxtaposition of mSanhedrin 9:5a and 9:5b. It is understandable that Rav Sheshet, no doubt perplexed (as people now are) by the mysterious bursting of the belly, would seek a solution by combining the two, but there seems to be no reason to do so in the Mishnah itself.

A few words about the nature of the *kipa*. The exact nature of this structure is unclear. Some translate it as 'dome' or 'vaulted chamber' (Kehati on mSanhedrin 9:5), which is an etymologically plausible translation. Hammer-Kossoy rejects this view, suggesting that vaulted architecture would be too expensive for such a lowly use.[7] This argument, however, fails to consider the climatic factors that affect architectural techniques. In temperate countries where wood is plentiful, the time and effort needed to construct a vault or dome would restrict its use to buildings of unusual importance, such as the impressive vaulted cathedrals of western Europe and capitols of the American states. In the Middle East, however, wood is

5 L.S. Beres and T.D. Griffith, "Do Three Strikes Laws Make Sense—Habitual Offender Statutes and Criminal Incapacitation," *Georgetown Law Journal* 87.1 (1998), 103-38.

6 See, e.g., A. Reich, "The Punishment of '*Kipa*' (Imprisonment) in Jewish Law" (Hebrew), *Mealiyot* 31 (1986), 31-41; M. Elon, "Response to Reich, 'Punishment of Kipa'" (Hebrew), *Me'aliyot* 31 (1986), 42-3; E. Waltz, "Ofyo shel Din Kipa" ['The Character of the *Kipa* Law'], *Ki Vam Hiyitani* 113 (2016), 102-14.

7 M. Hammer-Kossoy, "Divine Justice in Rabbinic Hands: Talmudic Reconstitution of the Penal System," PhD Diss. (New York University: 2005), 231.

scarce, and masonry is the primary construction material. Domes and vaults are necessary for constructing anything more than a modest structure, and even modest structures would be built with domes or vaults.[8] Moreover, the word *kipa* is used in many senses, varying from something as grand as the vault of Heaven to something so humble as a cellar,[9] so there is no lexicographical problem applying it to a lowly cell. Maimonides (*Commentary on the Mishnah* to mSanhedrin 9:5) describes it as a cell so narrow that a person can neither undress nor lie down in it; but this seems unlikely, for Rabbi Judah says it is large enough to hold several people (mSanhedrin 9:3), or even several oxen (bSanhedrin 79b), a size which would surely allow a person to undress and lie down.

Death by Bursting Belly. Can eating barley in any form cause a person's death? It seems that it can. The closest thing to a description of an actual case is the account found in *The Emigrants*, by Vilhelm Moberg. It is worth quoting this account in some detail:

> Anna had eaten herself sick on the barley porridge; it was too strong a fare for her after the famine food of the winter. Her stomach swelled up like a drum, firm and expanded. She let out piercing shrieks as the pain increased. . . . Berta [the healer] said the barley grains had swelled in the bowels of the little girl to twice their original size, thus causing something to burst. . . . Anna cried loudly and asked someone to help as the pain grew agonizing. . . . During the night she became delirious at intervals. . . . Her cries could be heard out into the byre . . . . Early in the morning the child died in her agony.[10]

8 S.L. Chernyshev and E. L. Elmanova, "The Fact of the Lack of Wood in the Formation of Muslim Architectural Style," (Russian and English), *Vestnik MGSU* 10 (2015), 7-20.

9 E. Ben-Yehuda, *Milon Halashon haIvrit haYeshana vehaHadasha* (Hebrew), (Jerusalem: 1908), s.v. *kipa*. Compare the Latin *fornix*, which refers to structures as noble as a triumphal arch and as lowly as a cellar. See H. Cancik et al., *Brill's New Pauly* (Leiden: 2006), s.v. *fornix*.

10 V. Moberg, *The Emigrants*, trans. G. Lannestock (New York: 1951), 105.
The Emigrants is admittedly a novel, but it is a 'documentary novel' based on extensive research, and complete with a bibliography (R. McKnight, "Introduction to the Emigrant Novels," in V. Moberg, *The Emigrants* (Minneapolis: 1995), xii-xiv). Moberg's research notes record that an incident of this kind actually occurred in his hometown of Algutsboda, Sweden, in 1846 (G. Eidevall, *Vilhelm Mobergs Emigrantepos: Studier i Verkets Tillkomsthistoria, Dokumentära Bakgrund och Konstnärliga*

In a more technical vein, Michelle Hammer-Kossoy suggests that such a death might be caused by a phytobezoar, an intestinal blockage caused by an accumulation of fibrous plant material.[11] Such deaths do in fact occur, though they are rare,[12] and it is unclear whether there is any well-documented case of a fatal bezoar caused by barley. However, if a person has been on a near-starvation diet, eating an excessive quantity of *any* food can cause death, as is known from the well-known tragic cases of concentration camp inmates who survived their imprisonment only to die after liberation by gorging themselves on food. This seems to have been the case in Moberg's account.

However, the Mishnah does not mention placing the prisoner on a near-starvation diet. Barring such a diet, it is hard to imagine a prisoner eating sufficient barley to cause such a fatal result. However, the latter section of the same Mishnah does seem to mention a near-starvation diet:[13]

> If a man committed murder but there were no witnesses, they must put him in prison and feed him with *the bread of adversity and the water of affliction* (Isa 30:20).

In the Gemara, Rav Sheshet claims that the two Mishnaic statements are mutually applicable, so that in both cases—the recidivist and the unwitnessed murderer—one first feeds the prisoner bread of adversity and water of affliction until the prisoner's stomach shrinks, and then feeds him barley until his belly bursts (bSanhedrin 81b). But, as Hammer-Kossoy notes, "This reading is forced, however, since there is nothing about either clause which indicates that it lacks important information."[14] Whatever its status among the *amoraim*, Rav Sheshet's interpretation must be understood as an addition not present in the original Mishnah.

Without the near-starvation diet, it seems impossible that a diet of

---

Gestaltning (Stockholm: 1974), 22.

11 Hammer-Kossoy, "Divine Justice," 249.

12 F. Caputo et al., "A Rare Case of Fatal Bowel Obstruction Secondary to a Colonic Bezoar," *American Journal of Forensic Medical Pathology* 39.1 (2018), 38-40.

13 I say 'seems,' because there is reason to reject the idea that it is a starvation or near-starvation diet, as I discuss below.

14 Hammer-Kossoy, "Divine Justice," 241.

barley could prove fatal for a healthy person. Surely, it is far-fetched in the extreme to suppose that a person would voluntarily eat the required quantity of barley. Nor is it likely that a sufficient amount could be force-fed, especially without the devices, such as rubber tubes, that are used today. The idea of a healthy person succumbing to death by barley must be counted as fiction.

It is true that there are additional passages in the Gemara that suggest that the punishment of the recidivist in the *kipa* indeed shortens the prisoner's life:

> Because he has been twice flagellated, Beth Din places him in a cell? - R. Jeremiah answered in the name of Resh Lakish: The reference is to flagellation for an offence punishable by extinction, so that he is already liable to death [at the hand of God], but the time of his death has not yet come: since, however, he abandoned himself [to sin, by transgressing a third time], we hasten his death (bSanhedrin 81b).

> Is there anything for which the Merciful One did not impose a penalty, for which we may kill? — And is there not? But we learned, *One who was twice flagellated is placed by the Beth Din in a cell*: thus, the Merciful One exempted him, yet we slay him! (bSanhedrin 82b).

In any case, the contention of the present argument is that such views represent a later interpretation of the Mishnah and is not its original meaning.

Additionally, from a twenty-first-century point of view, one might be hesitant to attribute to the *tannaim* such a torturous death as the one described by Moberg. This argument, however, seems to be a retrojection of contemporary sensibilities onto people of a very different time. The Mishnah (mSanhedrin 7:2) prescribed the penalty of death by burning for certain crimes, by means of forcing the convict's mouth open and dropping a burning 'wick,' described in bSanhedrin 52a as a bar of lead, into his mouth. This 'wick' goes into the convict's stomach and burns out his innards. This is surely a case of death by torture, yet the *tannaim* did not hesitate to impose it. It is not the torturousness, but the impossibility of the penalty, that grounds the argument against it.

One aspect of the Mishnaic punishment is missing from both Moberg's account and from the similar accounts of people dying from a phytobezoar. All these cases imply an internal rupture of some part of the digestive tract. The Mishnah, however, uses the phrase *kereiso mitbakaat*, which refers not merely to an internal rupture, but to the belly opening so that the person's innards are exposed, or even protrude. This meaning is attested in the Talmud:

> R. Levi said in R. Pappi's name in R. Joshua's name: After three days [from death] the stomach bursts (*nivkaat*) and it [its contents] lies cast out before his face and exclaims [to the mouth], 'Take what you have put in me' (bShabbat 151b).[15]

This presents a further reason to doubt the possibility of causing the bursting of the belly by means of barley: though the barley may cause an internal rupture, it is extremely far-fetched to suppose it might cause an external rupture that would allow the entrails to gush forth.

The bursting of the belly of a living person, in the absence of external trauma, does not seem to be a natural phenomenon. It can, of course, be caused by physical damage, such as by a knife, but the spontaneous bursting of the belly of a living human, even as the result of illness, seems to not be recorded. The abdominal wall is lined with powerful muscles—muscles that allow a boxer to withstand a blow to the belly and prevent its spontaneous eruption.[16] Medical science does identify a phenomenon called 'burst abdomen,' but this occurs only after a surgery that cuts through the abdominal wall. Although the wound is sutured, the sutures may fail, resulting in the protrusion of the entrails.[17] Eric Lyons argues that the bursting of Judas Iscariot's belly was a natural phenomenon, bringing as proof the example of a beached whale in Taiwan whose belly had burst.[18] But this occurs only after the whale had been long dead, as a result of decomposition

15 See also Rashi on bSanhedrin 45a (s.v. *minval*), where he notes that if a person subject to the penalty of stoning is dropped from too great a height, his body might burst (*keriso nivkaat*). Similarly, in bHullin 56a-57b, the Talmud, using the related root פקע, describes an incident in in which a person fell from a roof so that "his belly burst open and his entrails protruded."

16 Note that in the Moberg passage, though little Anna's belly swells up like a drum, it does not burst. If her abdominal muscles, weakened by starvation, were still strong enough to prevent an eruption of her innards, surely the muscles of a healthy adult are more than strong enough.

17 J.P. Chevrel, "Postoperative Burst Abdomen," in J.P. Chevrel (ed), *Hernias and Surgery of the Abdominal Wall*, 2nd ed. (Berlin: 1998), Chapter 8.II.A.

18 E. Lyons, "Did Judas Die Twice?," https://apologeticspress.org/did-judas-die-twice-1761/ (accessed 12 June 2022).

gases.[19] It would take from five to eleven days for this to occur in a human corpse and, in any case, the abdominal wall is so strong that even then, the gas of putrefaction would cause material to emerge from the nose, mouth, and anus before the belly bursts.[20] Jewish law would have required the prompt burial of the corpse of the prisoner long before this could happen. In sum, the bursting of the belly of a living person, without the application of a knife or similar instrument, does not occur as a natural phenomenon. This information can be gleaned from ordinary lay observation, and was available to the *tannaim* no less than to us. Spontaneous bursting of the belly is in the same category as a rod that blooms and bears almonds (Num 17:8), or a jar that yields many times its volume of oil (2 Kgs 4:1-7). It must be considered a case of Divine intervention, an instance of death at the hands of Heaven.

There is another consideration—ideological, in this case, not practical—that weighs against the idea that the *tannaim* would have proposed a barley diet that would cause the bursting of the belly. There is widespread (though not universal) consensus that the death penalties prescribed in the Mishnah are calculated so as to minimize the mutilation or disfigurement of the body. Burning and stoning are not done by the methods one might suspect—pelting with stones or burning at the stake—but by methods that leave the body intact.[21] If we accept that consensus, it is hard to suppose that the *tannaim* would have proposed a capital punishment that not only mutilates the body, but does so in a most degrading and gruesome manner.

Barley Diet as Punishment. Since the idea of death by barley appears to be fictional, I suggest that the barley diet is itself intended as a punishment, irrespective of its consequences. The word '*ad*' in the Mishnah—more specifically, the phrase '*ad she*' ('until')—must be taken as temporal rather than causal. Such usage is not hard to find elsewhere in the Mishnah:

> From what time in the evening may the *Shema* be recited? . . . Until the rise of dawn (*ad sheyaale amud hashahar*) (mBerakhot 1:1).

19 T. Parfitt, *Notes from the Other China* (New York: 2008), 44.

20 M. Wilson, *Life after Death: What Happens to Your Body after You Die?* (Cham, Switzerland: 2022), 101.

21 B. Berkowitz, *Execution and Invention: Death Penalty Discourse in Early Rabbinic and Christian Cultures* (Oxford: 2006), 25-64.

> R. Eleazar b. Azariah said: Lo, I am like to one that is seventy years old yet failed to prove why the going forth from Egypt should be rehearsed at night until (*ad she-*) Ben Zoma thus expounded it . . . (mBerakhot 1:5)

In both cases, *ad she-* is clearly temporal, not causal. Grammar is thus no bar to the reading proposed above.

Hammer-Kossoy points out that barley was considered an inferior food, primarily the diet of livestock, and thus a barley diet would humiliate the offender.[22] But this by itself, though true, does not clinch the point. After all, as Hammer-Kossoy notes in the same place, barley was also eaten by humans, especially poor people. It is hardly a cause for surprise if prisoners are given the same kind of diet that poor people eat. Even now, prisons do not spend excessive amounts on food for their inmates.[23] However, the diet of barley, I suggest, is more than a money-saving measure. A diet of barley was, in fact, a well-known punishment for disobedient soldiers in the Greco-Roman world.[24] The account of the Greek historian Polybius is especially striking. In his *Histories*, he describes the punishment of disobedient Roman troops.

> After one in ten soldiers, selected at random, are beaten to death, the rest receive rations of barley instead of wheat and are ordered to encamp outside the camp on an unprotected spot… and as the public disgrace of receiving barley rations falls on all alike, this practice is that best calculated both to inspire fear and to correct the mischief.[25]

This was such a well-known form of punishment that there was even a Greek word for it: *krithophagia*.[26] The *tannaim*, living under Roman occupation, would surely have been familiar with this punishment.

22 Hammer-Kossoy, "Divine Justice," 250-51 and footnotes there.

23 Lieberman, "Perushim baMishnayot" makes the same point (1970, 12, and note 13 there); Yehonatan Reiner, "Oneshin Shelo min haDin," 94, following Lieberman, describes the idea that death by barley is an innovation of the Gemara, not present in the Mishnah.

24 G. Bush, *Illustrations of the Holy Scriptures* (Philadelphia: 1865), 139; R.P. Vegetius, *Vegetius: Epitome of Military Science*, trans. N.P. Milner (Liverpool: 1996), 14; J.F. Donahue, *Food and Drink in Antiquity: Readings from the Graeco-Roman World: A Sourcebook* (London: 2015).

25 Polybius, *The Histories*, trans. W. R. Paton (Cambridge: 1966), 3:355.

26 H.G. Liddell and R. Scott, *A Greek-English Lexicon* (Oxford: 1845), s.v. κριθοφαγία.

The barley diet would have been perceived as a penal diet.

The significance of the "belly bursting." Since, as we have said, the idea that barley can cause a person's death seems improbable in the extreme, and that it certainly could not cause the belly to burst and the entrails to protrude, we must read the word *until* in the Mishnah as temporal rather than causal: that is, the Beit Din imprisons the convict and feeds him a penal diet of barley, and he eventually dies in a way that has nothing to do with the barley but is particularly gruesome.

This gruesome death has a meaning: it is a sign of Divine disfavor.

Before turning to this thought, I will first consider Saul Lieberman's proposal. He understands the words '*until his belly bursts*' to mean 'as much as he wants.' He cites a passage from Menahem Meiri's novellae on bSanhedrin 22b. The Gemara there considers whether *kohanim* can drink alcohol. In the days of the Temple, a priest under the influence of alcohol could not officiate. In the Gemara we read:

> Has it not been taught: Rabbi [Judah the Prince] said: In my opinion, priests should, by right, be at all times forbidden to drink wine, but what can I do, seeing that their calamity [the destruction of the Temple] has been to their advantage in the matter? (bSanhedrin 22b).

Meiri explains "their calamity has been to their advantage" as follows: Since the Temple has been destroyed, the *kohanim* have no occasion to officiate in the Temple, so they need not be concerned about being sober; a priest can therefore drink wine "until his belly bursts."[27] Surely, Lieberman interprets the phrase correctly in this context, but just as surely, the use is ironic. The corresponding phrase, in various translations, is used ironically in English as well.[28] The plain, unironic meaning of the phrase, both in English and Hebrew, is that the belly literally bursts. Should we then understand "until his belly bursts" ironically in our present context? Perception of irony is a delicate matter, and words meant ironically are all too often understood literally, and vice versa. To the present writer, our Mishnah seems to exclude Lieberman's ironic reading. Since the barley diet is a punishment, it seems unlikely that it would be offered in abundance. There is, moreover, reason to understand it literally.

27 Meiri, cited in Lieberman, "Perushim baMishnayot," 13.

28 An internet search for "until my belly burst" or "until my stomach exploded" retrieves many such examples; Google search, accessed 28 June 2020.

The bursting of the belly, without external trauma, is not a natural phenomenon, and must therefore be understood as a miraculous occurrence, or an act of God. There are numerous reports in Jewish and other sources of such deaths, seemingly all indicating Divine disfavor.[29] Some of the passages describing such a death are indeed post-Tannaitic. Those that postdate the Mishnah are cited here as evidence of an ongoing understanding that death by bursting belly is a sign of Divine disfavor. The first passage is from the *Tanakh*:

> Jehoram was thirty-two years old when he became king, and he reigned in Jerusalem eight years. He followed the practices of the kings of Israel doing what the House of Ahab had done, for he married a daughter of Ahab; he did what was displeasing to the Lord… A letter from Elijah the prophet came to him which read, "Thus says the Lord God of your father David: Since you have not followed the practices of your father Jehoshaphat and the practices of King Asa of Judah, but have followed the practices of the kings of Israel, leading astray Judah and the inhabitants of Jerusalem as the House of Ahab led them astray, and have also killed your brothers of your father's house, who were better than you, therefore, the Lord will inflict a great blow upon your people, your sons, and your wives and all your possessions. As for you, you will be severely stricken with a disorder of the bowels year after year until your bowels drop out." . . . After this, the Lord afflicted him with an incurable disease of the bowels. Some years later, when a period of two years had elapsed, his bowels dropped out (*yatzeu*, "came out") because of his disease, and he died a gruesome death… (2 Chr. 21:5-19).

It is quite clear from the prophet's words that this gruesome death is Jehoram's Divine punishment for his wicked deeds.

In the Gemara, a woman dies the same way for insulting a Sage:

> A certain woman of Nehardea came before Rav Judah for a lawsuit and was declared guilty by the court. "Would your teacher Samuel have judged thus?" she said. "Do you know him then?" he asked. "Yes, He is short and

29 Something similar was suggested in an inverted sense by Reuben Margaliot: Ordinary digestion is a miracle, which God withholds in the case of the recidivist, so that the undigestible barley kills him. R. Margaliot, *Margaliyot haYam, Masekhet Sanhedrin* (Hebrew), (Jerusalem: 1977), on bSanhedrin 81b, § 25 (p. 101), based on Exod Rabbah 24.1.

> big-stomached, black and large teethed." "What, you have come to insult him! Let that woman be under the ban!" he exclaimed. She burst open and died (bNedarim 50b).

A boy is similarly punished for idolatry:

> It was related of Elijah the Righteous, that whilst searching for those who were languishing with hunger in Jerusalem, he once found a child faint with hunger lying upon a dungheap. On questioning him as to the family to which he belonged, he replied, "I belong to such and such a family." He asked: "Are any of that family left?" and he answered, "None, excepting myself." Thereupon he asked: "If I teach thee something by which thou wilt live, wilt thou learn?" He replied, "Yes." "Then," said he, "recite every day, Hear O Israel, the Lord is our God, the Lord is one." But the child retorted, "Be silent, for one must not make mention of the name of the Lord." [He said this] because his father and mother had not taught him [to serve the Lord], and straightway he brought forth an idol from his bosom, embracing and kissing it, until his stomach burst, his idol fell to the earth, and he upon it, thus fulfilling the verse, And I shall cast your carcases upon the carcases of your idols [Lev 26:30] (bSanhedrin 63b-64a).[30]

In Flavius Josephus' *Antiquities of the Jews*, the wicked Zenodorus lies in the same manner.[31] Even more to the point, Josephus describes the death of the evil Catullus:

30 Some might dismiss this case as an example of Divine retribution. For example, Lieberman ("Perushim baMishnayot," 12, n. 14) considers the bursting of the belly, in this case, as a natural conclusion to the process of starvation. In any case, the boy seems to be innocent, since he is merely following the teaching of his parents, so why should he be punished at all? (Michael Schein, personal communication). Yet, this passage is presented as an example of the curses that will come upon Israel as a punishment of spurning God and His commandments, specifically citing a verse from the section of curses in *parashat* Behukotai. Though the boy himself may be blameless, the curses are collective and imposed upon Israel because of their sins, as Isaac Aboab notes (citing the tale of Elijah and the starving boy) in I. Aboab, *Menorat haMaor* (5.3.2.3), trans. B. Krief as *Le Candélabre de Lumière* (Marseille: 2006), 834-35.

31 F. Josephus, *The Jewish Antiquities*, Books 14-15, trans. R. Marcus (Cambridge: 1963), 429-31.

> [Catullus'] malady ever growing rapidly worse, his bowels ulcerated and fell out; and so he died, affording a demonstration, no less striking than any, how God in his providence inflicts punishment on the wicked.[32]

A startling parallel can be found in the *Tale of Ahikar*, described as "one of the earliest 'international books' of world literature, originally composed in Aramaic in the late 7th or early 6th century B.C. … The earliest version of *Ahikar*[33] has been scantily preserved in a very fragmentary Aramaic papyrus of the 5th century B.C.[34] In later times the work circulated in a great number of versions, written in various languages (Syriac, Armenian, Old Turkish, Old Slavonic, Ethiopic, etc.)…"[35] Parts of the *Tale* were incorporated into the apocryphal Book of Tobit (Tobit 1:21-22; 2:10-11; 11:18; 14:10). In the *Tale*, the pious Ahikar is betrayed by his nephew, Nadan. J. Rendel Harris, in his introduction to his edition of the *Tale* (jointly prepared with F.C. Conybeare and Agnes Smith Lewis) summarizes the conclusion of the *Tale* as follows:

> The wretched young man [Nadan] is tamed by preliminary discipline of flogging, followed by black-hole and bread and water, and his uncle enriches his mind with further instruction of a very personal character and application; and when, at the close of this preliminary treatment, Ahikar is preparing the extreme penalty for Nadan, the nephew simplifies the action of the play by swelling up and bursting asunder in a melodramatic manner, which satisfies all the instincts of Justice.[36]

Note that the same elements are present: flogging, imprisonment, a meagre diet, and belly bursting. The *Tale of Ahikar* contains, in addition, the elements of moral instruction and preparation for execution, the

32 F. Josephus, *The Jewish War*, trans. H.St.J. Thackeray (London: 1928), 633.

33 The name *Ahikar* is spelled variously in the sources drawn upon here. For the sake of uniformity, I have used the spelling *Ahikar* throughout.

34 The papyrus was found "among the remains of a Jewish colony of mercenaries at Elephantine," and was thus familiar to this part of the Jewish world, at least. Quote from I. Konstantakos, "A Passage to Egypt: Aesop, the Priests of Heliopolis and the Riddle of the Year (*Vita Aesopi* 119–120)," *Trends in Classics* 3 (2011), 85n.

35 Ibid., 84.

36 F.C. Conybeare and J.R. Harris, *The Story of Ahikar from the Aramaic, Syriac, Arabic, Armenian, Ethiopic, Old Turkish, Greek and Slavonic versions* (Cambridge: 1913).

latter of which is forestalled by Nadan's gruesome death.

The motif of Divine punishment by having the belly burst is found also in some early Christian sources. Although no claim is made that the *tannaim* knew of these texts, they testify to the persistence of the motif. The most famous example is that of Judas Iscariot, in the New Testament, Acts 1:18:

> Now this man [Judas] bought a field with the reward of his wickedness; and falling headlong[37] he burst open in the middle and all his bowels gushed out. (RSV)

According to St. Athanasius (ca. 296–298 to 373), Arius, condemned as a heretic, died in the same manner as Judas Iscariot:

> I conceive that when the wonderful circumstances connected with his [Arius'] death become known, even those who before questioned it will no longer venture to doubt that the Arian heresy is hateful in the sight of God… Arius, who had great confidence in [his ally] Eusebius and his fellows, and talked very wildly, urged by the necessities of nature withdrew, and suddenly, in the language of Scripture, "falling headlong he burst asunder in the midst"[Acts 1:18] and immediately expired as he lay, and was deprived both of communion and of his life together.[38]

His gruesome death (in the eyes of Athanasius) gave proof that God Himself had condemned Arius' heresy.

Similarly, in the Syriac *Life of St. Simeon Stylites* (ca. 390? to 459), composed shortly after his death, we read of the demise of a "wicked and evil" man of Antioch. The man first suffered from a bowel disease and "[h]is belly swelled up like a wineskin." Saint Simeon sent him some water, with the instruction:

> "If God knows that when he is healed he will turn away from his evil deeds, mercy will be shown him and he will recover. But if he would continue in his wickedness, he will never see this water at all." Taking the water they

37 Note that The Revised Standard Version indicates an alternative translation of "swelling up" in place of "falling headlong."

38 Athanasius of Alexandria. Letter 54, to Serapion. In P. Schaff (ed.), *Athanasius: Select Works and Letters*, https://www.ccel.org/ccel/schaff/npnf204.xxv.iii.iv.ix.html (accessed 2 July 2020), §§ 1, 3.

> went, and as they arrived at the door of his dwelling, he asked that he might be turned over in his bed, whereupon on a sudden his belly burst open, and his bowels gushed out so that he died. So he did not see that water at all, according to the word of the Saint.[39]

Thus, the man's evil intent is revealed by his grisly death.

In all these cases, evil action is followed by the spontaneous bursting of the belly. It is not always explicitly stated that the bursting of the belly is God's punishment for the evil action, but the implication is clear enough, seeing that bellies just do not burst by themselves.

As mentioned above, a corpse's belly in the grave bursts three days after death. Hammer-Kossoy notes that the convict resembles a corpse: He is "a person who is already dead while living." In this respect, the punishment resembles those of Korah and Miriam (Num 16:28-33; 12:4-12). In the convict's case, while above the earth, he resembles a buried corpse. In Korah's case, he goes down alive into to the grave; while Miriam is afflicted with a skin disease so that she resembles a corpse. Both are signs of Divine disfavor. In the case of Korah, it is quite clear:

> And Moses said, "By this you shall know that it was the Lord who sent me to do all these things; that they are not of my own devising: if these men die as all men do, if their lot be the common fate of all mankind, it was not the Lord who sent me. But if the Lord brings about something unheard-of, so that the ground opens its mouth and swallows them up with all that belongs to them, and they go down alive into Sheol, you shall know that these men have spurned the Lord."

The connection between Divine disfavor and punishment is less explicit in Miriam's case, but it is clear that her punishment is a direct result of God's burning wrath (Num 12:9). In the same way, the bursting of the belly, *without* any human causal factor, shows that the penalty is an act of God.

The bursting of the belly, then, seems to be merely one more case where God takes an active role in the administration of justice on earth. Aaron Kirschenbaum suggests that the administration of Jewish criminal justice is entrusted to three institutions: the rabbinic courts,

39 F. Lent (trans.), *The Life of Saint Simeon Stylites* (Merchantville, N.J.: 2009), 61-3.

the monarchy, and the Holy One.[40] In a situation where the first two are insufficient, the third one acts:

> [I]t was taught in the school of Hezekiah: From the day the Temple was destroyed, although the Sanhedrin was abolished, the four modes of execution were not abolished... He who is worthy of stoning either falls from the roof or is trampled to death by a wild beast; he who merits burning either falls into the fire or is bitten by a serpent; he who is worthy of decapitation is either delivered to the [gentile] Government or brigands attack him; he who is worthy of strangulation is either drowned in a river or dies of suffocation (bSanhedrin 37b).

In the case of the recidivist, the earthly court does what it can. If lashes of the whip fail to deter, the court protects society by imprisoning and punishing him with a punitive diet. Then the Holy One takes over and brings about a hideous death that displays God's condemnation of the sinner in an especially graphic way.

The bursting of the belly, though not labeled as such in this Mishnah, is an example of death at the hands of Heaven, a concept found in Tannaitic literature (see, e.g., mSanhedrin 9:6 and tZevahim 12:8). The present contention is that it does not have to be labeled as such, since, as argued above, the bursting of the belly is clearly not a natural phenomenon.

Bellies can, of course, burst from *external* natural causes; one such case is mentioned in a Baraita:

> R. Tarfon said, "If his hand touched the membrum[41] let his hand be cut off upon his belly." "But," they said to him,[42] "would not his belly be split (*kereiso nivkaat*)?" "It is preferable," he replied, "that his belly shall be split

40 A. Kirschenbaum, "The Role of Punishment in Jewish Criminal Law: A Chapter in Rabbinic Penological Thought," *Jewish Law Annual* 9 (1991), 123-43.

41 The reference is to masturbation, not simply touching the penis, as is clear from the Tosefta, cited below.

42 Current editions of the Talmud insert here the words, "'If a thorn stuck in his belly should he not remove it?' He said to them: 'No'," which seem out of place. They are relegated to a footnote in the English language Soncino Talmud, which I quote here, following the emendation of Rabbi Solomon Luria, *Hokhmat Shelomo*, ad loc. It seems that this passage has been moved up from later in the paragraph.

> rather than that he should go down into the pit of destruction" (bNiddah 13b).[43]

It appears that this, and its parallels, are the only other Tannaitic use of the phrase *kereiso nivkaat* (and its variants) outside of mSanhedrin 9:5 and its parallels. This passage clarifies that the phrase refers to an external bursting, not an internal rupture. Even here, the Gemara raises the possibility that what is prescribed in this case is not a punishment to be carried out by human hands, but a curse. The scope of the curse is unclear, but would fit in with the present contention if we were to understand the Baraita to say, "If a person's hand touches his penis, may his hand fall off and his belly burst!"—that is, may God bring it about. In this case, it would be similar to the case mentioned above of the curse placed upon the woman who insulted a Sage. Even if it is not a curse, the bursting of the belly here still constitutes a human punishment for a vile offense.

The Next Reference to the Kipa. After the statement under examination here, the Mishnah continues to discuss another case of imprisonment in a *kipa*:

> If a man committed murder but there were no witnesses, they must put him in prison *(kipa)* and feed him with *the bread of adversity and the water of affliction.*

As suggested above, I propose that the juxtaposition of these two texts is mnemonic. If so, there is no essential connection beyond the mention of the *kipa* in both. Although the focus of this paper is on the first part of this Mishnah, we may devote a few words to the second.

Some suggest that this implies a starvation diet, amounting to a death sentence for the murderer, but the origin of the italicized phrase argues against it. The phrase is taken from Isaiah 30:20, which should be read in the context of the previous verse:

> Indeed, O people in Zion, dwellers of Jerusalem, you shall not have cause to weep. He will grant you His favor at the sound of your cry; He will respond as soon as He hears it.

43 A parallel passage is found in the Tosefta, Niddah 2:8. The verb there is *nitpahat*, rather than *nivkaat*, but the meaning is the same. The same dictum is found in jNidda 2:1:2, again ascribed to Rabbi Tarfon, in words almost identical to those of the Tosefta, but again employing the verb *nivkaat.*

> My Lord will provide for you meager bread and scant water...

Surely God's favor would not amount to a starvation diet: the provisions are evidently modest, but sufficient to sustain life.[44]

Was It Really Practiced? As Hammer-Kossoy points out, one odd aspect of punishment in the *kipa* is that "There is no evidence that any of the laws about *kipah* were ever applied. Not a single case or even aggadic passage makes use of this term."[45] This is perhaps not surprising. Aaron Kirschenbaum goes so far as to argue that there is no undisputed case of anyone being put to death for a crime under Torah law.[46] It is, of course, not impossible that the punishment of the *kipa* could have been carried out in Mishnaic times. Whether this is a real possibility depends on the degree of power and authority held by the rabbis, a question very difficult to answer due to the sparsity of documentary evidence. If we are to believe Shaye Cohen, they had no power to enforce their decisions except by excommunication, which he seems to brush aside:

> It was a voluntary act for a Jew to accept the verdict of a rabbinic court or the authority of a rabbi. The tannaim had no means (aside from excommunication, about which the tannaim say little) to enforce their decisions and decrees. They were not the agents of the state. In sum: the rabbis did not control the religious and civil life of second-century Palestinian Jewry.[47]

Philip Alexander, on the other hand, considers that the power of excommunication gave the rabbis considerable control over their communities:

44 Compare the comment of Metzudat David: "The Omnipresent will put it into your heart to make do with meager bread and scant water . . . so that you will no longer be greedy for pleasures, as you are now."

45 Hammer-Kossoy, "Divine Justice," 228-29.

46 Kirschenbaum, "The Role of Punishment," 138n; ibid., "The Role of Punishment of Jewish Criminal Law: A Chapter in Rabbinical Penological Thought," (Hebrew), *Tel Aviv University Law Review* 12.2 (1987), Appendix, 267-73.

47 S. Cohen, "The Rabbi in Second-Century Jewish Society," in W.D. Davies, J. Sturdy, and W. Horbury (eds.), *The Cambridge History of Judaism*, vol. 3. (Cambridge: 1984), 971.

> Here rabbinic authority, as I have already hinted, looks weak, but the Rabbis had always the weapon of the ban (the ḥerem). They could call upon the community to boycott the offender, and, if the community, or even a substantial part of it, answered that call, the offender could have found life very difficult, and been forced into compliance.[48]

If Alexander is right, rabbis with such influence could have prevailed upon people to impose the penalty of *kipa* upon a recalcitrant criminal, especially since one can assume that members of the community would be sufficiently outraged so as to *want* to do something about a known habitual offender.

There remains, however, the lack of any written record of *kipa* ever being imposed. This fact, though highly suggestive, is not necessarily conclusive, as the penalty may have been imposed secretly. Writing at a slightly later period, Origen states:

> So now, when the Romans reign and the Jews pay them the half-shekel,[49] their ethnarch, with Caesar's acquiescence, has as much power as if he were the king of the nation. I know this because I saw it myself. Trials are held in secret, according to their law, and they carry death sentences.[50]

Origen lived from 185 to c. 253, but perhaps we may extrapolate backward to Tannaitic times. The fact that the punishment of *kipa* was irregular under Jewish law, and that Roman law (in theory) denied Jewish judges the authority to impose it, might have easily led them to refrain from making any record of such a *sub rosa* proceeding. Still, it would be surprising if there were no mention whatsoever of such an unusual occurrence. After all, if a barley diet (as proposed here) was

48 P. Alexander, "The Rabbis and Their Rivals in the Second Century CE," in J.C. Paget and J. Lieu (eds.), *Christianity in the Second Century: Themes and Developments* (Cambridge: 2017), 61.

49 The half-shekel, a tax originally paid to the Temple, was paid to the Romans after the Temple's destruction.

50 Origen, *Epistle to Africanus*, in *Sur les Écritures: Philocalie,* trans. N. de Lange (Paris: 2008), 565-67 [my translation from De Lange's French]. H.-P. Chajes remarks that there are no reports of such cases, beyond that of Origen himself. "[I]f they actually happened," he adds, "they are excesses and abuses that it was thought possible to commit with impunity in certain eras, but which, at other times, were seriously repressed." H.-P. Chajes, "Les Juges Juifs en Palestine, de l'An 70 à l'An 500," *Revue des Études Juives* 39.77 (1899), 52 [my translation].

one that would sustain, not end, the life of the prisoner, a person might be confined to a *kipa* for decades. One would think that during that time the prisoner's family and friends would appeal for his release, and that some notice of such an appeal would have been recorded. Be that as it may, for the purposes of this paper I will assume that it was never imposed; or, alternatively, that it was imposed on rare occasions (as Chajes suggests) as an irregular measure, something forbidden that a judge could nonetheless, on occasion, inflict with Caesar's acquiescence.

The Kipa and Time. On this assumption, the penalty of *kipa* thus falls into the category of non-applied law, as described by Chaim N. Saiman.[51] Non-applied law falls on a continuum from the impossible to law that is applied every day, and everything in between. The case of the *kipa* appears to be possible, aside from the possible lack of criminal jurisdiction of the rabbinic court. Still, as proposed here, it seems not to have been applied, or was at most applied rarely and irregularly. Yet, the Mishnah in question describes the penalty of the *kipa* in bland present-tense language, as if it were a normal, everyday thing, as is the case with most of its non-applied laws. Various explanations have been proposed.[52] A number of sources mention the apparent timelessness of the Mishnah.[53] From the very start, the Mishnah speaks about past and present in the same voice:

> From what time in the evening may the *Shema* be recited? From the time when the priests enter [the Temple] to eat of their Heave-offering until the end of the first watch. So R. Eliezer. But the Sages say: Until midnight. Rabban Gamaliel says: Until the rise of dawn. His sons once returned [after midnight] from a wedding feast. They said to him, "We have not recited the *Shema*." He said to them, "If the dawn has not risen ye are [still] bound to recite it. Moreover, wheresoever the Sages prescribe 'Until midnight' the duty of fulfilment lasts until the rise of dawn." The duty of burning the fat pieces and the members [of the animal offerings] lasts until the rise of dawn; and for all [offerings] that must be consumed the same day, the duty lasts until the rise of dawn. Why then have the Sages said: Until midnight? To keep a man far from transgression (mBerakhot 1:1).

51 C.N. Saiman, *Halakhah: The Rabbinic Idea of Law* (Princeton: 2018), 29-43.

52 See references in Saiman, Halakhah, 256 n. 11.

53 Saiman, Halakhah, 51; H. Cohn, "The Penology of the Talmud," *Israel Law Review* 5.1 (1970), 55; H. Maccoby, *Philosophy of the Talmud* (Hoboken: 2013), 160.

The Mishnah speaks about present events and past events in the same present voice, as if there were still priests who were purifying themselves to eat heave-offerings (*teruma*), fat pieces, and parts of sacrificial animals offered in the Temple, which had long ceased to exist. Note the different effect that would have been produced if this Mishnah had been written using the past tense for the past:

> From what time in the evening may the *Shema* be recited? From the time when the priests used to enter to eat of their Heave-offering during the time when the Temple existed until the end of the first watch.

This altered version gives the impression that the time of eating heave-offering was something that one might have to look up in a book. The original version gives the impression that the time of eating heave-offering is something that the reader or hearer would be familiar with, almost as if by experience. The current author is reminded of the famous quote from William Faulkner: "The past is never dead. It's not even past."[54] Or, more prosaically, the statement of Oxford historian Francis Young:

> [W]hat is patently obvious from his stories is that [M. R. James] experienced the past as something alive (or 'undead') in the present. Every half decent historian has had this experience: for a moment, the past seems more real than the present, and the absence of the dead an absurdity. I remember experiencing this powerfully one day after a morning spent in the Suffolk Record Office in Bury St Edmunds. I was walking back through the Great Churchyard (a place James knew and loved as well), and I found myself momentarily uncomprehending of the fact that people who seemed so alive to me in my research were nothing but dust under the ground.[55]

In the words of the Mishnah:

> In every generation a man must so regard himself as if he came forth himself out of Egypt, for it is written, *And thou shalt tell thy son in that day saying. It is because of that which the Lord did for me when I came forth out of Egypt* (mPesahim 10:5).

54 W. Faulkner, *Requiem for a Nun* (London: 1919), 85.

55 F. Young, "Why Historians Need Ghosts," https://drfrancisyoung.com/2015/01/19/why-historians-need-ghosts/, 2015 (accessed 29 July 2022).

The penalty of *kipa*, though not practiced at the time, seems like a reasonable proposal for something that might be done in the future. It is stated, however, in the present tense: it is for readers or hearers who can see the future as something real.

Yet Mishnaic time does not stand still. It has a direction; there is a before and after. In the last-quoted Mishnah, there is a time *before* the Exodus and *after* it. Maccoby, seeming to contradict his previously cited statement, says that "In the Aristotelian universe, Time is an illusion. In the Jewish universe, on the contrary, Time is real..."[56] Some would even go so far as to say that it was the Jews who *invented* the idea of linear time, as opposed to the cyclical time of pre-literate people, for whom time is an endlessly repeated cycle.[57] This proposal is no doubt exaggerated,[58] but the Mishnah does clearly present history as having a direction and describes how various *halakhot* fell into desuetude:

> When murderers became many the rite of breaking the heifer's neck ceased. When Eleazar b. Dinai came (and he was also called Tehinah b. Parisha) they changed his name to Son of the Murderer. When adulterers became many [the rite of] the bitter water ceased; and R. Johanan b. Zakkai brought it to an end, for it is written, *I will not punish your daughters when they commit whoredom nor your daughters-in-law when they commit adultery, for they themselves* [*go apart with whores . . .*]. When Jose b. Joezer of Zeredah and Jose b. Johanan of Jerusalem died, the 'grapeclusters' ceased, as it is written. *There is no cluster to eat, my soul desireth the first-ripe fig*. Johanan the High Priest did away with the Avowal concerning the [Second] Tithe. He made an end also of the 'Awakeners' and the 'Stunners'. Until his days the hammer used to smite in Jerusalem; and in his days none needed to inquire concerning *demai*-produce (mSota 9.9-10).

The Mishnah continues in this vein, toward the end of the chapter, ending with anticipations of the Messiah and the resurrection of the dead.

How, then to reconcile time and timelessness?[59] Time is represented

56 Maccoby, *Philosophy*, 27.

57 T. Cahill, *The Gifts of the Jews* (Thorndike, Maine: 1998), 13-14, 136-44.

58 B. Albrektson, *History and the Gods* (Lund: 1967).

59 Compare Eliezer Schweid's discussion of the parallel issue with regard to the Jewish Holidays in *The Jewish Experience of Time: Philosophical Dimensions of the Jewish Holy Days* (Northvale, N.J.: 2000), 11-20.

by the geometrical figure of a line; timelessness by a circle, in which events repeat but no progress is made, as in the case of the timelessly circular motion of the Aristotelian heavens or the corresponding endless round of the seasons. These two geometric time-metaphors might seem incompatible, but they can be reconciled: time as represented by a helix, such as a spiral staircase on which one only ascends. Like the timeline, the helix is linear and unidirectional. Like the circle, one circles back to the same point one occupied in the past, only one level higher. The climber can look down and see the lower rounds of the staircase and say, "I'm at the exact same place I was before," or look up and say, "I'm at the place where I will actually be when I come around again." The legalist can look down and see the application of obsolete *halakhot* almost as if they were current, having the sense that he is witnessing them being carried out; or look up and see the future application of *halakhot*, such as those imposing confinement in a *kipa*, and have the sense that it is virtually present and the prisoner sitting in it, eating his barley-bread. If a much later incident may be adduced, the situation is reminiscent of the account of Rabbi Shmelke of Nikolsburg who, on one occasion when acting as *sheliah tzibur*, is said to have recited the Song of the Sea with such fervor that his hearers felt themselves entering the sea and lifted the hems of their kaftans to prevent them from getting wet.[60] Without doubt, the intense study of Mishnah could bring about a similar sense of reality of things not present.

This approach will work for *halakhot* that once were practiced, or might be practiced in the future. For impossible *halakhot*, or *halakhot* so hedged in by limitations as to be impossible to apply, this approach will admittedly not work. The punishment of *kipa* can be seen as falling in the former category. The punishment of recidivists is needful and might indeed be practiced at some future time when the successors of the *tannaim* will have the authority and power to impose it. This future, vividly conceived, seems in a way present now, and is expressed in present-tense language as if it *were* happening now.

60 Y. Buxbaum, *Jewish Spiritual Practices* (Northvale, N.J.: 1990), 536, citing M.M. Walden, *Ohel Yitzhak* (Piotrków: 1914), 74.

The Jewish Law Annual, Vol. XXII

Dwercules, Jewish Law, and the Doctrine of Legal Error*

Hanina Ben Menahem**

I. Dworcules' Theory of Law

Recently, scholars of Jewish law who wished to characterize the workings of Jewish law turned to Ronald Dworkin's writings for inspiration. These scholars seem impressed by his jurisprudential theory, and more specifically by his theory of adjudication, and consider him a kindred spirit. I do not share this sense of affinity between Jewish law and Dworkinian thought; over thirty years ago I published an article entitled "Is there always one uniquely correct answer to a legal question in the Talmud?" arguing against this alleged affinity.[1] In this paper, I wish to reiterate my reservations by focusing on the role of the doctrine of error in Dworkin's philosophy and in Jewish law. Let me make two preliminary remarks.

First, it goes without saying that one can find, in Dworkin's account, distinctions and insights that are applicable to Jewish law. This, however, does not imply that there is any particular affinity between Jewish law and Dworkin's theory, as these shared insights can also be found in **other** accounts of the law, and are not specific to Dworkin's **own** theory of law. Those who seek to establish an affinity between Dworkin's theory of law and Jewish law must do so based

* This paper is based on a lecture delivered at the Harvard Jewish Law Conference in 2012.

** Hanina Ben Menahem is a professor of law (emeritus) at the Faculty of law, The Hebrew University, Jerusalem.

1 "Is There Always One Uniquely Correct Answer to a Legal Question in the Talmud?" *Jewish Law Annual* 6 (1987), 164–75.

on features that are characteristic of law **as conceived by Dworkin**. Secondly, Dworkin is a prolific writer who has, over the years, gradually enlarged and fortified his account of the law. Moreover, his theories have been subject to extensive interpretation and elaboration. To avoid getting into debates about the correct interpretation of Dworkin's theory, let us imagine a legal philosopher, Dworcules by name, who holds the propositions I am about to discuss. (Should someone discern some overlap between Dworcules and Dworkin, well, so be it.) These Dworculean theses may overlap to some degree, meaning, they do not constitute the tightest and minimal possible version of this theory. Nevertheless, I am listing them in this way rather than reducing them further, as this is how they often appear in this 'expansive' form in Dworcules' writings.

My presentation has two parts. In the first part, I present an outline of Dworcules' theory, drawing attention to the prominent role played by the doctrine of error. In the second part, I turn to Jewish law and argue that a doctrine of error, as conceived by Dworcules, is **at odds** with the general orientation of Talmudic legal thinking, and hence, Dworcules' theory is inapplicable in the context of Jewish law.

An Outline of Dworcules' Legal Theory

1. **The legal system is a coherent web of norms.** This is a fundamental element of Dworcules' theory of law, which asserts that the binding part of the output of the community's legal creativity is coherent and consistent. This proposition does not posit that legislators and judges always act in a coherent way, but rather, that only those products of their activity that cohere with the rest of the system have a normative import. Coherence is a primary value in Dworcules' moral philosophy, and it is the standard that determines the limits of the legal system. Rules and legal determinations that are incompatible with the system's coherent core are not part of its norms.

   Dworcules is deeply concerned with the ways by which the system's coherence can be made manifest. Therefore, he devotes much time and energy to the provision of a suitable theory of interpretation. Different judges will generate different accounts of the law's coherent core, but this, Dworcules claims, does not prove that coherence is a subjective concept. The diversity of judicial accounts of the law's core demonstrates only that explication of the core is an onerous intellectual task.

2. **The system's coherence is secured by filtering the system's output.** According to Dworcules, this coherent core is identified by examining the system's output and extracting those principles that qualify as political morality. This process aspires to identify a coherent web of norms that pass the test of political morality, while filtering out some legal determinations from the past. To this end, Dworcules invokes his doctrine of mistake. (See [3] below.) Dworcules assigns this exceedingly difficult task to Hercules.

3. **Erroneous determinations, that should not be included in the system's coherent core, are identified through a doctrine of mistake.** Past legal determinations that are incompatible with the system's core are labelled "mistaken," and lose their normative status. We can distinguish between two types of mistaken determinations: those that were valid for their own time only, but have no gravitational force – that is cannot be used as precedents for other cases, and those that were altogether mistaken, and must be excised. Dworcules realizes, of course, that it is dangerous to allow judges to declare past legal activity (both precedents and statutes) erroneous, and therefore ignore it, as this could undermine an even-handed application of the law. Hence, he sets guiding principles that govern recourse to the doctrine of mistake, and cautions judges to be very careful before concluding that a mistake has been made. Nevertheless, the doctrine of mistake is fundamental, and much of Dworcules' account of the law, and his theory of adjudication, hinges on it.

    Indeed, rejection of this proposition would lead to the collapse of several other Dworculean theses. For example, consider the following thesis:

4. **Every legal question has one uniquely correct answer.** The "uniquely correct answer" is that which is derived from, and in accordance with, the system's coherent core. It is not necessarily the best answer in terms of morality but is, rather, the uniquely correct answer that is supplied by the system. Granted, this uniquely correct is not always arrived at; but the quest for correct answers motivates all judicial activity and should be the system's guiding principle. Clearly, the quest for uniquely correct answers makes sense only if the system is indeed coherent, and therefore generates only one answer. Logic dictates that anything can be derived from a non-coherent web of norms. A coherent picture, as noted above, can only be secured by invoking a doctrine of mistake.

5. The proposition that every question has one uniquely correct answer leads to the principle that **there is no legal question for which the law does not provide an answer**. Dworcules claims that there are no lacunae. He does not state this explicitly, however, it follows from the "one uniquely-correct answer" doctrine. If every legal question has one uniquely correct answer, then judges never need resort to extra-legal material, as all legal questions can be addressed through exclusively legal materials. In the same vein, Dworcules upholds the proposition that judges need not, and do not, have strong discretion.

   The following Dworculean propositions are less connected to the doctrine of mistake, and their relevance to our present discussion will become manifest when we turn to a discussion of Jewish law.

6. **Judges must decide cases by relying on a pre-existing set of norms.** This thesis, too, expresses the idea that judges must rely exclusively on the system's coherent core, and should ignore not only extra-legal material, but also legal determinations that lack "gravitational force."

7. **Litigants have a legal right to be judged in accordance with the law**; they are claiming a right, not pleading for a favour. The Dworculean theory of rights ensures that litigants are treated exclusively in accordance with the law. No infringement of their rights is allowed, even to secure the well-being of society. The judge's role is limited to determining the scope of the litigants' rights and ensuring that these rights are respected. Whether or not a litigant has a right to a favourable decision is determined according to the system's coherent web of norms.

8. **Judges are not allowed to base their decisions on policy considerations.** This is a major tenet of Dworcules's theory of adjudication. This thesis identifies legitimate considerations, which reflect principles, and render the judge's decision backward-looking (pre-existing rights), from considerations that reflect policies, and render the decision forward-looking (potential consequences).

9. **Citizens are governed by rules, not by individuals.** This proposition, which essentially encapsulates all the preceding propositions, offers support for the lay understanding that judges are the law's servants, not its masters.

II. The Model of Error Implicit in the Talmud

Let us now look at some central Talmudic sources that are part of the canon, and have shaped our understanding of the philosophy of Jewish law. This examination will demonstrate that almost none of Dworcules' claims about the nature of law cohere with Talmudic law.

I want to start by pointing out that propositions (6)-(9) above are all inconsistent with Talmudic jurisprudence. Elsewhere I addressed the Talmudic doctrine of judicial deviation,[2] according to which (1) judges need not decide cases submitted to them on the basis of a pre-existing set of norms; (2) are allowed to base their decisions on policy considerations; and (3) litigants do not have the right to be judged exclusively in accordance with the law. This means that citizens are governed by individuals, not by rules. These tenets clearly suggest that the determination that a ruling is erroneous cannot be made by simply comparing it to the sources of the law. One might, then, wonder what room is left for a doctrine of legal error in Talmudic law.

Indeed, what **is** the Talmudic doctrine of legal error? The Talmudic doctrine of judicial legal error is discussed primarily in three *sugyot*: bSanhedrin 33a, the *sugya* of the rebellious elder (mSanhedrin 11, bSanhedrin 88a-b), and the first chapter of tractate Horayot. Other references to legal error do not change the picture. These three main sources have generated an enormous body of literature, which is beyond the scope of this paper. Here, I will give an overview of the Talmudic doctrine of error. These sources create the illusion that the doctrine of error occupies an important place in Talmudic jurisprudence, with far-reaching consequences. We will see that the significance of these consequences has been exaggerated, and the import of the doctrine is, in fact, rather modest.

The Talmudic doctrine of judicial error is based primarily on a procedural test, not a substantive one. That is, a judge can be said to have erred only if his **method** of reaching the decision is defective, in the sense that he did not know some relevant legal material or legal practice. No error can be ascribed to a judge based on the substance of his decision. A judge who issued a ruling that does not accord with the law, not because he was unaware of the law, but because he believed that his ruling was appropriate, is not considered to have made a mistake; nor is his ruling erroneous, however much it deviates from the law. I set aside cases of self-ascribed error—cases in which the judge

2 Hanina Ben Menahem, *Judicial Deviation in Talmudic law, Governed by Men, Not by Rules* (Chur: 1991).

himself retracts his decision, claiming to have erred in his reasoning. I return to these cases below.

A key issue in considering the doctrine of error is the manner in which an alleged error can be identified. One such identifying mechanism, found in most legal systems, are the appellate courts that are charged, among others, with the identification and rectification of legal errors. This mechanism is not recognized by Talmudic law. The explanation is straightforward. Since it is almost impossible to conclusively determine, based on external evidence, that the judge was not aware of a pertinent legal norm—recall that this is the characterization of judicial error in Jewish law—courts of appeal cannot establish that an error has been made. This corroborates my claim about the nature of judicial legal error. An error can only be determined by the judge's own admission. Consider the following example:

> A certain man misappropriated a yoke of oxen from his fellow, went and did some ploughing with them, and also sowed some seeds with them, and at last returned them to their owner. When the case came before R. Nahman, he said [to the officers of the court]: Go forth and appraise the increment [to the field]. But Rava said to him: Were only the oxen instrumental in the increment, and did the land contribute nothing to the increment? He replied: Did I ever order payment of the full appraised value of the increment? I surely meant only half of it. He, however, rejoined: Be that as it may, since the oxen were misappropriated, they merely have to be returned intact, as we have indeed learned: "all robbers have to pay in accordance with [the value] at the time of the robbery." [Why then pay for any work done with them?] He replied: Did I not say to you that when I am sitting in judgment you should not make any suggestions to me, for Huna our colleague said with reference to me that King Shapur and I are [like] brothers in respect of civil law?[3] The person [who misappropriated the pair of oxen] is a notorious robber, and I want to penalize him (bBaba Kama 96b).

Note that here the judge's ruling diverges from the mishnaic rule that "all robbers have to pay in accordance with [the value] at the time of the robbery," but this divergence does not impair the ruling's validity since it does not result from unfamiliarity with the mishnaic norm. Note, also, that the judge does not consider the mishnaic ruling mistaken. In fact, both the mishnaic ruling, as well as the judge's ruling, are binding. Lastly, note that the robber cannot request to be judged in accordance

3 Meaning, both have the authority to deviate from the law when they deem it warranted.

with the mishnaic ruling.

I must now say a few general words about the *sugya* in Horayot, the *locus classicus* for judicial error. This *sugya* contemplates a case in which the court, after issuing a ruling, recognizes that it has erred. However, the nature of the mistake is unclear: was it a self-ascribed error, a case in which the court had second thoughts and sought to retract its ruling, or was it a case in which the court was made aware of some relevant legal source that had somehow escaped its notice? The language of the *sugya*—"the thing being hidden" (Lev 4:13)—suggests the latter, but is not conclusive.

At the outset, let me caution that any comprehensive account of this complex and elusive *sugya* will remain unsatisfactory. One difficulty stems from the fact that several key words in the *sugya* are used to denote different things. For example, the Hebrew word "*horu*" ('they ruled'), which in most cases denotes a judicial ruling permitting something, can also mean 'they taught.' The *sugya* unquestionably distinguishes between these two types of High Court activities: teaching the law (without recommending any specific course of action), and issuing rulings that mandate or prohibit a specific behavior. Though the *sugya* is generally understood as issuing legal rulings, the cases it brings seem to demonstrate teachings, not rulings. For example, "[The law concerning] the Sabbath is not found in the Torah, [the law concerning] idolatry is not found in the Torah..." (bHorayot 4a). In order to transform the Talmudic examples into court rulings, we must assume that the ruling formulated as "you are **allowed** to do X" (a permission—granting ruling, for example, to eat this piece of meat) or formulated as "you are **obliged/forbidden** to do X" (a duty—imposing ruling, for example, the prohibition against building a fence on the Sabbath).

My reading of this *sugya*—which, I expect, will be somewhat controversial—is that it accords with the principle that when the High Court issues rulings that impose a duty, all are obligated to comply with its directives, whether they agree with them or not. Accordingly, this *sugya* is fully in line with that of the rebellious elder, which mandates strict obedience to the High Court's rulings, even though that elder is to be treated more severely than an ordinary individual. It is of crucial significance that the Talmud never questions the relationship between the two *sugyot*; apparently, it never felt that there was any tension between them. The Talmud does **not** understand the *sugya* in Horayot as challenging that of the rebellious elder, a claim supported by the fact that the *sugya* in Horayot explicitly mentions the rebellious elder.

The Mishnah distinguishes between a learned individual and a layman. If the court's ruling was acted upon by only **some** individuals (as opposed to the whole community), these individuals are exempt from bringing a sin-offering. If, however, the person acting on the court's ruling was learned, and had believed from the outset that the ruling was mistaken, then he must bring a sin-offering. The Talmud ponders the question of why the learned individual must bring a sin-offering, given that he was aware of the court's mistake, and hence cannot be considered to have erred inadvertently; under these circumstances, a sin-offering seems to be inappropriate. The Talmud's contrived reply is that a sin-offering is nonetheless allowed because the learned individual erred regarding the "precept of obeying the words of the Sages" (טעה במצוה לשמוע דברי חכמים), mistakenly thinking that one is duty-bound to follow **all** court rulings.

Some scholars, my former self included,[4] inferred from this reply that one can identify judicial mistakes by reading them directly off the rulings themselves. This goes against my preceding analysis. Further, they inferred the far-reaching conclusion that such mistaken rulings are not binding and should not be adhered to. According to this reading, this *sugya* is not compatible with that of the rebellious elder. This putative discrepancy between the two *sugyot*, in turn, allows all kinds of forced distinctions. While some of the traditional exegetes conclude that there is no categorical obligation to obey the High Court, this view is primarily suppored by contemporary scholars. *The drive to show that Talmudic thinking is sensitive to individual autonomy, a rather modern idea, plays a central role in the adoption of this anachronistic reading of the sugya in Horayot.*

My critique of this 'libertarian' reading is three-tiered. First, as has been pointed out by many commentators, the Talmudic discussion here appears to be rather limited in scope: it covers only rulings that permit something that is considered prohibited. Consequently, the learned individual's mistaken belief was that he had to follow court decisions permitting acts he believed to be forbidden. That is to say, the Talmud is informing us that a learned individual should not rely on a lenient ruling if he believes it to be mistaken. The obligation to follow the court's ruling does not entail an obligation to act to one's own advantage.

The eighteenth-century scholar R. Haim Ben Atar summarizes the *sugya*:

Man is commanded by God to do all that he is told by the Sages [i.e., the

4 Ben Menahem, *Judicial Deviation*, 170.

> High Court], and in so doing … he is observing a precept. And why then do they say that he erred inadvertently–he did nothing wrong! And it must be said that since the Sages do not oblige him to consume the prohibited fat, which they ruled on, but rather give him permission to do so, if he wishes, if he believes that it is forbidden to eat that prohibited fat, he can refrain from eating it without thereby violating a ruling of the Sages. … his mistake was that he thought that it was a precept incumbent upon him to listen to the Sages and deliberately eat it, despite the fact that he thought it was forbidden [he thought] that he was duty-bound to actually act on the ruling of the Sages.[5]

This reading, to which Maimonides apparently subscribed, is supported both by the many examples adduced by the Talmud in Horayot to illustrate court activities, all of which refer to rulings that permit rather than prohibit, and by the repeated use of the verb "*horu*," which primarily denotes rulings permitting something.

Second, even if we read the *sugya* as referring to both permission-granting rulings and duty-imposing rulings, as some scholars claim, the sin-offering of the learned individual is due only after the court has admitted its mistake. The learned individual's claim that the court is mistaken is of no consequence until the court itself recognizes its mistake. This is highly significant.

The court's assertion tells us, retroactively, that its ruling should not have been followed. The Talmud projects our present knowledge (that the court has retracted its ruling because it was mistaken) onto the past; It claims that the learned individual erred regarding the scope of the obligation to defer to the Sages (טעה במצוה לשמוע דברי חכמים).

That is to say: we deem him to have erred in thinking that he had to follow a ruling that, by virtue of the court's retraction, turned out to be mistaken. His knowledge of the error is of no consequence until the court issues its retraction.

However, I think there is a more logical way to respond to the argument that the *sugya* does not endorse a categorical obligation to obey the High Court. The claim that the learned individual was mistaken, regarding the precept of obedience to the words of the Sages, is introduced to present his behaviour as involving an element of inadvertency. This, in turn, explains why he must bring a sin-offering. It seems problematic to infer conclusions regarding the obligation to obey court rulings from such a contrived, incidental, and ad hoc explanation. Furthermore, this explanation is at odds with what we know about Talmudic law in general, and indeed, many commentators

5 Haim b. Atar, *Hefetz Hashem* (Amsterdam: 1732).

and halakhic authorities reject this inference.

Let me recapitulate: according to the Talmudic approach, one legal authority can hardly ascribe error to another. Jewish law deems whatever is decided by competent halakhic adjudicators to be legally binding, and the legal discourse very rarely refers to the construct of error with regard to past decisions.

I wish to qualify the above account of the Talmudic doctrine of error. As I argued in my study of Talmudic judicial deviation, the Babylonian Talmud and the Jerusalem Talmud uphold different philosophies of the judicial process. The Babylonian Talmud's policy of permitting judicial deviation, of which I spoke earlier, is related to its policy of absolute compliance with all judicial rulings.

> Right and left: even if they show it before your eyes that left is right and right is left, listen to them.[6]

Without the latter, the former would be meaningless. This means that there would be very few cases that ascribe error to a ruling on the basis of its substance, as opposed to the manner in which it was arrived at by the court.

The Jerusalem Talmud's approach to the judicial process is different. It requires that the court manifest total fidelity to the law, and hence does **not** uphold an absolute obligation to obey legal rulings. Therefore, deviant rulings can be deemed erroneous. For example:

> Could it be the case that if they say to you that right is left and left is right, you would listen to them!? Therefore, Scripture teaches "to go to the right hand or the left"—that they will tell you of right that it is right and of left that it is left (jHorayot 1:1 [45d]).

In light of our discussion of the limited role that the doctrine of error plays in Talmudic legal culture, we may suggest to reject Dworcules' theory of error, while retaining the rest of his legal theory. Well, we cannot. As I noted above, the rejection of Dworcules' doctrine of mistake entails the rejection of his additional propositions. It entails, for instance, rejecting his first thesis: the halakhic system is *not* coherent, and coherence is *not* its ultimate objective. The following much-cited

6 *Sifre On Deuteronomy*, edited by Louis Finkelstein, (Re-published by The Theological Seminary of America, New York 1969), 207.

Talmudic sources will help clarify this:

> Was it not in fact taught: The law is always in accordance with the view of the house of Hillel, but he who wishes to act in accordance with the view of the house of Shammai may do so, and he who wishes to act in accordance with the view of the house of Hillel may do so; [he, however, who adopts] the more lenient rulings of the house of Shammai and the more lenient rulings of the house of Hillel is wicked, [while of one who adopts] the strictures of the house of Shammai and the strictures of the house of Hillel, Scripture said: "But the fool walketh in darkness" (Eccl 2:14). One should, rather, act either in accordance with the house of Shammai with respect to both their lenient and their strict rulings, or in accordance with the house of Hillel with respect to both their lenient and their strict rulings (bEruvin 6b-7a).

This source demonstrates that individuals are expected to act coherently, but the system itself is not required to do so. In the same spirit, the following source explicitly seeks to record rejected legal opinions, for future reference:

> And why do they record the opinion of the individual against that of the majority, since the law may only be decided according to the opinion of the majority? So that if a court approves of the opinion of the individual, it may rely on him. (mEduyot 1:5)[7]

That is, Talmudic law prefers to support the judge's decision-making authority, and rejects the desideratum, endorsed by Dworcules, to keep the law completely coherent.

One final point before my concluding remark. The lack of coherence, the difficulties, and the complications that the Talmudic Sages retain also indicates their approach to the question of lacunae. The claim that lacunae exist can be understood in two different ways. One is to say that the issue under consideration has been overlooked by the system; another is to say that the issue under consideration is indeed addressed, albeit ambiguously, and there is no legal material that can decisively settle the matter. Regarding the first possibility, I agree with Dworcules that if something has been overlooked, this does not constitute a lacuna; however, my reasoning differs from his. Dworcules claims

7 The Mishnah further records Rabbi Judah's minority view that minority views should be ignored.

that a coherent system can generate answers to any legal situation. I argue that in any normative system, including law, if something is not addressed by the system then one should be at liberty to act as they wish. This may be undesirable, but until a norm is established, this is the legal situation. The second understanding of lacunae, however, that would also be rejected by Dworcules, **is** consistent with Talmudic jurisprudence: where the complexity of the corpus of legal materials can generate contradictory legal arrangements, there is no legal basis for determining which is correct.

Conclusion

We have seen that the doctrine of mistake is vital to Dworcules' conception of the law. It plays a central role in his notion of a coherent legal system and in the desideratum of reaching such coherence at all costs, as well as in the no-less important thesis that every legal question has one uniquely-correctly answer. According to this theory, the doctrine of mistake is the primary instrument for critiquing legal decisions that are deemed inappropriate. Invoking the doctrine of mistake implies taking on a judgmental role regarding past decisions, and undermining positions with which one does not agree. To put it in deliberately extreme terms, one could even say that ascribing error to one's opponent is a violent act of silencing. By contrast, Jewish law does not presuppose either the coherence of the system in its entirety, or the availability of uniquely correct answers. As we have seen, Jewish law ascribes error only in cases where the court itself recognizes its mistake, and furthermore, it restricts error to a particular type of mistake, namely, ignorance of a binding legal source. Rarely is the concept of error used to discredit past decisions in light of the current court's own political morality.

The Talmudic discourse that is committed to the ideal of "both are the words of the living God" differs markedly from the discourse of error. Controversy, the hallmark of Talmudic legal culture, allows (and encourages) diverse views to remain within the system, whether or not they are accepted, without requiring that they be labeled "mistaken"; in other words, it allows divergent views to be tolerated. Moreover, due to its interpretive nature, halakhic creativity emerges in successive layers, injecting contradictory and incompatible assertions into the system. The result is that there is no coherence in the system, but this is the price it pays for the open and inclusive dialogue that it endorses.

The Jewish Law Annual, Vol. XXII

On the Plaintiff's Duty to Avoid Harm in Rabbinic Law

Amy Birkan*

Introduction

Rabbinic law is replete with rulings that counter-intuitively exonerate a defendant from liability for predominant forms of harm that she, or her property, causes. In the course of this article, I will show that these striking instances of acquittal stem from a fundamental doctrine in the Rabbinic system wherein the plaintiff bears an independent responsibility to be vigilant and anticipate common forms of harm, in order to forestall them. So, while liability is predicated on negligence in the Rabbinic system,

* The author holds a PhD in Jewish Thought from Hebrew University, specializing in Rabbinic legal theory, and carried out postdoctoral studies at the University of Toronto Law School. She has recently completed an LLB at Hebrew University and is presently an intern with the Ministry of Justice.

the law's focal point is primarily the plaintiff's negligence. Scholars such as Albeck and Westreich posit that liability in the talmudic system is predicated on the tortfeasor's negligence; however, I argue that the key gauge for determining liability is the plaintiff's ability to have avoided the injury. This article comprises three sections.[1] The first identifies an implicit duty tannaitic law imposes on the plaintiff to avoid injury caused by a pit negligently left exposed by the defendant (mBaba Kama 5:6), typical forms of harm caused by the defendant's animal (Tooth and Foot, mBaba Kama 2:1-2), obstacles created by the defendant in the public domain ("He Situated a Jug in the Public Domain," mBaba Kama 3:1) and collisions (mBaba Kama 3:4-6). The second section treats the amoraic approach to a plaintiff's duty to prevent harm in tort law, limiting it in certain cases, such as the negligently exposed pit (bBaba Kama 54b, jBaba Kama 9:6), yet fixing an express duty that requires a plaintiff to be vigilant in the public domain ("He Is Required to Look Where He Is Going," bBaba Kama 27b, jBaba Kama 3, 1/2). The third section of the article aims to identify the doctrine underlying what is perhaps the main principle of the Rabbinic tort system, "the plaintiff must distance himself from harm," by considering it in light of contemporary tort legal theory.

1. The Plaintiff's Duty to Avoid Harm in Tannaitic Law

1.1 The Negligently Exposed Pit (*Bor*)

Rabbinic law emphasizes the plaintiff's responsibility to avoid harm occasioned by the defendant's negligence, rather than fault the defendant for creating the hazard in the first place. This is modeled by the tannaitic case of the pit, a paradigm for indirectly producing harm:

> If he had covered it properly and nevertheless an ox or an ass fell into it and died, he is exempt, but if he had not covered it properly and an ox or an ass fell into it and died, he is liable…
>
> [If] Into it fell an ox, the deaf, a fool or a youth, he is liable,
>
> [If] A boy or a girl or a bondman or a bondwoman fell therein, he is not liable (mBaba Kama 5:6).[2]

1 This article is not intended as a critical analysis of talmudic material but as a conceptual analysis of Rabbinic tort rules and doctrines.

2 Translation based on H. Danby, *The Mishnah: Translated from the Hebrew*

Two distinct duties are created by the Mishnah. The apparent rule fixed in the *reisha* is that a defendant has a duty to cover a pit she digs or owns in the public domain,[3] while the *seifa* implicitly establishes a second duty through listing victims whose injury is recoverable and more importantly for our purposes, the victims it omits from this list. The *seifa* limits the defendant's liability to the injuries of animals, children, the deaf, and the insane.[4] The victim glaringly absent from the list is the average person, the *bar daat* injured by the pit. Note that the very Rabbinic terms for plaintiff – not defendant – *bar daat* and *pike'ah,* translate roughly as "[the] perceptive."

While the Mishnah does not reveal a ratio or principle for its decision to exempt the defendant from liability to most persons, its ground may be inferred from a parallel in the Tosefta (tBaba Kama 6:14):[5]

---

with Introduction and Brief Explanatory Notes (Peabody, Mass.: 2012), 399, with minor changes. Danby incorporates the Bavli's stipulation from bBaba Kama 54b into his translation of the Hebrew text, rendering it as "an ox that was deaf, foolish or young" rather than "into it fell an ox, the deaf, etc."

3 The context for *bor,* the negligently exposed pit, is disputed among the *tannaim.* Opinions vary as to whether it is situated on private grounds, or in the public domain but connected to the tortfeasor's land. The predominant understanding found in the Kaufman and Parma manuscripts of the Mishnah, as well in tBaba Kama 6:14, is that the pit is situated in the public domain, the reasonable context for such legal discussion. According to mBaba Kama 5:5, "If a man dug a pit in the public domain, and an ox or ass fell into it and died, he is liable." Here the defendant's negligence conditions his liability for damage caused by the pit, where the lack of any legal tie between him and the pit (since being situated in the public domain it is not technically owned by him) is deemed irrelevant.

4 Laws addressing the defendant's liability for human accidents pertain to injury alone, as a negligent pit-owner is never culpable for human deaths (tBaba Kama 6:14):

"And they will also split [the value of] the carcass. Excluded is [recovery for] vessels as they have no value [once shattered], excluded is recovery for human [death], as they have no value in death."

5 The *Mekhilta de'Rabbi Yishmael* does not address the case of human injury in its exposition of the biblical verses treating the negligently-exposed pit (*Masekhta deNezikin,* 11, 287-89 in the Horowitz-Rabin edition). This may well be accounted for by the tendency of the Mekhilta to append legal material to biblical verses, and the verses in themselves deal exclusively with animal injury and make no mention of human injury. The biblical verses that establish liability for the uncovered pit (Exod 21: 33-34) refrain from mentioning human injury, which may indicate that the tannaitic

> An ox, a deaf, a fool, a youth, a blind ox, and a pedestrian at night, he is liable.
>
> A boy or a girl, a bondman or bondwoman, he is exempt.

In contrast to the Mishnah, the Tosefta adds "pedestrians walking at night" to the list, evincing that the defendant's liability is specific (and limited to) victims with a reduced capacity to perceive, owing either to internal constraints as in the case of a child, or external constraints such as darkness.

While neither the Mishnah nor the tosefta outright state that a *bar daat* is denied recovery, two baraithas in bBaba Kama expressly exempt the tortfeasor from any degree of liability for the ordinary person injured by the pit:

> Into it fell a (*bar daat*) - he is exempt.

And:

> Into it fell an ox, a deaf, a fool, a youth, a blind person, and a pedestrian at night, he is liable.
>
> An alert person walking in daylight - he is exempt (bBaba Kama 54b).[6]

Here, it is important to note the several functions of the Rabbinic ruling, *patur* ('exempt'). Though the ruling clearly exonerates the defendant from liability, the exoneration is often the upshot of an implicit primary decision to hold the plaintiff accountable for the injury. Rather than frame the law as 'the plaintiff is barred from recovery,' the Talmud rules 'the defendant is exempt,' which is its vehicle for imposing a substantive duty or burden on the plaintiff to avoid harmful conditions generated, or occasioned by, the defendant.

In the present case of Pit, the law denies the plaintiff recovery not in order to exempt the negligent pit owner; rather, it is the reverse. The "he is exempt" rule is the means through which the law shifts the burden to prevent accidents from the defendant to the plaintiff. This is not only its role *prima facie*, but is a central way in which such rulings

doctrine of contributory negligence reflects ancient biblical law.

6 These baraithas are cited according to their version in the Hamburg manuscript.

are grasped by the *amoraim*.[7]

In the case of Pit, if the defendant has breached the law by leaving it uncovered, why exempt him from liability? Nor can the defendant's peculiar acquittal be attributed to the *grama*[8] doctrine of non-liability for producing harm indirectly,[9] since the negligent pit-owner is liable for injuries sustained by animals, children, etc., which would be precluded under *grama*.[10]

Rather, the case of Pit involves two competing duties: the defendant's duty to cover the pit, and the plaintiff's duty to observe and avoid it.

Damage archetype Pit establishes the principle that a plaintiff's duty to be vigilant overrides the tortfeasor's duty to not create obstacles and even traps in the public domain; and as in the common law's doctrine of contributory negligence,[11] it bars a plaintiff from recovery.[12]

7 One source that illustrates that the ruling "he is exempt" imposes a burden on the plaintiff to avoid harm caused by the defendant is in the *sugya* on the issue of nuisance, "One who [tills or builds] along a border," (bBaba Batra 17a-18b). This case sets the parameters of the tortfeasor's rights to cultivate her land together with her responsibility to not harm her neighbor with emissions. There, the Bavli consistently treats the Mishnah's choice to exempt the tortfeasor from liability as a direct expression that it is the plaintiff who is burdened with the responsibility of prevent the damages he suffers. One of the key precepts the Bavli applies in its Nuisance law (*Hilkhot Nizkei Shekhenim*) is that "The plaintiff must distance himself from harm."

8 *Grama* is a halakhic term for a result that is brought about indirectly, and that was not certain to occur.

9 Under the *grama* doctrine, the indirect manner that causes the damage precludes the imposition of liability.

10 The defendant's liability for the injuries of animals, minors, the mute, and the insane shows his acquittal in the case of the average plaintiff cannot be attributed to a doctrine of non-liability for causative harm (*grama*), or to the fact that the tortfeasor does not legally own (*zikat baalut*) the medium that causes the damage. If the rulings for the pit were predicated on either of these policies, the tortfeasor would not be accountable for the damages sustained by the impaired, minors, and animals in the pit.

11 Until the Law Reform (Contributory Negligence) Act 1945 amendment, the common law ruled that a finding of contributory negligence barred recovery.

12 Relatedly, in the context of nuisance law, the Bavli formulates the maxim that "The plaintiff must distance himself from harm," which succinctly captures the tannaitic tendency to place the primary responsibility for the

What emerges is that Rabbinic law is concerned with two distinct responsibilities, the defendant's responsibility of care toward the plaintiff and the plaintiff's responsibility of care toward herself.

Shalom Albeck considers Rabbinic tort a negligence-based system in which the only criterion for determining liability is negligence on the part of the defendant.[13] Under this theory, liability is conditioned solely by the defendant's negligence, and in accordance, the only circumstance that leads to an acquittal is *ones* (circumstances beyond one's control), as where the defendant produces injury through involuntary conduct. To Albeck, 'involuntary conduct' in this context means that the defendant could not have foreseen the harm that would ensue from the given act.

However, Rabbinic law frequently acquits defendants from liability for the apparent harmful effects of conduct. Rulings of this nature pose a serious problem for Albeck, who goes to great lengths to explain why the defendant could not have anticipated obvious outcomes.[14] This article argues that exemptions of this sort are simply unrelated to the defendant's conduct, but rather, to negligence on the part of the plaintiff. By contrast, Albeck does not identify the plaintiff's role in harm prevention as a legally relevant consideration, and certainly does regard this as the primary benchmark in Rabbinic tort.

Medieval scholar Nahmanides observed that a defendant's acquittal is often entirely unrelated to the nature of his act, but rather derives from the law identifying the plaintiff as the *causa causans* of the injury. Nahmanides criticized the Tosafists for their oversight in failing to recognize that negligence on the plaintiff's part is an integral and independent legal factor.

For example, Rabbinic law applies a doctrine of absolute liability, in contexts involving the damage archetype *adam hameizik* (a 'person who causes damage'), and holds the defendant perpetually liable for any injury caused by the body, whether accidentally or deliberately, while awake or asleep (mBaba Kama 1:6), even by involuntary conduct. Yet,

---

avoidance of injury on the plaintiff. Nuisance is an independent branch of tort that operates on standards not entirely congruent with general tort policy, and therefore exceeds the scope of this article. However, nuisance laws well reflect the tannaitic tendency to accentuate the plaintiff's role in harm prevention.

13 S. Albeck, *Pesher Dinei haNezikin baTalmud* ['An Explanation of the Tort Law in the Talmud'], (Hebrew) (Tel Aviv: 1965).

14 Albeck's theory on the Rabbinic tort system is treated in further detail below, at 9-10.

in set cases, such as "He Was Sleeping and the Other Came and Slept by Him" the law acquits the defendant for injury directly produced by the body. To account for this acquittal the Tosafists frame a new legal category – 'major involuntary acts' – Nahmanides protests:

> And they [the Tosafists] answered he is not liable for **major involuntary acts** (*onasin gedolim*) and support this with the Yerushalmi's ruling in "He Was Sleeping and the Plaintiff Came and Slept by Him." But it [the case] does not constitute support [for their category], **as in it the plaintiff was negligent towards himself**. And also regarding their understanding of "The Beam Carrier Walked Ahead and the Vat Owner Behind," **and that entire Mishnah**. And likewise, their explanations for "persons are not prone to look where they are going" - **all these [exemptions] are unrelated to *adam hameizik* and are owing to the factor that the plaintiff acted negligently towards himself.**[15]

Nahmanides identifies the plaintiff's negligence as the source for the defendant's acquittal in "He Was Sleeping." In lying down by the sleeping defendant, the plaintiff assumed the risk that the other might injure him in his sleep.[16] Thus, two distinct doctrines are operating and competing in "He Was Sleeping," the defendant's absolute liability for all injury produced by the body, and the plaintiff's duty to pre-empt harm; and it is the latter that prevails. Note the amoraic idiom Nahmanides adopts for contributory negligence, "the plaintiff acted negligently towards himself," has a similar tone to the language used by Park B. in *Bridge v. Grand Junction Ry., 3 M. & W. 244 (Ex. 1838)*: "He is the author of his own wrong."[17]

The ruling in "He was sleeping" is particularly significant for appreciating the weight of the Rabbinic doctrine of contributory negligence since it takes precedent even within the category of *adam hameizik*.[18]

15 *Hidushei haRamban*, bBaba Metzia, chap. 2.

16 Had both gone to sleep at the same time, the defendant would be liable for injuring the plaintiff in his sleep. Certain cases presented in this article may also be understood under the doctrine of voluntary assumption of risk, such as the present case.

17 James Fleming Jr. cites this case in "Contributory Negligence," *Yale Law Journal* 62 (1953), 693, n. 14.

18 "He Fell off a Roof in Unforeseeable Winds" (bBaba Kama 27a). The class of 'a person who damages,' *adam hameizik*, is an exceptional branch of tort

1.2 The Plaintiff's Duty to Avoid Typical Injury Caused by the Defendant's Animal (Damage Archetypes Tooth and Foot)

In addition to the obligation or burden to avoid obstacles, Rabbinic law requires potential plaintiffs to anticipate and avoid common types of injury prone caused by others' animals. This is modeled through the archetypes 'Tooth,' which refers to damage sustained by the animal consuming or contaminating produce, and 'Foot,' which refers to damage sustained by the animal crushing articles in its path. As Tooth and Foot are paradigms for animal harm they are, by definition, foreseeable, and can be anticipated just as readily by the plaintiff and defendant. Yet, notwithstanding this factor, and the consideration that it is the defendant who derives benefit from owning the animal and whose property actually causes the injury, she is acquitted from all Tooth and Foot injury liability as it occurs in the public domain:

> How does Foot typically injure while walking? The animal is prone to walk and to crush…
>
> How does Tooth typically eat what is suited for her? An animal is prone to eat fruits and vegetables…
>
> **Where do these laws apply? On the plaintiff's property. But in the public domain he is exempt** [author's bold] (mBaba Kama 2:1-2).

After characterizing (damage archetypes) Tooth and Foot, the Mishnah drastically limits liability and allows recovery exclusively where such injury occurs on the plaintiff's property. In all other contexts, the defendant is exempt from Tooth and Foot liability. If the defendant's animal helps itself to the plaintiff's produce,[19] or crushes a vessel while

---

and the only one governed by a policy of absolute liability, *adam muad leolam*. In general instances of tort, an agent will only be accountable for damage when it is caused through negligence. Thus, there is a policy of absolute liability that renders the tortfeasor accountable for the plaintiff's injury when he himself is blown off the rooftop by unforeseeable winds. In contrast, if it is his property that swept off the roof, for example, if "He Placed Jars on the Roof to Dry" (bBaba Kama 29a), liability will be contingent on whether or not the act of placing them on the roof is deemed negligent. Apart from the category of 'a person who damages,' in the absence of negligence there is no liability.

19 While the law exempts the defendant from liability for Tooth, it prohibits unjust gain. Therefore, when Tooth serves as a substitute for the animal's

walking through the public domain,[20] the damage is not recoverable.

That is, the upshot of the Mishnah's rule is that the defendant is not bound to keep animals at a distance from the plaintiff's commodities or direct animals around the plaintiff's vessels; rather it is the plaintiff who must obviate injury by keeping her belongings out of the animals' way. This drastic curb on liability renders the defendant solely accountable for the damage archetype 'Horn,' signifying an animal's aggressive act, which is regarded as uncharacteristic by Rabbinic law and accordingly unforeseeable behavior. Even in instances of Horn, the defendant is liable only if the animal is *muad*,[21] namely, a repeat offender.

The law's counter-intuitive rulings for Tooth and Foot in the public domain shift the responsibility for preventing predominant injury caused by animals from the defendant to the plaintiff.

---

feeding (*hanaa*), the defendant is required to compensate the plaintiff (mBaba Kama 2:3). The Bavli sets compensation for feedings at the minimal rate of cheap barley or straw:

"And if it benefited, he pays." How?

Raba said the value of cotton, Rava said the value of cheap barley.

Rashi explains (*dmei amir*) -

If it ate barley until it was satisfied, he does not pay him [its actual value] rather he pays as though it had eaten straw, for he may claim "I cannot afford to feed it barley, only straw" (bBaba Kama 20a).

The Yerushalmi similarly sets compensation for feedings at the rate of straw and adds that when the animal eats produce that is harmful to it, such as wheat, the defendant does not compensate the plaintiff (jBaba Kama 2, 4/2) at all. Moreover, liability for Tooth is contingent on the animal feeding to the point of satiation. There is no liability when the animal picks produce or pokes its mouth and nose inside the plaintiff's basket and contaminates its content. The plaintiff's responsibility to keep her produce beyond the animal's reach is tempered by the separate doctrine of unjust gain ('One may not prosper through damage one causes').

20 Also see tBaba Kama 3:4 and bBaba Kama 5b on the defendant's exemption from Tooth and Foot in the public domain.

21 Saul Lieberman notes that the only animal damage the defendant is consistently responsible for is Horn and its aggressive acts: "And so, with an animal he is liable in any location when it intended to cause damage, and not for its pleasure." S. Lieberman, *Tosefta kiPeshuta, Bava Kama* ['The Plain Reading of the Tosefta, Baba Kama'] (New York: 1992), 30. Note that the liability for Horn is itself contingent upon the animal being *muad*. There is no liability for damage caused by an animal's first Horn offense. Since the defendant's liability is limited to Horn, he or she is not liable for the majority of damage caused by their animals.

1.3 Tooth and Foot on Common Property

The principle that requires the plaintiff to protect her property from damage typically caused by animals applies to common property as well. Yards were customarily used to both keep animals and store belongings. Yet, rather than require the defendant to adopt reasonable measures to prevent an animal from damaging the plaintiff's property, the law again leaves it up to plaintiffs to ensure that their belongings are beyond the animal's reach.

The formative Mishnah that establishes liability for harm caused by one's property or animals includes a limiting clause:

> [And the defendant is liable for damage caused] In every location, apart from property particular to the tortfeasor,
>
> And property belonging to both the plaintiff and tortfeasor (mBaba Kama 1:2).

The law aligns common property with the defendant's property where liability is naturally most limited. While the issue of liability for Foot and Tooth damage on common property is disputed in the Bavli (bBaba Kama 13b), R. Isaac Alfasi and Maimonides (Monetary Damage 1:9) align it with the public domain and exempt the defendant from liability.

Maimonides bases the ruling in a theory of rights:

> If it [the animal] caused damage in the public domain or on property belonging to neither the defendant or plaintiff or in a courtyard that belongs to them both, which is particular for storing fruits and keeping animals, and in pathways between fields and the like, if it [the animal] damages through Tooth or Foot he is exempt since it has a right to walk there and it is typical for an animal to eat and crush while it walks (ibid.).

Maimonides understands the tortfeasor's liability, at least for Tooth and Foot, as contingent on the defendant acting outside the scope of her rights; since she has a right to keep her animal in the shared yard, she is not liable.[22] However, considering the issue of Tooth and Foot liability

22 Maimonides, like the Mishnah, refrains from explicitly stating that the plaintiff is responsible for ensuring she is not harmed by the tortfeasor's animal in all locations apart from her own property, though Maimonides' decision to acquit the tortfeasor from liability for Tooth and Foot in accordance with the Mishnah affirms this.

from the perspective of rights rather sharpens the question at hand and necessitates a precept. Why is it that when both the defendant and the plaintiff act within their respective rights, it is the plaintiff who has the burden of obviating foreseeable damage caused by the defendant's property?[23]

1.4 Contemporary Scholarship on Foot and Mouth

As mentioned, according to Albeck, Rabbinic tort law founds liability solely on the defendant's negligence and only circumstances of *ones* (unforeseeable harm), lead to an exemption. This is precisely how Albeck accounts for the ruling on Foot and Mouth:

> In the public domain and on shared grounds both plaintiff and defendant are present. As a result, each can be aware of the other's activity and it is up to the plaintiff to understand he may be injured by the defendant's activities, and he must take precautions, and if he has not, he has deviated from the norm and been negligent towards himself.
>
> The defendant was entitled to think the plaintiff had thought of the [potential] injury and adopted precautions, while [the defendant] only acted as is customary. Therefore, the defendant is *annus* and acquitted. When the defendant's activities are common and others can be aware of them, he is exempt even when the plaintiff's activities are common as well.[24]

Albeck maintains that when both the plaintiff and the defendant engage in common activities – whether in the public domain or on shared grounds – it is up to the plaintiff to consider the damages he may incur. Why? Intuitively, and from the standpoint of justice, oughtn't the defendant be required to consider the damage he may cause the plaintiff? Moreover, Albeck does not classify the plaintiff's requirement to consider and adopt measures against foreseeable injury as an independent legal consideration. Rather, for Albeck the plaintiff's omission to do so merely paves the path for typifying the defendant's conduct as "involuntary," that is, the defendant could not have foreseen

23 Or, in legal terms, why does the law give the tortfeasor a right to use shared property in a manner that will invariably harm the plaintiff who also acts within her rights? Legal rights also do not account for the defendant's exemption when both parties are on land that belongs to neither of them which includes trespass, the first context Maimonides mentions.

24 Albeck, *Pesher Dinei haNezikin baTalmud*, 103.

that the plaintiff would omit to adopt precautions, and accordingly the result of this omission, the injury was unforeseeable.

Avishalom Westreich similarly characterizes Rabbinic tort law as a defendant-based negligence regime; however, he provides a different ratio to account for the defendant's acquittal in the cases of Tooth and Foot. Westreich classifies the Tooth and Foot rule as an exception to the Rabbinic tort standard, based in exegesis:

> In the Bavli's view this law [exemption from Tooth and Foot damages] is not founded on standard considerations that characterize other rulings, rather its source is 'external,' an exceptional homily on Scripture and its content is limited to this source. It [the rule] does not comprise a fundamental negation of other tort considerations that influence a defendant's liability or acquittal. Rather, exemption from Tooth and Foot in the public domain is an exceptional law founded on a homily which removes it from this legal system.[25]

According to Westreich, the Tooth and Foot rule is an aberration to the Rabbinic tort system that neither represents nor conforms with its standard doctrine.[26] This is, however, a difficult claim, since Tooth and Foot are paradigms for *all typical harm* caused by the defendant's animal, so accordingly, Tooth and Foot constitute the standard. To Westreich, the case of "One Who Situates a Jug in the Public Domain" models standard tort principles (mBaba Kama 3:1). There, liability is imposed on the defendant when the plaintiff runs into the jug set down in the public domain. I argue below that mBaba Kama 3:1 which finds the defendant liable for the accident, comprises the exception to Rabbinic tort law, and (*author*: which) is governed by principles foreign to tort law.

25 A. Westreich, "Hermeneutics and Developments in the Talmudic Theory of Torts as Reflected by Exceptional Cases of Exemptions," PhD Diss. (Bar Ilan University: 2007), 134.

26 In his article, "Law and Beyond-Legal and Extralegal Aspects of Talmudic Tort," *26 Shenaton ha-Mishpat ha-Ivri (2009-2011)*, 203, Westreich suggests that the defendant is exempt from Tooth and Foot in the public domain as there he has no duty of care towards the plaintiff for such harm. However, this presents the law in the language of responsibility rather than revealing its underlying principle. Why doesn't the defendant have a responsibility to protect the plaintiff from the foreseeable harm her animal is likely to cause?

1.5 Collisions in the Public Domain

As mentioned earlier, in the damage paradigm *adam hameizik*, a doctrine of absolute liability applies for any damage a defendant directly causes with his body or force (mBaba Kama 1:6). Yet, in mBaba Kama 3:5 which deals with a series of cases of collision in the public domain, the defendant is acquitted in most circumstances:

> This one [approached] carrying with his vat, and this one with his beam, the one's vat was broken by the other's beam,
>
> He is acquitted - for this one has a right to walk, and this one has a right to walk.
>
> The beam owner walked ahead, and the vat owner behind him, the vat was broken on the beam.
>
> The beam owner is acquitted.
>
> But if the beam owner halted, he is liable.
>
> And if he warned the vat owner, "Stop," he is acquitted.
>
> The vat owner walked ahead and the beam owner behind him, the vat was broken by the beam,
>
> The beam owner is liable.
>
> But if the vat owner halted, he is acquitted.
>
> And so too with, "This one approached with a flame, and the other with his linen."

The Mishnah models its precept for collisions through its first case. When the defendant and plaintiff approach one another in the public domain and the plaintiff's vat is broken by the defendant's beam, the latter is exempted from liability.

Adding to the counter-intuitive nature of this ruling, the Mishnah chooses to illustrate its standard with a situation wherein it is the defendant who transports the dangerous load. Intuitively, we would expect the party that carries a hazardous object through the public domain to be required to exercise heightened care.

The ruling for "this one [approached] carrying with his vat, and this one with his beam" also cannot be attributed to the law's consideration for the cumbersome nature of the load the defendant carries, or to the fact that it might be easier for the plaintiff to perceive and avoid it, since the defendant is likewise exempted in the Mishnah's final case where the defendant carries a flame and the plaintiff some fabric. It is the plaintiff who must avoid the flame, not the defendant who must take care not to ignite the linen.

The Mishnah states the principle for its rulings: "since each has a right to walk." The legal norm, then, is that when two parties act within their rights, it is the plaintiff's duty to avoid harm, a norm that prevails over the defendant's absolute liability under *adam hameizik*. However, the Mishnah does not offer a reason for this. It limits the defendant's liability to circumstances that do not afford the plaintiff a chance to forestall harm, as when the defendant, walking ahead of the plaintiff transporting a beam abruptly halts without issuing a warning.[27]

1.6 Obstacles Placed in the Public Domain

The ruling for "One Who Situates a Jug in the Public Domain" (mBaba Kama 3:1) marks an antithesis to the laws reviewed thus far, since the defendant is liable for damage the plaintiff incurs upon running into it. Moreover, while in Pit the obstacle or trap created by the defendant is particularly dangerous and difficult to perceive, here the jug is plainly visible.[28] Furthermore, in Pit the defendant is acquitted, although her failure to cover the pit breaches express law. It is argued that the precise function of this Mishnah is to establish a prohibition for parties to situate objects in the public domain, which derives in considerations

27 The subsequent Mishnah prioritizes contributory negligence over the defendant's absolute liability for *adam hameizik*, when the defendant and plaintiff collide in the public domain (mBaba Kama 3:6). The defendant is exempt for the damage he causes with his body, even while involved in the more dangerous activity, such as when he is running and the plaintiff is walking. In this case, there is a dissenting view. According to the minority view of R. Issi Ben Yehuda, relayed in a *baraitha* (bBaba Kama 32a), the defendant is generally liable for damages he causes while running through the public domain since he is the party deviating from standard conduct. Towards Sabbath eve, when running is commonplace and permitted, R. Issi Ben Yehuda acquits the runner.

28 As many pits were cisterns used to collect water, an exposed pit in the public domain rendered the population susceptible not only to injury, as in the case of a dry pit, but to drowning as well (bBaba Kama 50a).

unrelated to general tort principles.

In *The City in Roman Palestine,* Daniel Sperber describes the narrow passages typical of Roman marketplaces:

> In those places where the side streets were so narrow as to allow no more than a single carriage to pass by, the rising tide of outspread merchandise blocked the passage of traffic.[29]

The ruling in mBaba Kama 3:1 apparently departs from standard tort principles for pragmatic purposes, so as to keep narrow public passages clear. This notion is reinforced by the *seifa* of mBaba Kama 3:1 and the two Mishnahs that follow it (mBaba Kama 3:2-3), that hold the defendant liable for damage caused by shards of a broken vessel and discarded materials. That standard tort law is not applied in Mishnahs mBaba Kama 3:1-3 is evident from the fact that the defendant is liable for damage produced by debris despite the lack of ownership. These regulatory rules mark an exception to liability principles and aim to keep public routes clean and unobstructed.

2. The Plaintiff's Duty to be Vigilant in Amoraic Law

2.1 Hazards and Traps Contra Obstacles in the Public Domain

In contrast to tannaitic law, amoraic law requires the defendant to compensate the standard victim, a *bar daat,* injured by the Pit. Interestingly, both the Bavli and the Yerushalmi present the defendant's liability towards the standard victim as self-evident, though it contradicts every tannaitic source on Pit liability, all of which deny the *bar daat* recovery and include no dissents.[30] As mentioned above, mBaba Kama 5:6 acquits the negligent pit-owner from liability in an indirect way, by omitting the *bar daat* from the list of victims entitled to recovery:

> Into it fell an ox, a child, a mute, an insane person and a minor - he is liable.

29 D. Sperber, *The City in Roman Palestine* (Oxford: 1998), 12.

30 *Pikeah,* an 'Alert Person,' is a synonym for *bar daat* in Rabbinic law, where both terms are employed interchangeably. However, they are used only in reference to the plaintiff, not the defendant who is consistently designated as the *meizik,* the 'injurer.'

Rather than read the terms 'mute,' 'insane,' and 'child' as nouns, both the Bavli and Yerushalmi treat these terms as adjectives that describe the ox that falls into the pit:

> An ox that is mute, an ox that is insane, an ox that is a youth (bBaba Kama 54b; jBaba Kama 5, 9/6).

The farfetched nature of this reading highlights the degree of its departure from the Mishnah's actual law.

However, reading the nouns as adjectives that describe the ox is critical to the amoraic interpretation, since it constrains the list of compensable injury to animals, blurring the absence of the *bar daat* from the list of human victims entitled to recovery.[31] At the same time, this reading results in 'an ox that is alert - he is exempt': the pit-owner is solely liable for injuries incurred by animals with coexisting circumstances.

Rava, apparently with intentional irony, takes the implicit grounds on which tannaitic law denies the standard person recovery and applies it to the 'alert' ox:

> Rather Rava said, "An ox that is mute, an ox that is insane, an ox that is a youth [he is liable], but an ox that is alert he is exempt. On what grounds?" We say to it, "You are required to look where you are going" (bBaba Kama 54b).

The law says to the ox, as it were, 'You ought to have been paying more attention.' It is the ox's negligence that is considered the cause of its fall into the pit, rather than the defendant's failure to cover it.[32] Thus, in amoraic Pit law, the *bar daat* is entitled to compensation, while animals, rather than persons, are expected to look before stepping:[33]

> a. The Bavli's Precept, "He [the Plaintiff] Is Required to Look Where He is Going"

31 See also bBaba Kama 28b and bBaba Kama 43b for the pit-owner's liability to the average person, the *bar daat* injured by the pit.

32 The Bavli exempts the pit owner solely for the deaths of the average animal, bBaba Kama 28b.

33 Ravina, in a dissenting view, seems to uphold tannaitic Pit law and denies the *bar daat* recovery. In bBaba Kama 54b he adamantly maintains that two baraithas that expressly bar the alert person from recovery are to be read literally and not in reference to alert animals.

The Bavli's determination to extend recovery to the standard plaintiff injured in Pit damage does not mean it fundamentally disagrees with the tannaitic doctrine of contributory negligence. On the contrary, the Bavli not only recognizes the plaintiff's obligation to be vigilant in the public domain, it formalizes this in the positive legal precept "He is required to look where he is going."[34]

The Bavli's decision to extend recovery to the *bar daat* in the case of Pit may derive from the categorical distinction it draws between hazards and traps on the one hand, and obstacles, on the other, considering it too harsh to fault the plaintiff for neglecting to notice a pit. Under this distinction, the Bavli imposes liability for injury caused by hazards and traps, that are difficult to perceive and capable of causing severe harm.[35] The doctrine of contributory negligence in the Bavli applies in contexts involving accidents caused by obstacles.

The Bavli's endeavor with respect to the Mishnah "He Situated a Jug" is to develop the tacit tannaitic doctrine of contributory negligence into a formal legal principle and establish the plaintiff's obligation to be vigilant. The Bavli questions the Mishnah's choice to fault the defendant for the plaintiff's stumble into the jug:

> And another came and stumbled on it and broke it - he is exempt.
>
> Why is he exempt? He is required to look where he is going (bBaba Kama 27b).

34 Among the key conclusions of his work, Leib Moscovitz concludes that many amoraic conceptions and principles are not independent innovations, but rather articulations of implicit tannaitic doctrines and precepts (L. Moscovitz, *Talmudic Reasoning: From Casuistics to Conceptualization* [Tubingen: 2002], 356). While the *amoraim* do make certain legal innovations or extrapolations, one distinct legal accomplishment was lending formal linguistic expression to precepts, doctrines, and principles implicit (but not articulated) in tannaitic law. See B. Porat, "The Philosophy of Jewish Law: A Methodological Reflection," 30 *Diné Israel* 30 (2015), 179, 182 nn.14 and 17 (2015). The amoraic precept "He must look where he is going" well illustrates this tendency, as the Bavli employs it to transform the tacit tannaitic doctrine of Contributory Negligence into a formal legal principle.

35 The notion that the Bavli distinguishes between hazards and obstacles is supported by its classification of dangerous items left out in public as Pit, holding the defendant liable for damage such loads cause (see "His Rock, His Knife, His Load," bBaba Kama 28b).

The Gemara assumes that the plaintiff ought to be responsible for the accident and transforms the pedestrian into the tortfeasor.[36] Just as the Bavli faults the pedestrian in a case where the defendant situates a jug in the public domain, it imposes *okimtot* - provisos - to account for the Mishnah's insistence that the jug owner is responsible for the accident. Through these provisos the Sages define the scope of the plaintiff's obligation to be alert in the public domain:

It was said in the name of Rav's academy, he [the tortfeasor] filled the entire [passage of] the public domain with jugs.

Shmuel said, in the dark, they taught.

R' Yohanan said, in a corner (bBaba Kama 27b).

In Rav's conception of contributory negligence, the plaintiff is virtually always required to observe and avoid obstacles. It is only when the defendant obstructs the entire passage with jugs that the pedestrian is not faulted for the collision, and under such circumstances, a plaintiff may even purposely break vessels to forge a passage. Shmuel qualifies the plaintiff's obligation to be perceptive to the daytime, while the jug owner will be liable for accidents caused by obstacles at night, similar to the tannaitic rulings in tBaba Kama 6:14 and bBaba Kama 54b. R' Yohanan applies the contributory negligence doctrine both during the day and at night, and acquits the pedestrian solely when the defendant creates an obstacle in a precarious place where it is not visible, such as around a bend. The Bavli does, however, include an alternate position that does not impose any obligation on the pedestrian to perceive and avoid obstacles, one it attributes to the Sages of Israel. These Sages focus on the way in which pedestrians tend – rather than ought – to conduct themselves. Since "it is not typical

36 Shanna Strauch Schick uses "He Placed a Jug" to demonstrate that the *amoraim* adopted a policy of strict liability for *adam hameizik*, and the pedestrian is liable for running into the jug owing to this precept ("Intention in the Babylonian Talmud: An Intellectual History," PhD Diss. (Yeshiva University: 2011), 48). Here, however, the pedestrian does not first falter and then knock over the jug. Rather, the case discusses which of two parties is liable for an accident, the one who creates an obstacle or the agent who fails to perceive it, as indicated by the name of the case. Moreover, the Sages explain their rationale for faulting the pedestrian, attributing the damage to her negligence.

for persons to be discerning ['*mavhin*'][37] along the routes," the creator of the obstacle, the jug-owner, is liable for the pedestrian's accident.[38] Nevertheless, the Bavli concludes its discussion with concrete cases wherein both Shmuel and Rava fault the pedestrian for stumbling into and damaging the other's belongings (bBaba Kama 27b), indicating that the ruling ultimately adopted bars pedestrians from recovery in contexts involving obstacles, finding that inadvertence on their part was the cause of the accident.

Note that in its discussion on accident prevention in the public domain the Bavli does not even address the defendant's conduct, and specifically negligence on the defendant's part for setting out obstacles at night or around a bend. It solely focuses on the principle of contributory negligence, of which the defendant's liability is an offshoot. In the rare instance where the plaintiff is relieved from the obligation to be vigilant,[39] the defendant will be liable, and not the other way around.

In marked contrast to the Bavli, the Yerushalmi does not require the pedestrian to be alert, nor does it record any dissenting view that applies the principle "he is required to look where he is going."[40] Rather,

37 This term implies observation, a level of attention higher than merely looking.

38 The Nimukei Yosef (bBaba Kama 27b) offers a theory to explain pedestrians' tendency to not to notice obstacles: "*It is not typical for pedestrians to be discerning*: As a person is full of thoughts and owing to the trepidations of his heart it is not customary for him to look while he is walking which is why they say specifically of the stumbled [pedestrian] who did not perceive [the jug] that he is acquitted." In contrast with animals whom amoraic law considers prone to notice obstacles (bBaba Kama 54b), humans tend to be preoccupied with serious matters, which may preclude careful observation. It is not that plaintiffs are perceived as being absent-minded, says the Nimukei Yosef, rather, on the contrary, they are absorbed by serious thought and concern.

39 The dispute on bBaba Kama 29 as to whether an accidental slip of a jug from a party's hands is to be classified as negligence or as an involuntary act may be underscored by a fundamental question on human conduct. Are slips and stumbles inherently indicative of inadvertence on an agent's party, which heightened attention would have prevented, or are slips and stumbles an invariable component of human conduct? Perhaps we must also consider whether it is worthwhile for a party to try to prevent each and every slip, given the costs of extreme attention to minor detail contra a *de minimus* rule.

40 While the Yerushalmi's discussion of the "He Placed a Jug" case (jBaba Kama 3, 1/2) includes key features found in the Bavli's discussion,

as relayed in the Bavli, the Sages designate the creator of an obstacle liable for the accidents it causes, on the ground that pedestrians are not prone to be perceptive along routes.

3. The Theory Underscoring the Rabbinic Doctrine of Contributory Negligence

Steve Friedell observes that in contexts of causative harm legal systems generally tend to limit a defendant's liability: "Although it may seem counterintuitive, wrongdoers are not liable for most of the damage they cause. The law leaves most of the burden of torts on the victims because it would be neither just nor practical to hold culpable defendants liable for all the harm they cause…To do otherwise would expose a wrongdoer to liability to an indefinite number of people for an indefinite amount of time."[41]

While Steve Friedell's observation is made in reference to the limited scope of liability in instances of indirect harm caused by *grama*,[42] the argument of the present article is that the Rabbinic tendency to limit a wrongdoer's liability applies just as well in paradigmatic cases of direct harm.[43]

At the same time, it is difficult to attribute, perhaps even to reconcile the Rabbinic tort system with an efficiency theory, as proposed by Benjamin Shmueli and Yisrael Yuval.[44] For example, concerning the Tooth and Foot rule that prevails in both tannaitic and amoraic law, simply requiring the defendant to muzzle an animal while in the

---

including the stipulations set on the Mishnah, the Sages' names, etc., it approaches the case from a different angle. The Yerushalmi assumes that pedestrians are prone to inadvertence while walking through the public domain and are under no duty or burden to exercise heightened care.

41 S. Friedell, "Nobody's Perfect: Proximate Cause in American and Jewish Law," *Hastings International and Comparative Law Review* 25/2 (2002), 111.

42 Friedell enumerates several methods adopted in Rabbinic tort to reduce the defendant's liability for the direct damage she causes, S. Friedell, "Some Observations on the Talmudic Law of Torts," *Rutgers Law Journal* 15 (1983), 904-5.

43 In "The State's Liability in Torts and the Exception of 'Discretion' in Jewish Law," (*Jewish Law Association Studies* 24 [2013], 284-302), Michael Wygoda considers assorted models of the Rabbinic system that might serve as a basis for limiting the liability of a state in torts.

44 See Y. Sinai and B. Shmueli, *Maimonides and Contemporary Tort Theory* (New York: 2020).

marketplace is an efficient and inexpensive means of preventing costs the plaintiff will incur for consumed and contaminated foods.

The present article proposes that the seemingly counter-intuitive Rabbinic bent to limit tort liability and consistently require the plaintiff to be perceptive to anticipate and avoid injury derives from a theory of individualism.

Froom v. Butcher involved a car accident for which the defendant was obviously and concededly the only party at fault, while the plaintiff's injuries were seriously exacerbated by the fact that he refrained from wearing a seat belt. Seat belt cases raise the fundamental question of what legal principle determines that the plaintiff's damages are reduced when the defendant is the only party accountable for the accident. In Lord Denning's words, "In these seat belt cases, the injured plaintiff is in no way to blame for the accident itself... The accident was solely caused by the negligent driving of the defendant. Sometimes outrageously bad driving. It should not lie in his mouth to say: 'You ought to have been wearing a seat belt'."[45] Lord Denning clarified that in cases of contributory negligence, the court was not asking what caused the **accident**, but rather, what caused the **damage**.[46] Lord Denning cites the definition of 'seat belt' in the Motor Vehicles (Construction and Use) Regulations 1973 as "a belt intended to be worn by a person in a vehicle and designed to prevent or lessen injury to its wearer in the event of an accident." Exercising prudence may be understood as a proverbial seatbelt, "Every time that a car goes out on the road there is the risk of an accident. **Not that you yourself will be negligent. But that someone else will be. That is a possibility which a prudent man should, and**

45 *Froom v. Butcher* [1976] 1 Q.B. 286, 292.

46 In *Jones v. Livox Quarries* (1952) 2 Q.B. 608, Lord Denning establishes that contributory negligence depends on foreseeability: "Just as actionable negligence requires foreseeability of harm to others, so contributory negligence requires the foreseeability of harm to oneself" at a standard of prudence rather than ordinary care. This, while bearing in mind that others may act negligently: "A person is guilty of contributory negligence if he ought reasonably to have foreseen that, if he did not act as a reasonable, prudent man, he might be hurt himself; and in his reckonings he must take into account the possibility of others being careless," 615. Implicit in "he ought reasonably to have foreseen" is the objective test of reasonable foreseeability determined in *Vaughan v. Menlove* (1837) 132 E.R. 490 and not a subjective 'bona fide to the best of his judgment' test based on the capacities of the specific plaintiff.

will, guard against."[47]

Justice Yizhak Englard has observed that the Rabbinic legal system is composed of laws whose purpose is to promote justice and order, as well as laws oriented towards instilling virtue.[48]

It is argued that the Rabbinic doctrine of contributory negligence, which consistently deflects the burden of anticipating and avoiding injury to the plaintiff,[49] may be in view of training the plaintiff on a micro legal level, to act as her own best sentinel, by being perceptive. This training disciplines the plaintiff on a macro level, to formulate her own tests for avoiding injury – as she defines it – in other realms, as well as the touchstones for concluding as to their effectiveness.

The doctrine of contributory negligence – the plaintiff's duty of care towards herself – is implicit in the common law duty of care, as established by Lord Atkin in *Donohue v. Stevenson*, in connection with the rule "love thy neighbor as thyself." "The rule that you are to love your neighbour becomes in law, you must not injure your neighbour; and the lawyer's question, Who is my neighbour?": "The answer seems to be - persons who are so closely and directly affected by my act that I ought reasonably to have them in contemplation as being so affected when I am directing my mind to the acts or omissions which are called in question."[50]

We may say that the doctrine of contributory negligence derives from Hillel's maxim "If I am not for myself, who will be for me?"

Francis Bohlen grounds the doctrine of contributory negligence in a fundamental conception of self-reliance, wherein it is the plaintiff's inability to have independently prevented the injury that marks the very starting point of legal intervention:[51]

47 *Froom v. Butcher*, 295.

48 *Mavo leTorat HaMishpat* ['Introduction to Jurisprudence'], (Hebrew) (Jerusalem: 1990), 22.

49 The burden imposed on the plaintiff in Rabbinic tort may be classified as ancillary to biblical law "וְנִשְׁמַרְתֶּם מְאֹד לְנַפְשֹׁתֵיכֶם" (Deut 4:15) and the Rabbinic doctrine of self-care established by virtue of it, bShabbat 82a.

50 *Donoghue v. Stevenson* [1932] A.C. 562, 580.

51 It is the plaintiff who sets the legal system in motion by filing a claim, and the notion of self-reliance may underscore the common law rule that no one can sue on behalf of the plaintiff. According to John C.P. Goldberg and B.C. Zipursky ("Torts as Wrongs," *Texas Law Review* 88 [2010]) the tort mechanism in general, and the plaintiff's claim of "redress" in the form of claiming compensation in particular, are colored by a strongly personal hue.

> The civil law conception that an individual may do what he pleases with his own is tinged by the peculiarly English characteristics of independence and self-reliance, and so becomes supplemented in the common law by the more intensely individualistic conception that he is also his own first bulwark against outside interference, and that the function of remedial law takes on where the power of self-protection ceases.[52]

Wrongdoers and pitfalls are inevitable. Rabbinic law requires plaintiffs to avoid the injurious results of both, by serving as their foremost sentinels against harm.

Fleming ("Contributory Negligence," 699) likewise identifies the 'philosophy of individualism' as the foundation for a contributory negligence burden.

52 See Francis Bohlen, "Contributory Negligence," *Harvard Law Review* 21(4) (1907-1908) 233, 253, and also at 254: "Unless each man was to be regarded as his brother's keeper, unless he was to be unduly burdened with eh duty of practically insuring the world against the results of his conduct, it was necessary that the correlative duty of self-protections should be extended as a counterpoise and corrective. It was manifestly unfair that the whole burden of protective caution should be thrown on one of the two parties, or that any man should be required to take better care for others than such persons are bound to take of themselves. The duty of care for others manifestly should be no higher than the duty of self-protection. To hold otherwise would be to unduly burden business and enterprise, to make of those engaged therein the guardians of those apt to be affected by their operation, and at the same time to rob of self-reliance, and so enervate and emasculate and in effect pauperize the latter by accustoming them to look to others for protection and by removing from them all responsibility of their own safety… the plaintiff can ask from others no higher respect for his rights than he himself pays to them."

The Jewish Law Annual, Vol. XXII

Third Parties' Intervention in Jewish Law: New Friends (*Amicus*) in the Rabbinical Courts Litigation

Yitshak Cohen* and Shai Farber**

* Yitshak Cohen is an Associate Professor of Law, Ono Academic College, Law School. Visiting Scholar, Columbia Law School (2012–2014). Visiting Professor, McGill University (10/2013). Visiting Professor, Masaryk University (11/2017). Ph.D., Bar Ilan University Law School.

** Dr. Shai Farber is a senior lecturer in the Department of Criminology at Emek Jezreel Academic College and an adjunct lecturer at the Faculty of Law at Bar Ilan University.

Introduction

This article discusses the proper use and adoption of the *Amicus Curiae* practice in Jewish law and in rabbinical courts. The main argument of the article is that the *Amicus Curiae,* in all matters regarding the law in rabbinical courts in Israel, should, in fact, serve as an "*amicus*" – meaning, as a "friend" – of the rabbinical court, one that assists with the resolving of different issues, in a professional and objective manner, without bias towards one of the formal litigants. Rabbinical judges, or *dayanim,* base their decisions on the Jewish Halakhah (religious law). They search for the 'true' halakhah - a decision based on the substantive truth as it had occurred, and not solely on the truth that can be learned from the admissible evidence - in each issue they face.

In some cases (mostly in cases involving fundamental legal issues), this practice requires the receiving of information from a source external to the panel. Sometimes, this information is fundamental legal-halakhic information that enables the rabbinical judges to consult with other expert scholars who are not part of the judicial panel. Other times, this is factual information that cannot be extracted from the formal litigants.

This article illustrates that even today, rabbinical courts make use of several legal practices that assist the court in receiving information from external sources. These practices are used in an obscure manner. The rabbinical courts oftentimes call these practices "consulting an outstanding scholar," "court trustee," "court expert on Judaism inquiries," or "*yada arikhta*" (Aramaic, literally meaning 'long arm'). This article argues that, while such practices are desirable in Jewish law and necessary in the rabbinical courts, they pose difficulties relating to the law of evidence, procedural law, ethics, and problems that point to a conflict between the rabbinical courts and the adversarial approach practiced in the common law.

In place of these obscure practices, the article suggests formally adopting the *Amicus Curiae* practice according to a dedicated model tailored to the rabbinical courts. This can help solve some of the difficulties that currently arise and regulate the information received from external sources. This will also help improve the rabbinical court's decisions and direct them as much as possible to the true halakhah, the substantial truth. The *Amicus Curiae* is a proper (though not perfect) solution to the current practices used in the rabbinical courts, in their efforts to reveal the truth and acquire information from external sources. Finally, considering the growing necessity of the *Amicus Curiae*, the article suggests an initial version of regulation of the *Amicus Curiae* in the Rabbinical Courts' Regulations.

The first chapter presents the positive law regarding the role of the *Amicus Curiae* in Israeli law. In addition, we will present the different models of the *Amicus Curiae* ("the classic model," "the supporting model" and "the lobbyist model") and their use in Israeli law. The second chapter reviews the unique characteristics of Jewish law which adopting the *Amicus* can complement: the demand for absolute truth in Jewish law, and the rejection of the *res judicata* doctrine and the expertise required of the *dayan*, the religious judge. The third chapter discusses the existing practices that assist the rabbinical court in its pursuit of the truth: consulting an outstanding scholar, a court trustee, a rabbinical court expert on Judaism inquiries, and the *yada arikhta* ('long arm'). The fourth chapter describes the problems that rise from the use of these practices, as mentioned above. The fifth chapter reviews the different justifications for integrating the *Amicus* in rabbinical courts. The sixth chapter suggests an initial framework for the regulation of the *Amicus Curiae* in rabbinical courts and presents a criticism of the suggested outline. The final chapter summarizes the article.

1. *Amicus Curiae* - General

A Background

Amicus Curiae (Latin, *Amicus* – friend; *Curiae* – of the court) is a legal practice that allows third parties, who are not formally part of the legal proceedings, to present their opinion to the court through a written brief, called an "*Amicus* Brief." Courts usually only allow written briefs, but in some cases, *Amicus* can deliver an oral argument. Generally, third parties who are interested in affecting legal proceedings make various uses of the *Amicus* practice.[1]

The *Amicus* practice is primarily used by third parties (such as a professional association, an individual, a commercial company, or a rights organization), who introduce legal or factual arguments that have not been presented to the court by the formal parties.[2] In some cases, *Amici* (the plural of *Amicus*) are third parties that request to join the proceedings in order to introduce arguments relating to the effects of the proceedings on a broader level, or on other parties not represented in the proceedings. Sometimes, it is the court that initiates the inclusion of *Amici* in the proceedings, in order to present information from different fields such as religion, economy, philosophy, sociology, or environment, when this information is not readily available to the formal litigants or when they are not interested or able to introduce it to the court.[3]

The final type of *Amicus*, used mainly in the USA but also to some extent in Israel, is when the third party has an interest in the legal outcome and they request to join the proceedings to convince the court, as *Amici*, to side with the party they support (the "Modern *Amicus*").[4]

Not only are there different types of *Amici*, but many countries assign different roles to the *Amicus Curiae* in legal proceedings. For example, in England and other common law countries, the *Amicus* is usually a neutral and objective third party invited by the court to present a written brief on an issue debated by the court.[5] In the USA,

1 See: J.D. Kearney and Th.W. Merrill, "The Influence of *Amicus Curiae* Briefs on the Supreme Court," *University of Pennsylvania Law Review* 148 (2000), 743-4; N. Hakman, "Lobbying the Supreme Court—An Appraisal of 'Political Science Folklore'," *Fordham Law Review* 35 (1966), 15.

2 See, generally, E. Angell, "The *Amicus Curiae*: American Development of English Institutions," *International and Comparative Law Quarterly* 16 (1967), 1017.

3 Kearney and Merrill, note 1 above.

4 J. Bellhouse and A. Lavers, "The Modern *Amicus Curiae*: A Role in Arbitration?," *Civil Justice Quarterly* 23 (2004), 187. H.A. Anderson, "Frenemies of the Court: The Many Faces of *Amicus Curiae*," *University of Richmond Law Review* 49 (2015), 361. For a comparative study see Sh. Farber, "The *Amicus Curiae* Phenomenon – Theory, Causes and Meanings," *Transnational Law and Contemporary Problems* 29 (2019), 1.

5 See E. Metcalfe, *To Assist the Court: Third Party Interventions in the UK* (2009), 13. See *R (E.) v. Governing Body of JFS* [2009] *UKSC* 15, [2010] 2 AC 728 (appeal taken from England).

the main use of *Amicus Curiae* is by interested third parties that turn to the court on their initiative in order to submit a brief that clearly supports one of the formal parties.[6]

In Israel, the *Amicus Curiae* practice was adopted in 1999 by the Supreme Court in the *Kozaly* case.[7] This case set the criteria to be examined when adding a third party as an *Amicus*: the potential contribution of the *Amicus'* opinion to the proceedings; the type of proceeding and procedure; the formal parties; the stage at which the request of the *Amicus* was submitted; and the nature of the issue at hand.[8] Since its adoption into Israeli law, many requests to join the proceedings as *Amicus Curiae* have been submitted to the court in all legal fields, to most of the courts in Israel.[9] However, *Amicus Curiae* have not been formally practiced in rabbinical courts, at least not to date.

The *Amicus Curiae* practice became popular in the last few years also in international commercial arbitrations. Several significant international organizations have adopted the practice of accepting briefs from *Amicus Curiae,* including (1) the World Trade Organization ("WTO");[10] (2) The

6 Regarding the *Amicus Curiae* practice in the USA, see Kearney and Merrill, note 1 above, 743; P.M. Collins, Jr., *Friends of the Supreme Court: Interest Groups and Judicial Decision Making* (New York: 2008); J. Harrington, "*Amici* Curiae in the Federal Courts of Appeals: How Friendly Are They?" (Note), *Case Western Reserve Law Review* 55 (2005), 667.

7 7929/96 *Kozaly v. The State of Israel* 53(1) PD 529, 555 [1999] (Isr.).

8 Ibid. The court stated that these are the main criteria, but not exclusive ones. See also Sh. Farber, *Amicus Curiae,* note 4 above.

9 E.g., CA 9384/01 *El Nasasra v. Israeli Bar Association* 59(4) PD 637 [2004] (Isr.); as per our inquiry in two legal databases – Nevo and Pador (lastly inquired December 2019); (Be'er Sheva District Court) 49319-12-14 *Levi Pirsk v. Kav Tzinor Eilat Ashkelon Inc.*, Nevo Legal Database (by subscription) (Isr.) (Aug 9, 2016); (Tel Aviv District Court) 22050/03 *Israeli Bar Association Tel Aviv v. Arnona Nihul Nehasim VeYeutz (1965) Inc.* (Feb 2, 2004) Nevo Legal Database (by subscription) (Isr.).

10 Despite considerable reservations, the WTO adopted the *Amicus Curiae* procedure in dispute settlement and in appellate proceedings at the Appellate Body. The authority to approve the use of *Amicus Curiae* in arbitration proceedings was first debated in two precedential decisions: United States – Imposition of Countervailing Duties on Certain Hot-Rolled Lead and Bismuth Carbon Steel Products Originating in the United Kingdom, Appellate Body Report, WTO Doc. WT/DS138/AB/R (May 10, 2000) (hereinafter Hot-Rolled Lead case), and European Communities – Measures Affecting Asbestos and Asbestos-Containing Products, 40 I.L.M.

North American Free Trade Agreement (NAFTA);[11] (3) The International Center for Settlement of Investment Disputes ("ICSID");[12] and (4) The International Chamber of Commerce ("ICC").[13] The central justification behind the *Amicus Curiae* Practice in international arbitrations is that sometimes commercial arbitrations deal not only with the commercial interests of the formal parties, but include important public matters as well: human rights, minority rights, environmental rights, animal rights, and the political rights of third parties.[14]

1193 (WTO Appellate Body 2001). In both cases, *Amicus Curiae* requests to join the proceedings were submitted to the Appellate Body. Although the formal parties to the proceedings argued that the Appellate Body does not have the authority to accept *Amicus Curiae* briefs, the arbitrators of the Appellate Body ruled that they are indeed authorized to accept them, stating that "We are of the opinion that we have the legal authority under the DSU to accept and consider Amicus Curiae briefs in an appeal in which we find it pertinent and useful to do so." Hot-Rolled Lead case, ¶ 42. In light of the many issues that arose during the years in connection with *Amici's* desire to join arbitration proceedings, the WTO was driven to implement a reform of the subject and establish, in 2010, rules regulating this issue. K.F. Gómez, "Rethinking the Role of Amicus Curiae in International Investment Arbitration: How to Draw the Line Favorably for the Public Interest," *Fordham International Law Journal* 35 (2012), 510; see also J. Robbins, "False Friends: Amicus Curiae and Procedural Discretion in WTO Appeals Under the Hot-Rolled Lead/Asbestos Doctrine," *Harvard International Law Review* 44 (2003), 317.

11 *Methanex Corp. v. United States,* NAFTA Arb. (Jan. 15, 2001); B. Legum, *Introductory Note to Methanex Corporation v. United States of America,* 44 I.L.M. 1343, 1343 (2005).

12 Rules of Procedure for Arbitration Proceedings, ICSID Convention, Regulations and Rules r.37 (Apr. 10, 2006), http://icsidfiles.worldbank.org/icsid/icsid/StaticFiles/basicdoc/basic-en.htm; *Aguas Argentinas S.A. v. Arg. Republic,* ICSID Case No. ARB/03/19, Order in Response to a Petition for Transparency and Participation as *Amicus Curiae* (May 19, 2005), 21 ICSID Rev. (2006), 342.

13 See E. De Brabandere, "NGOs and the 'Public Interest': The Legality and Rationale of *Amicus Curiae* Interventions in International Economic and Investment Disputes," *Chinese Journal of International Law* 12 (2011), 85.

14 Idem; see also L. Bartholomeusz, "The *Amicus* Curiae Before International Courts and Tribunals," *Non-State Actors and International Law* 5 (2005), 236. However, as it relates to *Amicus* practice in arbitration proceedings, it is important to remember that an arbitration proceeding is by nature a process of consent and free will between two parties. Therefore, *Amicus* cannot be forced on the formal parties as such coercion contradicts the

B The *Amicus* on Issues of Religion and State and in the Judgments of the Israeli Rabbinical Courts

Various *Amici* have tried to influence the courts on issues regarding religion and state, and on issues that directly regard the activity, authority, conduct, and decisions of the rabbinical courts, as well as the interpretation of Jewish law in the Israeli legislation. We describe below four major examples of different *Amici* activity in this field – two cases in which *Amici* tried to change the ruling of the rabbinical courts, and two in which the *Amici* requested that the Supreme Court enforce the rabbinical court's ruling.

First, the Supreme Court addressed the issue of whether the State Rabbinical Court has the authority to annul a conversion (to Judaism) if it concluded that the conversion was obtained by deceit. Several non-governmental organizations requested to join the petitioner (the converted) as *Amici* in the request for further hearing: "Brit Ne'emanei Torah VaAvoda," "Hiddush – for Religion Freedom and Equality," "Kolekh – Religious Women Forum," "Itim – the Jewish Life Advocacy Center," and "The Ruth and Emanuel Rackman Center."[15] The five organizations submitted written briefs as *Amici* and argued, each organization for its purposes, that the rabbinical court's ruling should be negated. Itim argued that the rabbinical court's authority to annul a conversion in case of deceit has a substantial impact on the converts and causes fear and constant uncertainty. The Rackman Center described the impact of the ruling on converts, and particularly on the children of women converts, as a result of possible divorce extortions and withholdings of a *get* (Jewish divorce document). The Rackman Center further argued that annulling the petitioner's conversion contradicts the public interest, especially since the petitioner has children. The authority to annul conversions should be limited considering the International Convention on the Rights of the Child.[16]

Second, the *Ragchova* case addressed the legality of non-Orthodox conversions.[17] Several converts arrived in Israel from various places in the world, and after some time in Israel, underwent private (non-State)

---

rationale of the arbitration process.

15 HCJ 18/15 *Plonit v. Special Rabbinical Courts for Conversion* (Apr. 30, 2015), Nevo Legal Database (by subscription) (Isr.) (hereinafter: *Plonit* case).

16 The arguments of the "*Amici*" were considered in the court's decision, but eventually the request for further hearing was denied. *Plonit* case, ibid.

17 HCJ 7625/06 *Ragchova v. Minister of Interior* (Mar. 31, 2016), Nevo Legal Database (by subscription) (Isr.).

conversion. The Supreme Court, in an extended panel of nine judges, addressed the question of whether the converts should be seen as Jews in the terms of the Law of Return. The petitioners requested that the converts be recognized as Jews. "Itim," as an *Amicus*, supported the petitioners. It argued that conversion in a known Jewish community, in Israel or abroad, is sufficient for recognizing the convert as a Jew in terms of the Law of Return. They further argued that recognizing only those converted by the State is an infringement on the freedom of religion and the right to equality of those who choose to convert privately. The Supreme Court ruled in favor of the petitioners. In its decision, the court considered the *Amici*'s arguments and ruled that the Law of Return applies to persons who arrived in Israel before conversion and underwent a conversion process during their stay in Israel.[18]

In two other cases, the *Amici* requested the court to affirm the rabbinical court's rulings. In one, addressing the rabbinical court's authority to arrest those who refuse their wives a divorce for an unlimited period of time, six women's rights organizations submitted a joint *Amicus* Brief to the Supreme Court.[19] The *Amici* argued in favor of the rabbinical court's ruling to arrest the resisting husbands. The Supreme Court did not formally accept the request to join as *Amicus*, but read the brief and heard their arguments.[20]

Similarly, in a case regarding the rabbinical court's authority to impose social sanctions (based on Rabbeinu Tam's excommunication methods) for those who withhold a *get*, the latter petitioned against the sanctions to the Supreme Court.[21] "The Legal Clinics of the Academic Center for Law and Science" requested to join the proceeding as an *Amicus* and argue in favor of the rabbinical court's ruling. The Supreme

18 The term "converted" in the Law of Return should be interpreted as relating to those converted in a known Jewish community, in compliance with that community's criteria. The court ruled that the recognition should not be limited to those converted by the State conversion process alone.

19 HCJ 4072/12 *Ploni v. the Great Rabbinical Court* (Apr. 7, 2013), Nevo Legal Database (by subscription) (Isr.).

20 Ibid. In most courts in the world, "*Amici*" are allowed to submit a written brief, and only on rare occasions are allowed to present oral arguments. Some courts forbid the oral arguments of "*Amici*" completely. See, for example, Ark. Sup. Ct. R. 4-6(b) ("*Amici Curiae* attorneys will not be permitted to participate in oral arguments").

21 HCJ 5185/13 *Ploni v. Great Rabbinical Court in Jerusalem* (Feb. 28, 2017), Nevo Legal Database (by subscription) (Isr.).

Court denied the request and dismissed the petition.[22]

To summarize, the cases described above show the potential impact of the *Amicus Curiae* on the conduct and authority of the Israeli rabbinical courts. Different organizations have made attempts to influence the rabbinical court's rulings, as *Amici*, mainly through Israeli law. In this manner, different organizations have tried to present their philosophies in court, and affirm or change the rabbinical court's rulings.[23]

Nonetheless, we believe that in the future, organizations will attempt to influence the rulings of the rabbinical courts by joining the proceedings in the rabbinical courts as *Amici*. Interest groups (such as women's rights organizations or religious organizations) may request to join the proceedings as *Amici*. It is our opinion that there is no legal hindrance barring organizations, which have the desire to influence various issues discussed in rabbinical courts (such as non-Orthodox conversions, arrests for those who refuse divorce, etc.), from requesting to join the proceedings as *Amici*. The *Amicus Curiae* practice is the result of the judicial ruling, and the rabbinical courts are authorized to include parties as *Amici*. In other words, we believe that it is likely that *Amici* requests will be submitted to rabbinical courts in the future and that the latter will need to decide in which type of *Amicus Curiae* they are interested.

The Amicus practice is been used not only in Judgments of the Israeli Rabbinical Courts but also in rabbinic arbitration in other jurisdictions, especially in the USA. For example, the "Beth Din of America" is a mediation and arbitration organization that has earned a reputation, among Jews across the ideological spectrum, for handling dispute resolution with confidentiality. The Beth Din regularly arbitrates a wide range of disputes among parties, ranging in value from small claims to litigation involving several million dollars. These cases include commercial disputes, such as employer-employee, landlord-tenant, business interference, breach of contract, breach of fiduciary duty, investor mismanagement, defective merchandise and unfair competition disputes; communal disputes, such as rabbinic contract disputes and other congregational issues; and familial issues, such as with family business, inheritance, and matrimonial disputes. The *dayanim* who preside over cases include leading authorities on Jewish law, as well as lawyers and businessmen who are familiar with secular

22 Ibid., decision from 6.3.2016.

23 See the above discussions (notes 10-12) relating to fraudulent conversions, non-Orthodox conversions, and arrests and social sanctions against those who withhold a *get*.

law and contemporary commercial practices.[24]

C The *Amicus Curiae* Models

Before looking into the *Amicus* practice in rabbinical courts, we conduct a comparative and theoretical survey of the different models of the *Amicus Curiae*. In our opinion, the most fitting model for the rabbinical courts, which best aligns with the halakhah, is the "Classic (neutral) *Amicus*." Meaning, it constitutes a third, uninterested party, called upon by the court to help with its decision.

Generally, there are three *Amicus* models, each with its own characteristics and functions. The first is the "Classic *Amicus*."[25] Sometimes, the court might need professional information or external assistance with a legal or factual issue that cannot be supplied by one of the formal litigants. At other times, the court requires more information on the issue at hand, and the formal litigants – certainly the one that anticipate 'losing' on account of this information - are not interested in supplying it, as the resulting decision might be contrary to their interests. In such cases, the court may request the independent and objective assistance of a third party. The "Classic *Amicus*" does not represent either party's interests; it participates in the proceeding strictly to assist the court.[26]

24 For further reading, including on the issue of court procedures see: "Rules and Procedures of the Beth Din," http://s589827416.onlinehome.us/wp-content/uploads/2015/07/Rules.pdf

25 The origin of the "classic *Amicus*" is debatable. As its Latin name suggests, the origin of the *Amicus* was probably Roman, given that Latin was the Roman Empire's official language. Some argue that the *Amicus* practice was common among the elite in the Roman judicial system. However, the origin of the *Amicus* is probably more complicated. While there are some similarities between the *Amicus* and practices that were common in the Roman Empire, the evolution of the *Amicus* is rooted in social and historical processes that occurred in the common law, first in England and later in other common law countries. S. Krislov, "The Amicus Curiae Brief: From Friendship to Advocacy," *Yale Law Journal* 72 (1963), 694. For more on the historical roots of the amicus in Roman law and common law, see Shai Farber, "The Historical Roots of the Amicus Curiae: The Reproduction of a Legal Procedure in the Common Law," 144 Zmanim (2022). (Heb.)

26 Courts use this model of *Amicus* when the issue at hand relates to the public interest. In such cases, the court wants to have as much information as possible regarding the relevant interests, as well as an understanding of the possible outcomes of the decision on populations beyond the formal

The problem with this model is that the court might develop an independent position, or make certain requests of the represented parties, sometimes contrary to the parties' position. On the other hand, this model can be viewed as the court's desire to reach the truth, to see the full picture, where it requests and receives assistance (such as consulting with a scholar on a halakhic matter), from an unbiased third party.[27]

The second model is the "Supporting Model." This refers to use of a third party, unrelated to the formal litigants, who has some interest in the outcome of the case. This type of *Amicus* will usually request to join the proceedings and influence the interests promoted by the decision.[28] In some countries, state attorneys make use of this model when presenting the public interest to the court, as *Amicus*, while there normally is no obligation to do so.[29] When there is a statutory obligation that a state representative be present in the hearing, the representative is not considered an *Amicus Curiae*, as it is not voluntary. The "Supporting *Amicus*" differs from the "Classic *Amicus*" in that the former is appointed to represent the public interest, not its own position.[30]

The third model is the "Lobbyist Model." In this model, the *Amicus* has a distinct interest in the outcome of the case, and he seeks to present his opinion and position in order to influence the court's decision. This *Amicus* requests to join the proceeding on his own initiative. He is

---

parties. To achieve this, the court requests a third, professional party to present this information. The model is sometimes referred to as "the lawyer of the court." See P.M. Collins, Jr., P.C. Corley, and J. Hamner, "Influence of Amicus Curiae Briefs on U.S. Supreme Court Opinion Content," *Law and Society Review* 49 (2015), 917.

27 S. Ch. Mohan, "The Amicus Curiae: Friends No More?," *Singapore Journal of Legal Studies* (2010), 352.

28 See, e.g., *Morelle Ld. v. Wakeling* [1955] 2 QB 379 (CA), in which the court requested the Attorney General of England to join as an "*Amicus*" and present the State's position in a dispute between two private litigants. D.C. Thompson and M.F. Wachtell, "An Empirical Analysis of Supreme Court Certiorari Petition Procedures: The Call for Response and the Call for the Views of the Solicitor General," *George Mason Law Review* 16 (2009), 242.

29 In Hong Kong, courts appoint "*Amici*" in one-sided civil requests, such as the liquidation of corporations. In such cases, there is no legal obligation for a state representative to be present, and he is considered an *Amicus*. Another example can be found in *Re S. China Strategic Ltd.* [1997] H.K.L.R.D. 131 (C.F.I.), in which the court appointed a representative of the Department of Justice as an *Amicus*.

30 Thompson and Wachtell, note 28 above.

not a formal party to the proceedings, and his rights and obligations are different from those of the formal litigants, but his goal is clear: to present a one-sided position in support of one of the formal litigants, to influence the court's discretion.[31]

It is our opinion that the model most fitting for the rabbinical courts is the "Classic Model" (the "Neutral Model"). This is the model that best fits the halakhah by which the rabbinical courts abide. The rabbinical courts should formally adopt the *Amicus Curiae* practice in its "Classic Model" form – an uninterested, unbiased, and external third party, usually an expert of some kind, who assists the court independently and objectively.

In the following chapters, we present the distinction between the regular legal system and the Jewish law system, as relating to judicial conduct. Then, we will present the practices used by rabbinical courts to receive information from sources external to the panel. Finally, we will discuss the reasons for this conduct, the problems arising from such practices, and how the *Amicus Curiae* practice can resolve these problems.

D The Distinction between *Amicus Curiae* and Expert Witness

Some may argue that the adoption of the *Amicus Curiae* practice in the rabbinical courts is unnecessary, as civil courts have another solution, the expert witness. We would like to present the proper distinction between the use of the *Amicus Curiae* and the use of an expert witness. This distinction will help explain why the current legal status quo needs to be altered and why the rabbinical courts' provisions cannot rely on the regulations relating to expert witnesses.[32] Our proposed use of *Amicus Curiae* is substantially different from the common use of the expert witness and its provisions.

The first difference relates to the essence of these models. Generally, an expert witness is one who attends a hearing to present his expertise

31 P.M. Collins, Jr., "Friends of the Court: Examining the Influence of Amicus Curiae Participation in U.S. Supreme Court Litigation," *Law and Society Review* 38 (2004), 828.

32 There have always been consultations with external sources in religious law, though this consultation seems to aim primarily at promoting modesty among judges. See bSanhedrin 38b, and Rashi's commentary. In other words, adopting the *Amicus* in Jewish law is, to some extent, simply naming the current practice and resolving some of its accompanying problems.

in a certain matter. Unlike a regular witness, who testifies to facts as are known to him, the expert witness presents the implications of the facts that were presented to the court. Usually, an expert witness is appointed in cases that require professional knowledge, where the court does not, on its own, have the knowledge necessary to make a decision on the matter (such as that provide by a doctor or an architect, for example). Also, the expert witness' testimony is usually submitted to the court in writing, and the opposing party has the right to submit a counter opinion.[33]

Second, the role of the *Amicus* is usually to present an interest, point of view, position, opinion, or perspective that should be heard by the court (such as the opinion of a scholar expert on a religious issue). Generally, the *Amicus* is not a witness, and the evidence law does not apply to him.

The third difference also has to do with the law of evidence and testimony. Like a regular testimony, the parties are usually allowed to examine the expert on his opinion. The *Amicus*, on the other hand, is not considered a witness, and therefore the law of evidence does not apply to him and he cannot be examined. Nonetheless, his opinion is handed to the formal litigants who are granted the right to present an alternative opinion. This distinction can be seen in the *Plonit* case, in which the rabbinical court consulted with a rabbi and with people whom the court sent abroad to make certain inquiries. These consultations did not require the interpretation of the facts from an expert standpoint, but rather mere assistance to the court.

The fourth difference relates to procedural aspects. Oftentimes, courts require external information in fields in which expert witnesses, in their formal definition, cannot be applied.[34] Additionally, not every *Amicus* has an expertise that is admissible in court. Unlike an expert witness, the expertise of the *Amicus* is not examined by the court, and it is not a criterion for submitting a brief.[35] *Amici* may present their

33 Like regular testimony, the parties usually have the right to examine the expert witness. In many cases, the court appoints a "neutral" expert, with or without the parties' agreement. See, e.g., L. Kaplow and S. Shavell "Accuracy in the Assessment of Damages," *Journal of Law and Economics* 39 (1996), 191.

34 *Daubert v. Merrell Dow Pharmaceuticals, Inc.*, 509 U.S. 579 (1993); D.E. Bernstein, "Expert Witnesses, Adversarial Bias, and the (Partial) Failure of the Daubert Revolution," *Iowa Law Review* 93 (2008), 451.

35 The *Amici*'s 'qualification' to submit briefs has been criticized. See, for example, M. Rustad and Th. Koenig, "The Supreme Court and Junk Social

position without relying on scientific knowledge, and even when presenting scientific knowledge, their information need not undergo a process of scientific evaluation.[36]

In conclusion, the *Amicus Curiae* practice in the rabbinical courts is not meant to substitute the use of expert witnesses who testify on the implications of facts presented to the court. Rather, it is meant to fill a legal void of a different type, relating to the receiving of legal or factual information from an external source. The lack of regulations in the rabbinical courts necessitates such a practice, even regarding the appointment of an expert witness.[37]

2. Characteristics Specific to Jewish Law and the Necessity of the *Amicus Curiae*

A Prioritizing Truth over Stability

Civil law does not consider halakhic truth as a goal, since it is not bound to the halakhah (religious law). It is bound only to the civil law, that authorizes it to decide on specific matters without ensuring that their decision conforms with any higher, mystical truth.[38] Of course, the civil judge makes an effort to uncover the substantive truth – the facts of the matter at hand, as they occurred – but once the truth is decided according to the rules of evidence, that becomes the legal truth in civil law. This legal truth replaces the substantive truth, and the case will be decided according to the former.[39]

The judge should not then be concerned if the outcome is not compliant with the meaning of the legislator. It is possible that, for the sake of values (such as privacy), the legal truth will outweigh

---

Science: Selective Distortion in Amicus Briefs," *North Carolina Law Review* 72 (1993), 91, in which the authors argue that courts in the USA must take precautions when relying on information presented by *Amici* as they can sometimes present information in an exaggerated or unreliable manner.

36 See A.O. Larsen, "The Trouble with Amicus Facts," *Virginia Law Review* 100 (2014), 1757, relating to the problematic aspects of relying on information presented by *Amici*.

37 The sole regulation we have found regarding the matter is regulation no. 82, which only relates to the expenses of witnesses and experts, while not defining the expert's role or function.

38 HCJ 130/66 *Segev v. Rabbinical Court of Zafed* 21(2) PD [1966] (Isr.).

39 See, generally, H. Cohen, *The Law* (Jerusalem: 1997), 114.

the substantive truth.[40] The court might decide to ignore evidence and refuse to determine its findings based on it if, for example, it was obtained illegally. In such a case, the court may determine the legal truth based on the evidence it was willing to allow, and base its judgment on the legal truth even though it may have reason to believe that the substantive truth would lead to a different outcome.

This is not the case in Jewish law. Legal and substantive truths may differ from each other in the Jewish law, as well; though the religious judge must do everything possible to avoid making judgment that counters the halakhah, meaning, one that contrasts the substantive truth. The Jewish law instructs the *dayan* to sidestep the legal procedures and the rules of evidence in order to uncover the substantive truth, the facts of the matter as they had occurred.[41] As Rabbi Yaakov b. Asher states, "The judges are obligated to decide according to the truth, even though the judge is not a prophet and cannot know a person's thoughts, because a scholar is preferable to a prophet."[42] Meaning, a scholar, the judge, is required to uncover the truth with the accuracy that a prophet, who can uncover the thoughts of a man.[43]

Uncovering the truth in legal proceedings is a central obligation in the halakhah. A *dayan* may not give judgment based solely on the evidence brought before him, if he suspects there is more evidence

40 For instance, when evidence is obtained illegally. see, e.g., CA 1581/92 *Avraham Avi Valentine v. Dorit Valentine* 49 (3) PD 441 [1993] (Isr.).

41 See, e.g., Maimonides, Rules of Testimony, Chapter 3, halakhah 12; N. Rakover, *Rule of Law in Israel* (Jerusalem: 1989), Chapter 4, 107 and onward.

42 Tur, *Hoshen Mishpat*, 65.

43 However, there are other opinions regarding what is the factual truth toward which the *dayan* should strive. In the words of the Talmud (bShabbat 10), Hagaon meVilna writes: "The *dayan* must be proficient in the nature of the world so that there will be no deceived judgment. If the *dayan* is not knowledgeable in these matters - no truth will come out. That is, even if he rules truth, it will not be true. Therefore, the *dayan* should be proficient in both ... wise in matters of Torah and wise in matters of the world." It can even be said that this kind of truth, to which Rabbi of Vilna refers, is easily achievable in rabbinical courts today. These courts typically structure their arbitration agreements to provide the parties with "a compromise close to the law itself," results that do not necessarily conform to the requirements of struct justice or absolute truth. Perhaps it can indeed be said that a wise man is better than a prophet because it is not factual truth alone that rabbinical courts seek, but rather a form of constructive or legal truth requiring legal analytical skills with which a prophet is not necessarily equipped.

yet to be discovered. This obligation sometimes requires that the *dayan* deviate from the rules of evidence, even if those rules are written religious rules. Moreover, in Jewish law, the judge's ruling has significant implications; thus, oftentimes, the truth will outweigh other values (such as the right to privacy). In contrast, in civil law, which prioritizes individual rights, uncovering the truth would normally be outweighed by other values that are fundamental to individual rights.[44] This reflects the inquisitorial system customarily applied in the rabbinical courts. Uncovering the substantial truth requires that the *dayan* be knowledgeable of the ways of the world, that he thoroughly examine the testimonies, inquire, investigate the facts, etc.[45]

Another distinction between Israeli law and Jewish law relates to elements considered when seeking the truth, and to the legitimacy of the outcome. The Cohen Boslik case portrays this distinction.[46] In this case, Aharon Cohen, a *cohen* (Jewish priest), and Leah Boslik, a divorced woman, married "privately" This marriage was forbidden by Jewish law, and was therefore enacted without the presence of a State-endorsed rabbi. According to Jewish law, the marriage is valid even though it is forbidden. The newlywed couple requested a declarative judgement from the District Court declaring that they are married. The District Court, in a judgment given by Judge Kister, concluded that the marriage is questionable since it was conducted in contrary to the "Jerusalem Ban."[47]

The couple appealed to the Supreme Court. Judge Zilberg delivered a judgment, in which he states that regarding the distinction between civil law and religious law, Judge Kister left the question unanswered:

> A judge must come to a final conclusion regarding the issue brought before him. From a strictly legal standpoint, a "questionable marriage" has no legal ground in the Israeli law, unlike in Jewish law. When the questionability stems from differences between legal Jewish scholars, the judge must reach a clear conclusion, as in any other legal issue.[48]

44 H. Shein, "More on the truth The Legal Law," *Parashat Neso* 319, Shaarei Mishpat Academic College Publishing (2008).

45 P. Zavihi, *Shut Ateret Paz,* Part 1, 3, 3.

46 CA 238/53 *Cohen and Boslik v. Attorney General* 8 (4) PD [1953] (Isr.). (hereinafter: Boslik case).

47 CF 4/53 *Cohen and Boslik v. Attorney General* (Oct. 4, 1953), Nevo Legal Database (by subscription) (Isr.).

48 Ibid., 21.

A judge in the civil court is authorized to decide the couples' status, and his decision is final (subject to appeal). His decision determines the legal truth, even if it differs from the substantial truth. The civil judge may not leave the issue unresolved, but must determine whether the marriage is valid. He must give an operative order to the population registry. Unlike the civil judge, though a religious judge in the rabbinical court has the authority to give a decision and determine the legal truth, he is also bound by the religious rules, and thus by the substantial truth.[49] Therefore, he may reach the conclusion that the marriage is "questionable" and leave the issue unresolved.

To summarize, the pursuit of the substantial truth is central and necessary in the Jewish law. Therefore, the *Amicus Curiae* practice is essential in the rabbinical courts as it can help uncover the truth, the central goal of the halakhah and Jewish law.

B *Res Judicata* and the Finality of the Proceedings

The priority of uncovering the truth in the Jewish law leads to another distinction between the Jewish and Israeli law. This distinction, which affects the practice of *Amicus Curiae* in rabbinical courts, is found in the Rabbinical Courts' Regulations.[50] According to these regulations, the principles of *res judicata* and the finality of the proceedings do not apply in the rabbinical courts. If new evidence comes to light, the *dayan* must retract his decision and reopen the case.

In the *Winter* case, the *dayan* Goldschmidt attempted to moderate the regulations which clash with such central principles of the civil law.[51] According to his interpretation of the regulations, the case should only be reopened if the rabbinical court ruled in contradiction to an explicit halakhah (religious rule), or if, on a matter on which the scholars disagree, the court decided according to one opinion, while the common opinion is known to be otherwise.[52] In any other case, the ruling would stand.[53]

49 See sec. 12 of the *Dayanim* Law, 1955; Y. Sinai, *Applying Jewish Law in Israeli Courts* (Tel Aviv: 2009).

50 Art. 128-129 of the Rabbinical Courts' Regulations, 1973.

51 HCJ 1/60 *Winter v. Be'eri* (Jun. 16, 1961), Nevo Legal Database (by subscription) (Isr.).

52 Maimonides, Sanhedrin, Chapter 6, 2.

53 *Shulchan Arukh*, Hoshen Mishpat, 25, 1-2; Rema, ibid., 3; Sm"a, ibid., 14; Sha"kh, ibid., 14.

The *dayan* Goldschmidt explains that in rabbinical courts, it is customary for the *dayan* to ask the litigants, at the end of the arguments, whether they have any additional arguments or evidence. Once the litigants answer that they have nothing to add, the court does not accept any more arguments.[54] Judge Goldschmidt argued that it is rare that a litigant requests to contradict a ruling, either due to a mistake in halakhah, or due to new evidence relating to facts. According to judge Goldschmidt, reopening a case in which the judgement is based on a mistake in halakhah, where it contradicts the common opinion, or in light of new evidence (if this evidence was not available to the litigant during the proceedings), does not contradict the principle of *res judicata*.[55]

While we do not disagree with the above, we think that this demonstrates how the pursuit of the truth is prioritized in rabbinical courts, even over legal certainty. The halakhah requires the *dayan* to uncover the truth, even if this means reopening a case that has already been concluded and the legal truth determined. This differs from civil law which prioritizes legal certainty and stability over truth. Some have argued that rabbinical courts require the authority to reopen a case because of Jewish law posits that one rabbinical panel does not inquire into another's decision, and that Jewish law does not accept the appeal procedure.[56] Therefore, Jewish law authorizes the *dayan* to retract his own judgement. These religious rules strengthen the need for *Amicus Curiae* to assist the rabbinical court in uncovering the truth in the first instance.

C The Expertise Required of the *Dayanim*

Another aspect of Jewish law that points to a need of the *Amicus Curiae* practice in rabbinical courts, one that also has to do with the pursuit of the truth, is the requirement of the *dayan* to be well-versed in the ways of the world and not solely in the halakhah. The *dayanim* must be educated, and acquire knowledge in medicine and science, to be able to base their

54 Judge Goldschmidt refers to regs. 65 and 68 of the Rabbinical Courts' Regulations, 1960. The relevant regulations today are regs. 72-74 of the Rabbinical Courts' Regulations, 1993.

55 *Winter* case, note 51 above.

56 R. Yaakobi, "Hahatira laemet ve'irurim bevatei hadin harabaniim" ['The Uncovering of the Truth and Appeals in Rabbinical Courts'] (Hebrew)," *Parashat Vayera* 398 (2012). Regional rabbinical courts are not obligated to decide according to the rulings of the State rabbinical court, reg. 5(d) of the Ethical Regulations for *Dayanim* (2008); HCJ 214/64 *Basan v. Rabbinical Court* 18 (4) PD 309 [1964] (Isr.).

decisions on their own knowledge and not on that of expert witnesses.[57] This requirement is emphasized by the centrality of the truth in the Jewish law and the need to give judgement based on the substantial truth.

Moreover, rabbinical courts have recently faced several issues and matters which they had never faced before. These new matters require expertise and knowledge, and oftentimes also the assistance of sources external to the panel. For example, technological advances raise complex, new issues,[58] on which the rabbinical courts need to decide.[59] In order to properly manage these new matters, the rabbinical courts should develop new practices, primarily the *Amicus Curiae*.

3. Existing Practices in Rabbinical Courts for Obtaining Information from Sources External to the Panel

A Consulting an Outstanding Scholar

In this practice, unique to the rabbinical courts and Jewish law, the court turns to a scholar, not involved in the judicial system, for his opinion on whether the court's decision is correct in terms of the halakhah. This usually consists of turning to a highly considered authority in the Jewish law, in order to receive a kind of public approval for the judgement. This practice is foreign to civil law, as the civil court's ruling is always correct.[60]

Not only does Jewish law allow consultations with scholars external to the panel, it requires it:

> If the *dayanim* have a question regarding the case, they can ask and they do not need the litigants' permission to do so. The one providing the answer will answer directly to the *dayanim* and not to the litigants. This is because the litigants argue before the *dayanim* and not before the person providing

57 Maimonides, Sanhedrin, chapter 2, 1.

58 Some argue that technological developments are redefining human activity. See J. Tidmarsh, "Unattainable Justice: The Form of Complex Litigation and the Limits of Judicial Power," *George Washington Law Review* 60 (1992), 1683; L.H. Rosenthal, J.C. Francis, and D.J. Capra, "Managing Electronic Discovery: Views from the Judges," *Fordham Law Review* 76/1 (2007), 2.

59 See, e.g., Case 1123955/1 *Plonit (minor)* (Nov. 6, 2017), Nevo Legal Database (by subscription) (Isr.).

60 D. Heshin, "Hityaatzut shoftim" ['Judge Consultations'] (Hebrew), *Parashat Hukat* 350 (2009).

> the answer... Rather, the *dayanim* encounter a question and ask a scholar greater than them what the halakhah or the right answer is, and therefore the litigants should not mind that the scholar was asked.[61]

Moreover, a *dayan* who chooses to not consult a scholar greater than himself, but to rely solely on the ruled halakhah, is considered wicked. Such a *dayan* is viewed as one who doesn't take responsibility for his judgement and imposes it on his predecessors.[62]

A case from the rabbinical court in Safed is a good example of this practice.[63] In this case, the husband was badly injured and was hospitalized for seven years. The husband was not functional and there was no way to communicate with him. The *dayanim* visited him in the hospital and heard the doctors' expert opinions on his state.[64] The rabbinical court ruled to permit the woman to remarry, by "stepping into the husband's shoes" and becoming his messengers to divorce the woman, using the rule "*zakhin le'adam shelo befanav*" ('one can act in a person's interest in his absence'), allowing one to accept or do a positive thing for another without their presence or knowledge.[65] Realizing that this ruling is rather innovative and precedential, the *dayanim* consulted, *ex ante*, in writing, other scholars who were considered "outstanding scholars."[66]

At the basis of the Safed rabbinical court's use of this practice was *Arukh HaShulhan*'s statement that a *dayan* should not decide based on his own opinion alone but should consult with other scholars. According to him, a *dayan* who bases his decision solely on his own opinions is "reprimanded from above."[67]

Later, an anonymous person, unrelated to to the case, submitted

61 *Arukh HaShulkhan*, Hoshen Mishpat, 13, 11.

62 Maimonides, Sanhedrin, chapter 20, 8; Ba"ch, Hoshen Misphat, 10.

63 Case 861974/2 *Plonit v. Ploni* (May 20, 2014), Nevo Legal Database (by subscription) (Isr.) (hereinafter: the *Safed* case).

64 HCJ 9261/16 *Plonit and Mevoy Satom Organization v. Great Rabbinical Court in Jerusalem* (Mar. 30, 2017), Nevo Legal Database (by subscription) (Isr.).

65 mEruvin 7, 11; Talmudic Encyclopedia, "*Zakhin laadam shelo befanav*," vol. 12, 135; M. Vigoda, *Shlichut* ['Agency'] (Hebrew), (Jerusalem: 2014), 769 and onward.

66 The *Safed* case, note 63 above. As far as we know, the outstanding scholar's opinion was not submitted in writing and was therefore not passed on to the litigants.

67 *Arukh HaShulhan* 17, 139.

a request to the rabbinical court of Safed to retract its decision.[68] The court denied the request, while stating that it is possible for a scholar to present objections or halakhic remarks relating to the legitimacy of the *get* (Jewish divorce document), under special circumstances, even though the scholar is not a formal party.[69] Meaning, the consultation of a scholar is required even after judgement has been given.

This kind of practice does not exist in the civil court.[70] The rabbinical court bases its statement on the Mahar"ik, who writes that even though one should not case aspersion upon the *get* (according to Rabbeinu Tam),[71] that restriction stands only in cases where the petitioner lacks established arguments for his request. However, a scholar who considers the rabbinical court's judgement to give a woman a *get* problematic is obligated to discuss his concerns with the court.[72] He is obligated toward Rabbeinu Tam's *dictum*, even at the risk that a new *get* must be enacted.

The rabbinical court dismissed the request and argued that objections relating to the *get* should be discussed with the rabbi who issued it, not by publicly speaking against it and questioning its legitimacy and effectiveness.[73]

This matter demonstrates that, through the pursuit of the truth, the rabbinical courts often consult scholars external to the panel, both to hear their conclusion on the facts of the case and to receive the public's approval (at least among the religious communities) of their judgements.[74]

B Court Trustee

Rabbinical courts receive factual information from external sources also

68 Case no. 86194/3 *Almoni v. Plonit and Ploni* (July 20, 2014) Nevo Legal Database (by subscription) (Isr.).

69 Ibid.

70 This, unlike the appeal procedure and the request for a further hearing procedure which are subject to certain deadlines. See sec. 18 of Basic Law: The Judiciary; and sec. 30 of the Courts' Law.

71 Mordechai, bGittin, *siman* 37. In Y. Colon Trabotto, *Sefer she'elot uteshuvot Mahar"ik* (Venice: c.1440-1480), 455.

72 Ibid.

73 Case 86194/3, note 68 above.

74 Case 970523/3 *Plonit v. Ploni* (Mar. 8, 2017), Nevo Legal Database (by subscription) (Isr.); Case 1082582/1 *Ploni* (July 27, 2016), Nevo Legal Database (by subscription) (Isr.).

through additional practices. One such practice is the "court trustee," in which the court appoints someone to take judicial actions in its place. For example, an appeal to revoke an inheritance order that the court granted to the defendants was submitted to the rabbinical court in Haifa.[75] The plaintiff claimed that the defendants, nephews of the deceased, received the inheritance by fraud, claiming that the deceased had no children. According to the plaintiff, the deceased was his father.

The rabbinical court appointed Rabbi Birnbaum as a trustee, to hear testimonies of those who knew the deceased and his wife, examine the validity of the deceased's and the plaintiff's documents, as well as photographs and any other material that could establish the claim and uncover the truth.[76] The rabbinical court did not refer to any specific regulation authorizing it to appoint a trustee who could independently obtain factual information. Rabbi Birnbaum's appointment as a trustee, charged with locating documents and bringing them before the court was understandable. However, this practice is unique to the rabbinical courts, where a trustee is appointed to examine witnesses in a foreign country and report his opinion of the testimonies to the court. The trustee seemingly becomes a "portable rabbinical court," coming in place of the *dayanim* to hear the witnesses and examine their testimonies.

The trustee's opinion was delivered to the litigants, who submitted their objections. The court passed the objections on to the trustee, who answered them, upon which another round of comments commenced. The trustee, Rabbi Birnbaum, did not appear in court, did not give testimony or present his opinion on the testimonies, and was not examined. The defendants requested a hearing of the evidence, in which they would examine the trustee. The rabbinical court replied that there was no basis for examining the trustee. According to the *dayanim*, Rabbi Birnbaum was appointed by the court as a trustee and was given detailed instructions regarding the information needed. They further stated that Rabbi Birnbaum did his job well, and the court saw no need to examine him on his opinion, considering the clear and persuasive manner in which he answered all objections.[77]

The rabbinical court's reply is not convincing. It is well known that any story can be presented in several manners. Any person, even an expert, sometimes "completes" the story on his own, using his life

75 Case 8732941/1 *Ploni v. Plonim* (Apr. 22, 2015) Nevo Legal Database (by subscription) (Isr.).

76 Ibid.

77 Ibid., 9.

experience, point of view, culture, etc. Thus, any testimony should be questioned until it withstands the cross-examination.[78] Nonetheless, the court accepted the claim and revoked the inheritance order given to the defendants several years earlier. This practice of appointing a trustee, is common in rabbinical courts,[79] although its validity and basis in Jewish law is unclear.

C Rabbinical Court Expert on Judaism Inquiries

Rabbinical courts can also appoint a court expert on the issue of determining a person's status as Jew to receive information from sources external to the panel. This is not an expert witness, rather someone whose role is unclear and ill-defined.[80] The District Rabbinical Court had to decide whether a certain woman is Jewish. The findings were received from the relevant foreign consul and given to the head of Judaism inquiries department in the rabbinical court's administration. The rabbinical court called the woman in for an inquiry, first sending her to Dr. Reiz, the rabbinical court expert on Judaism inquiries among immigrants from the USSR.[81] The woman's counsel requested the expert's academic certificate. The rabbinical court replied:

> Dr. Reiz's expertise in Judaism inquiries is unquestionable. Dr. Reiz examines thousands of cases each year and has accumulated extensive experience in the field. His caution and ability to present recommendations one way or another assists the court in its decision.[82]

The woman's counsel appealed to the Great Rabbinical Court and requested to deem the panel disqualified for determining the validity of the expert's findings prior to testimony and cross-examination. The court brought the request before the rabbinical court's legal advisor, who answered that there is no right to examine a rabbinical-court-appointed

78 Y. Levitt, *Cross-Examination* (1991); N. Zeltsman, "Early Testimony, Written Statement and the Cross-Examination in Criminal Law," *Iyunei Mishpat* 8 (1981), 584.

79 Case 32743/15 *Ploni v. Plonit* (May 21, 2015) Nevo Legal Database (by subscription) (Isr.); Case 273965/5 *Ploni v. Plonit* (Jun. 24, 2003) Nevo Legal Database (by subscription) (Isr.).

80 Case 7894-62-1 *Plonit v. Rabbi Asher Rentroyi* (Apr. 1, 2008) Nevo Legal Database (by subscription) (Isr.).

81 Ibid.

82 Ibid., 4.

expert. The rabbinical court's opinion on the witness' expertise cannot be used as grounds for disqualification. The court accepted the legal advisor's arguments and denied the request. The Great Rabbinical Court accepted the legal advisor's reasons as well, stating that:

> The rabbinical court, as any court, is entitled to appoint an expert without the litigants' approval. The court-appointed expert is more objective than one appointed by a formal party, who understandably anticipates a certain outcome. Normally, the court will rely on the expert's opinion and his findings and will not deviate from them without extraordinary factual or legal reason to do so. The preferable status of the court-appointed expert also means that he should not be examined on his opinion, without the court's permission.

The Great Rabbinical Court further wrote:

> Dr. Ze'ev Reiz – the rabbinical courts administration expert on the genealogy of *olim* (immigrants) from the USSR – is not a formal party, nor an external expert or one appointed by a party. He is employed by the rabbinical court's administration, as an officer of the court, to inquire into issues in this field. For many years, rabbinical courts have been assisted by professionals in fields that require specific professional knowledge. In any case, the authority to decide is the rabbinical court's solely. Courts employ various professionals, including legal assistants and assistance units. Judges are assisted by them regularly, even though the final decision remains in the court's hands.

The appeal was denied.[83] The statement above grants the expert a special status, wherein the parties could be prevented from cross-examining him, or even submitting a counter opinion.

It is interesting that in all the cases mentioned above, not once did the court reference a halakhic source that supports this type of practice. In addition, the court did not reference any regulation supporting or authorizing such a practice. Indeed, the court's statement has some reason. However, the counter argument – such as the litigants' agreement on the expert, or at least the opportunity to question the opinion – has reason and is supported by law. We further discuss this

83 Case 897216/14 *Ploni v. Plonit* (Jun. 27, 2018) Nevo Legal Database (by subscription) (Isr.).

issue in the following chapter.

D *"Yada Arikhta"* (the 'Long Arm')

Rabbinical courts also use a practice called the "*yada arikhta*" (literally, the 'long arm'), meaning, an officer of the court. The *Plonit* case addressed the status of social workers, employees of the Assistance Units.[84] The rabbinical court calls these experts the "long arm" of the court. They submit briefs and recommendations that are not judicial decisions, but professional recommendations. The court then decides whether to adopt the recommendations in full or dismiss them altogether, all the while acting in the child's best interest.

The social workers do not receive the high status of the Court Expert or Court Trustee, whose opinion is not usually examined.

In another case, the rabbinical court addressed the Welfare Services briefs. The Welfare Services are not part of the Assistance Units. The rabbinical court stated that these briefs are an exception to the rule of evidence, since they are, in fact, hearsay, and constitute an opinion submitted in a manner that does not comply with halakhic principles. However, the law considers the case workers trustworthy as they are professionals.[85]

The rabbinical court considers the testimony of a social worker problematic as it is hearsay, even though, in the other practices mentioned above, it seems to allow such testimony without hesitation. Using the *yada arikhta* practice to receive the assistance of external sources can be found in the *Plonit* case.[86] In this case, the rabbinical court addressed the matter of a private investigator desecrating the Sabbath, who had even installed a camera during the Sabbath. The camera documented the married woman acting inappropriately with a third party. The rabbinical court accepted this testimony, reasoning that even one who desecrates the Sabbath does not give false testimony. The court further stated that investigators are not witnesses *per se*, but rather assistants to the court in its pursuit of the truth. Since their testimony is supported by evidence, others are discouraged from contradicting it.

84 Case 897196/3 *Ploni v. Plonit* (May 15, 2017) Nevo Legal Database (by subscription) (Isr.).

85 Case 582804/1 *Plonit v. Ploni* (Sep. 2, 2010); *compare*, Case 1004499/4 *Ploni v. Plonit* (Apr. 7, 2016) Nevo Legal Database (by subscription) (Isr.).

86 Case 863355/1 *Ploni v. Plonit* (May 17, 2017) Nevo Legal Database (by subscription) (Isr.).

In another case, the court addressed the status of a court expert during a hearing regarding a child-related dispute in arbitration.[87] The rabbinical court provided that in matters relating to children, social workers are the experts, are appointed as the court's "long arm" or as officers of the court.[88]

Rabbinical courts have also used this practice when using a polygraph machine, stating that though the results of a polygraph test are not considered verified evidence, the polygraph expert is an officer of the court relating to the questions provided by the court. Therefore, refusing to respond to the court's questions as asked by the polygraph expert is viewed as if the defendant refused to respond to questions asked directly by the court.[89]

In conclusion, rabbinical courts commonly use the court trustee, court expert, and *yada arikhta*, alongside the consultation with an outstanding scholar, to receive legal and factual information from sources external to the formal proceedings. The rabbinical courts sometimes view the expert as a *yada arikhta*, as an officer of the court, and at other times do not. The distinction between an court officer, court trustee, court expert, and others, is unclear. What exactly is their purpose? What is the legal basis for these practices? Are they professional experts, or rather "mobile rabbinical courts"? These questions and more are at the center of the following chapter.

4. The Problems with the Rabbinical Courts' Existing Practices

The rabbinical courts use several practices, all of which are meant to help obtain legal or factual information from outside the panel. The first practice is the consultation with an outstanding scholar.[90] The second and third practices are "court trustee" and "court expert," both of

87 Case 970523/9 *Ploni v. Plonit* (Feb. 26, 2017) Nevo Legal Database (by subscription) (Isr.).

88 Ibid.; see also CA 627/89 *Reicher v. Reicher* (Dec. 31, 1989) Nevo Legal Database (by subscription) (Isr.).

89 Case 190175/15 *Ploni v. Ploni* (Apr. 22, 2012) Nevo Legal Database (by subscription) (Isr.); Case 190175/3 *Ploni v. Plonit* (May 15, 2017) Nevo Legal Database (by subscription) (Isr.); also Case 970523/9 *Ploni v. Plonit* (Feb. 26, 2017) Nevo Legal Database (by subscription) (Isr.); Case 1120357/2 *Religious Council of Safed v. Safed-Meiron Sfardi Poorhouse* (Mar. 7, 2018); Case 364474/1 *Plonit v. Ploni* (Apr. 30, 2009) Nevo Legal Database (by subscription) (Isr.).

90 *Plonit* case, note 63 above.

which are used mainly for obtaining factual information not provided by the litigants. The fourth practice is the use of professionals, in fields that require specific professional knowledge (such as case workers), as officers of the court (*yada arikhta*).

These practices are desirable in Jewish law as they assist the rabbinical court in the pursuit of the truth. They have many advantages, but also seem to raise various problems: ethical issues, problems relating to the rules of evidence, and clashes between the rabbinical courts and the adversarial system. Though the rabbinical courts apply Jewish law to matters in which the law authorizes them to do so, they are generally perceived to be bound by the rules of evidence and order of judgement of the civil law. The rabbinical court cannot relieve itself of the customary procedural rules of civil law. For example, the rabbinical court cannot accept testimony obtained through a violation of the Eavesdropping Law, 1979,[91] even though Jewish law permits it.[92] Moreover, it cannot accept testimony obtained through a violation of privacy, although the rabbinical court permitted it.[93] For example, the rabbinical court is obligated to respect "basic principles of just trials" and of "human rights" when applying interim remedies.[94]

A Ethical Issues

According to Israeli law, a judge is forbidden to consult with an external source, and may be disqualified for doing so. Similarly, a *dayan's* consultation with an external source can also, under certain circumstances, lead to his disqualification.[95] The case that first dealt with this was the *Terifus* case from 1951,[96] in which it was decided that a judge is prohibited from consulting with an external source, and this may even lead to his disqualification.

91 *Sefer Hahukim* (Israel's official Lawbook), 938.

92 HCJ 1135/02 *Vezgiel v. Great Rabbinical Court*, 56 (6) PD 14, 22 [2002] (Isr.).

93 HCJ 6650/04 *Plonit v. Netanya District Rabbinical Court*, 61 (1) PD 581 [2006] (Isr.), at par. 36 of Judge Barak's decision.

94 HCJ 3914/92 *Lev v. Tel-Aviv District Rabbinical Court*, 48 (2) PD 491, 503-504 [1994] (Isr.).

95 See, e.g., HCJ 152/51 *Terifus v. Attorney General*, 6 PD 17, 26. [1951] (Isr.).

96 Ibid.

Half a century later, the Israeli Supreme Court affirmed this decision in the *Ben Shushan* case.[97] Israeli law prohibits any consultation of a judge with an external source on any matter that requires expertise in a field that is not clearly and entirely legal. The case-law did not address the question of consultation with a legal expert on a purely legal question. However, as the late judge Haim Cohen writes in his book, *The Law*: "It is well known that, nowadays, judges do not consult, and are prohibited from consulting, even with their Rabbi... Judicial consultation is conducted solely within the judicial panel; it is all-right for a judge to consult someone external to the panel, on a legal question."[98] Meaning, judge Haim Cohen thinks that consultation with anyone external to the panel is prohibited.[99]

In other words, the current practice of the rabbinical courts, and especially where this practice is unknown to the litigants and they cannot voice their objections or present a counter opinion, can raise ethical issues, and, according to some scholars, even lead to the disqualification of the *dayan*.

B Problems Relating to Rules of Evidence

Some of the practices described above raise problems relating to evidence law. For example, when an outstanding scholar is consulted, he does not directly hear the witnesses and their cross-examinations, and probably does not look through their documents. He hears the details of the case indirectly from the *dayan*, which constitutes hearsay, and is therefore impermissible in civil law. As opposed to the trial court *dayanim*, the outstanding scholar does not have access to information garnered from the witnesses' facial expression, body language, etc. He cannot receive answers to his questions, as the witnesses only appear before the *dayan*.[100] According to the hearsay evidence rules, hearsay

97 HCJ 2672/01 *Ben Shushan v. The State of Israel*, 55 (4) PD 794, 797 [2001] (Isr.).

98 H. Cohen, *The Law* (Jerusalem: 1997), 241.

99 See, generally, M. Ben Dror, "Setting Rules for Judicial Conduct," *Hamishpat* 13 (2002); *American Bar Association Model Code of Judicial Conduct* (2007); B.P. Goldman, "Should the Supreme Court Stop Inviting Amici Curiae to Defend Abandoned Lower Court Decisions?," *Stanford Law Review* 63 (2011), Note, 909–11.

100 E. Harnon, *Law of Evidence A* (1970), 28; Sh. Elbak, *Mavo lamishpat ha'Ivi beyimei haTalmud* ['Introduction to Talmudic Time Jewish Law'] (Hebrew), (Ramat Gan: 1999), 332.

evidence is inadmissible if it is presented to prove the truth of the matter asserted. There are three main concerns regarding the credibility of a statement that consists of hearsay. First, that the person who had originally provided the statement, insulated from cross-examination, is not credible. Second, that the original statement is ambiguous, and even if not, its contents cannot be verified. Third, even if the person providing the statement is credible, and the statement is unequivocal, the contents of the statement may be unrealistic, for various reasons.[101]

In addition to the problems stated above, the scholar's opinion is not available to the formal litigants, and therefore they cannot dispute, refute, or disprove it, or submit a counter opinion. Furthermore, albeit some may argue that this does not constitute an injustice, as this practice has been common for many years, it appears to be an injustice. Modern law (and the rules of natural justice) grants the litigants the right to demand, and receive, all relevant information before the verdict.[102]

Moreover, the other practices used by rabbinical courts also raise problems relating to evidence. The court trustee and the court expert, who had supplied the court with information, did not appear in court, did not give testimony, did not present their impression of the testimonies, and were not exposed to cross-examination by the litigants.[103] For instance, the rabbinical court determined that the court expert on Judaism inquiries is neither a formal party to the proceedings nor an expert witness.[104] According to the court, the expert is employed by the rabbinical court's administration for professional issues, and the parties do not have the right to examine him. The Evidence Order authorizes the court to admit as evidence, in writing, the opinion of an expert in fields relating to science, research, art, or other professional knowledge, as well as a doctor's opinion regarding a person's medical state.[105] The Evidence Order further provides that the court is authorized to order the examination of the expert, and will do so upon a party's

101 N. Ben Tor, *Hearsay Evidence Rule and its Exceptions*, Vol. 1 (2005), 166.

102 Compare the known saying: "Justice must be seen to be done"; *Sefer Hamitzvot*, negative commandment 281.

103 There are three common purposes for cross-examination: a positive purpose, to obtain evidence in favor of the client; and two negative purposes, to weaken the evidence against the client by disproving key elements in the testimony and to destroy the opponent's testimony by refuting his credibility.

104 Case 7894-62-1, the *Plonit* case, note 80 above.

105 Sec. 20 of the Evidence Order [new version] (1971).

request.[106] Meaning, litigants have the right to examine any expert who submits an opinion relating to their case.

The practices of court trustee and court expert are not in full compliance with the rules of evidence. If they are a type of expert witness, why are they not susceptible to cross-examination? Why are the formal parties unable to object to their appointment or status, one that is somewhat equivalent to that of the court? In addition to these difficulties, the use of these practices does not comply with the Rabbinical Courts' Regulations that set clear procedural rules relating to such issues, which are quite similar to hearsay.[107]

C The Conflict between the Rabbinical Courts and the Adversarial System

Some of these practices point to a conflict with the adversarial system. For example, the court trustee is, in essence, a third and unrelated party, not appointed by the litigants or with their approval, conducting examinations and hearing testimonies that seem relevant to him. This is somewhat of a "mobile rabbinical court" (although it is not the court itself, but someone appointed by it).[108] This practice defies the adversarial nature of Israeli law. In Israeli law, including all tribunals bound by it, the judge serves as a passive authority who arbitrates between two parties who are solely responsible for presenting evidence to the court.[109] In an adversarial system, the judge's role is, generally, to give a verdict after ensuring due process and deciding upon the admissibility of the evidence brought before him. This is unlike the inquisitorial system, common in Europe, in which the judge has an active role in managing the process and obtaining evidence (including evidence that the parties refrained from presenting to the court).[110] There is a debate regarding

106 Sec. 26 of the Evidence Order [new version] (1971).

107 Reg. 68 of the Rabbinical Court's Regulations 1993.

108 Moreover, the formal litigants are not present during the testimonies and cross-examinations.

109 See, generally, R. Cooter and L. Kornhauser, "Can Litigation Improve the Law without the Help of Judges?," *The Journal of Legal Studies* 9/1 (1980), 139-63.

110 It is important to say that the US federal rule of procedure authorizes the court to appoint neutral, court-appointed expert witnesses. In this example, an inquisitorial aspect is shown to be part of an adversarial process. In truth, no system is entirely either one or the other, but is rather some hybrid combination along the adversarial/inquisitorial continuum.

the character of Jewish law, and many consider it more inquisitorial than adversarial.[111] However, it seems that the rabbinical court has gone too far with the inquisitorial approach, sending a third party to conduct the proceedings in its place in the absence of the formal parties.

In conclusion, the rabbinical courts use several practices to acquire information external to the panel: consultation with an outstanding scholar; appointing a court trustee; consulting a court expert; and the use of *yada arikhta*, professionals who serve as officers of the court. We have discussed the necessity of these practices in the rabbinical courts and their pursuit of the truth. However, rabbinical courts sometimes act as though it is the court that is responsible for obtaining evidence, rather than the formal parties, even appointing a third and unrelated party to obtain evidence. This conduct conflicts with the very basis of the adversarial system and raises a series of issues, including ethical ones, as well as problems relating to rules of evidence and conceptual problems relating to the system applied in rabbinical courts.[112]

5. Justifications for Integrating the *Amicus Curiae* in Rabbinical Courts

The characteristics of Jewish law, especially the centrality of the pursuit of truth and the halakhah, lead to the use of several practices that assist the rabbinical court. In our opinion, adopting the *Amicus Curiae*, in a specialized model adapted to the rabbinical courts, and in accordance with the procedural rules suggested below, can help resolve some of the problems raised by these practices.

First, the *Amicus Curiae* will serve as an appropriate practice for obtaining factual and legal information from sources external to the judicial panel, in a transparent manner. The *Amicus Curiae* can help minimize some of the problems mentioned in the previous chapter. Formally integrating the *Amicus Curiae* practice in the rabbinical courts can help bridge the gap between religious law and civil law.

111 See A. Shochetman, *Order of Judgment in Rabbinical Courts* (2011), 1013; A. Weis, "Behanhagat beit hadin klapei ba'alei hadin" ['The Rabbinical Court's Conduct Towards the Litigants'] (Hebrew), *Kovetz Darkei Horaa* (2006).

112 See, generally, R. David and J.E.C. Brierley, *Major Legal Systems in the World Today*, 2nd ed. (1978); M.A. Eisenberg, *The Nature of the Common Law* (1991); P.H. Rubin, "Why is the common law efficient?," *The Journal of Legal Studies* 6/1 (1977), 51-63; L.S. Simard, "An Empirical Study of Amici Curiae in Federal Court: A Fine Balance of Access, Efficiency, and Adversarialism," *The Review of Litigation* 27 (2008), 669.

Second, rabbinical courts are now facing new, complicated issues, that require extensive knowledge and expertise. We discussed how the *dayan* must be well-versed in various areas and should not have to rely solely on the witnesses. Considering the accelerated modern development and the high resolution of innovative, intricate, new fields of knowledge, it is difficult to expect the *dayanim* to be educated in all developing fields. The *Amicus Curiae* can assist the *dayanim* accomplish their work. The neutral *Amicus*, unbiased, not appointed by any of the parties, could be the expert where the *dayan* is not.

Third, the rabbinical court has trouble delineating the legal status of the professionals it appoints – employees of the rabbinical court, researchers of Judaism, and the outstanding scholars whom it consults – although their necessity to the rabbinical court's work is undeniable. Formally adopting the *Amicus Curiae* in rabbinical courts, alongside procedural rules tailored to the rabbinical court, can provide a suitable solution for the legal status of such practices.

The rabbinical court's reasons in the *Plonit* case,[113] where they refuse one party's request to cross-examine the court expert, can be applied to the use of the Classic *Amicus Curiae* practice in rabbinical courts. The "Classic *Amicus*" (the neutral *amicus*) is not a formal party, nor is it an expert who speaks on behalf of one of the litigants. The *amicus* is a third party, external to the proceedings, whose purpose is to assist the court, independently and objectively, on professional matters that require certain expertise. When making use of the *Amicus Curiae* practice, the final decision remains solely in the court's hands. Adopting the *Amicus Curiae* practice would regulate the existing legal status and would increase transparency, since details of the consultation would be available to the litigants. Formal use of the *Amicus Curiae* would resolve most of the problems listed in the previous chapters.

Fourth, adopting the *Amicus Curiae* practice will go a long way toward establishing procedural justice and enhancing the appearance of justice in the rabbinical courts.[114] Hearing the positions presented by different *Amici* (such as women's rights organizations or non-Orthodox rights organizations), even when not necessarily acceding to their position, may increase the appearance of justice in the rabbinical

113 Note 80 above.

114 See T.R. Tyler, "Psychological Perspectives on Legitimacy and Legitimation," *Annual Review of Psychology* 57 (2006), 375.

courts. The mere willingness of the court to hear the *Amici* reflects its appreciation of these people, leading to a greater acceptance of their subsequent judgement.

6. An Outline for the Regulation of the *Amicus Curiae* Practice in Rabbinical Courts and the Potential Critique of that Regulation

The rabbinical courts have designed various practices to assist them in the pursuit of truth. However, these practices raise several difficulties. Integrating the *Amicus Curiae* practice in the rabbinical courts in a tailored model, similar to the "Classic" model, may solve some of these issues. This practice is appropriate for the character of the halakhah, the basis of the rabbinical courts. In this model, the *Amicus* is a third, unbiased party, unrelated to the proceedings, usually an expert, who independently and objectively advises the court on a certain matter. A true friend, if you will, of the court, meant to serve only the court itself, and no one else.

Prior to suggesting an amendment to the Rabbinical Courts' Regulations, designed to formally integrate the *Amicus Curiae* practice in the rabbinical court, we must determine the status of these regulations and the procedural manner with which to amend them. According to Judge Rubinstein, every court has the authority to determine its own procedure; thus, the rabbinical courts have the authority to do so as well. However, once the procedure in the rabbinical courts has been determined, albeit not formally constituting primary or secondary legislation, the courts are bound by it. According to Judge Zilberg, the Rabbinical Courts' Regulations are legally binding, even if they are not published in the *reshumot* (gazette of Israeli laws). Judge Rubinstein states that the status of the Rabbinical Courts' Regulations should be considered similar to that of the Civil Procedure Regulations.[115]

Therefore, amending the regulations is not subject to an intricate procedure but is in the hands of the rabbinical courts themselves. We therefore suggest adding to chapter 6 of the Rabbinical Courts' Regulations (defining the course of the hearing), after reg. 60, the following excerpt:

115 HCJ 9261/16 *Plonit v. Great Rabbinical Court of Jerusalem* (Mar 30, 2017) Nevo Legal Database (by subscription) (Isr.).

> **Friend of the Rabbinical Courts**
>
> The president of the rabbinical court, or the head of the panel, is authorized, in an ongoing proceeding, to request that a third party, not a formal party and unrelated to the proceedings, submit a written brief, appear in court, or perform other actions in the court's name and according to its directive, in any matter perceived by the court as necessary, all in the name of justice or of the public interest.

This excerpt could provide solutions to most of the problems described in the previous chapter and assist the court (in particular, rabbinical courts in Israel) in its pursuit of truth. Also, this regulation would allow the application of some of the practices already used by rabbinical courts, as described above. This unique model of the *Amicus Curiae* is tailored to the rabbinical courts, their procedure, their conduct and goals, which differ from those of the civil courts. The suggested outline would allow a rabbinical court in need of professional expertise or external assistance on a factual or legal issue to obtain the information from a third party, unbiased and unrelated to the proceedings, independently and objectively. The suggested outline would allow the rabbinical court to receive legal-halakhic assistance from the *Amicus*, via a written brief or expert opinion. For example, through formal use of the *Amicus* practice, the rabbinical court could request an expert opinion from an outstanding scholar, while this opinion would be transparent and available to the formal litigants, who would be permitted to present a counter-opinion or request clarifications.[116]

Third parties could assist the court with factual information, as well, so long as the information is fully disclosed to the litigants. The court could appoint an *Amicus Curiae* to collect statements from abroad. This *Amicus* would be authorized to perform additional actions to assist the court. Unlike the current practices used in the rabbinical court, actions performed by the *Amicus* would be disclosed to the formal parties who would be allowed to confront them. We should clarify: we do not mean that the appointment of an *Amicus* by the rabbinical

116 Our proposed regulation could permit the use of an advisory opinion, whereby one rabbinical court panel could consult a different, duly assembled rabbinical court (as distinct from consulting a single outstanding scholar or expert), though the parties should be notified of such utilization and be provided with a copy of any written ruling relied upon, at least in circumstances where the litigants' names or identities are disclosed the advisory rabbinical court.

court requires the parties' consent.[117] We think that it is sufficient that the rabbinical court appoints an *Amicus* with reliable discretion, while granting the formal litigants rights regarding this appointment. First, unlike the case with the current practices, the formal parties would be allowed to question the *Amicus* and present a different opinion, thus undermining his opinion. Second, if they feel that the rabbinical court violated their rights by their appointment of *Amici*, the formal litigants would be allowed to submit an appeal.[118]

In addition, we suggest supplementing the above regulation by specifying the powers of the "friend of the rabbinical court." For example, the appointed *Amicus* would, if relevant, describe his relationship with the formal parties. It is also worth considering a regulation that would determine the budgetary source for financing these *Amici* (if necessary). We believe that at this initial stage, the *dayanim* should be allowed some flexibility to design the practice, and, after some time, further examine the issue.

Moreover, formally integrating the *Amicus Curiae* practice may help prevent third parties, who represent the interests of one of the formal parties or of other interested parties, from joining. It may also help exclude parties who have a direct interest in the case's outcome. *Amici* who present their interests to the court, such as non-governmental religious organizations with a certain point of view, would be acceptable; however, it is hard to see how an *Amicus* that represents the interest of one of the formal litigants would assist the court in its pursuit of truth.[119]

117 This is the custom in additional courts from around the world when appointing a neutral *Amicus*. See, e.g., *R (E.) v. Governing Body of JFS* [2009] UKSC 15, [2010] 2 AC 728 (appeal taken from England), in which the court addressed the question "Who is a Jew," and Lord Phillips appointed Jewish organizations as *Amici* to better understand the matter at hand. In international law, courts sometimes appoint *Amici* without receiving the parties' consent. See D. Berg, "The Limits of Friendship: The Amicus Curiae in Criminal Trial Courts," *Criminal Law Quarterly* 59 (2012), 67.

118 See, e.g., 25880-01-16 *Liberman v. The Reform Center for Religion and State* (2.9.2016).

119 The reality in some courts worldwide proves this notion. See, e.g., *Jaffee v. Redmond*, 518 U.S. 1, 35–36 (1996), in which Judge Scalia criticizes the growing pressure of *Amici* on judges, as this might lead to a distortion of justice. This view is part of the critique in the USA that calls for a more moderate use of *Amici*. Larsen, "The Trouble with Amicus Facts."

Our suggestion is not immune to criticism. One might argue that the current practices used by the rabbinical courts to obtain information from external sources may suffice. These practices have been in use since the founding of the rabbinical courts in Israel, and no criticism has been voiced. This serves as evidence that they are "tolerable." A potential answer to this critique is that the question of whether someone has criticized these practices or refuted them is irrelevant. Moreover, whether these practices have been criticized or not, the outline suggested above ameliorates the current legal status and somewhat ensures the litigants' rights.

To summarize this point: although the critique is reasonable, rabbinical courts could, through the flexibility of the proposed regulation, appoint *Amici* for the various uses for which the current practices are used.

In our opinion, when appraising the integration of the *Amicus Curiae* practice in the rabbinical courts, given the potential concerns and critiques, the advantages outweigh the disadvantages. Adopting the *Amicus Curiae* practice in rabbinical courts would provide a fitting solution to the difficulty of obtaining information, both factual and legal, from sources external to the judicial panel, and would do so transparently. The *Amicus Curiae* could serve as a legal bridge between the religious law and the civil law. Furthermore, this practice would assist the court in its work, *inter alia*, by providing it with the knowledge and expertise in areas it needs but lacks. In addition, our suggestion would effectively resolve the legal status of the existing practices currently used by rabbinical courts. Finally, our suggestion may increase the legitimacy of the rabbinical courts by making their judicial process more transparent.

Conclusion

This article addressed the formal integration of the *Amicus Curiae* practice in rabbinical courts. We believe that in the rabbinical courts (and in particular, rabbinical courts in Israel) – unlike in the adversarial system, in which the *Amicus* usually serves a certain agenda – the *Amicus* should serve in its literal meaning, as a neutral friend, assisting the court objectively and independently. In contrast to the civil law, the rabbinical courts' main goal is to uncover the substantial truth, subject to the halakhah. In addition to this goal, many of the cases recently brought before the rabbinical courts raise intricate issues in which the *dayanim* are not experienced. To properly do their jobs, they often need assistance that cannot be provided by the litigants.

In other cases, mainly ones that can have extensive implications and involve *halakhicly* controversial matters, the *dayanim* like to consult with outstanding scholars that are not part of the judicial panel. They do this for several reasons: First, the religious rule provides that they are obligated to consult with outstanding scholars more knowledgeable than themselves. Second, such a consultation provides them with additional validity towards certain groups in society. Alongside the development of the neutral and professional *Amicus,* we foresee that interest groups may wish to influence the rabbinical courts' decisions as *Amici* (but not in the neutral sense).

Dayanim use a series of practices to obtain independent information, such as "court trustees," "court expert," etc. However, the existing practices raise an array of difficulties relating to ethics, rules of evidence, and conceptual problems relating to the characteristics of the rabbinical court. On the other hand, formally integrating the *Amicus Curiae* practice in a tailored and adapted model, especially adapted for the Israeli Rabbinical Courts' Regulations, may resolve some of these issues and assist the rabbinical court in its work.

The Jewish Law Annual, Vol. XXII

Complicity and Accessory, Aiding and Abetting: The Contribution of Jewish Law to the Doctrine of Accomplice Liability

Yishai Kiel*

Introduction

Around midnight of March 3, 2008, three young men challenged each other to a dangerous car race through the streets of Jerusalem. During this race, one of the vehicles crashed, an accident that resulted in the death of two of the three men. The participant who remained alive was charged with manslaughter for the reckless killing of his two friends and with endangering human life in a traffic route. The first instance court acquitted the defendant of manslaughter, reasoning that, despite his reckless state of mind, he could not be deemed the proximate/legal cause of his friends' death since they had willingly and autonomously exposed themselves to danger. Nevertheless, the court found him guilty of the lesser offense of endangering human life in a traffic route. This ruling was overturned at the appeal to the Supreme Court, which found the defendant guilty of manslaughter by a majority of 2:1, with Justice Hendel dissenting. In a further hearing held by an expanded panel, the Supreme Court overturned the decision of the appellate panel by a majority of 6:1 and reaffirmed the ruling and reasoning of the first instance court.[1]

In his dissenting opinion on the appellate panel and concurring opinion in the further hearing, Justice Hendel turned to Jewish law

* Yishai Kiel, Ph.D. (Talmud and Iranian Studies, 2011; Hebrew University) and Ph.D./LL.D. (Law, 2020; Hebrew University) is currently an associate at Meitar Law Offices, specializing in civil and commercial litigation as well as international arbitration and cross-border dispute resolution. Kiel was a lecturer at Yale University and the Hebrew University of Jerusalem.

1 See Criminal Appeal 9647/10 (335/11) *John Doe v. State of Israel* (3.1.2013); Further Criminal Hearing 404/13 *John Doe v. State of Israel* (15.4.2015).

as a source of inspiration for his legal opinion which delved into the intricacies of criminal causation.[2] In this context, he explains that Jewish law distinguishes between a strict standard of "pure causation" (קשר סיבתי טהור) and a more lenient standard of "practical causation" (קשר סיבתי מעשי).[3] The strict standard of pure causation stemming from the classical-hermeneutic system of rabbinic criminal law necessitates the perpetrator's actions be the sole, intentional, direct, and unmediated cause of the death of another. "Practical causation," by contrast, is a more lenient standard that is, more or less, similar to contemporary standards of causation. While rabbinic law requires "pure causation" to determine the perpetrator's liability to death by the court, this does not mean that in the absence of such a standard, he or she is to be set free. If the standard of "practical causation" is met, the court can label the perpetrator a murderer and punish them by an array of practical punitive measures.[4]

2 See par. 15 of Hendel's dissent on the appeal and par. 4 of his concurrence in the further hearing. See also M. Vigoda, "Manslaughter Charges in the Case of a Participant in a Car Race," Department of Jewish Law, Ministry of Justice (11.6.2014 [updated 18.1.2016]) (Hebrew).

3 For this classification see, e.g., Maimonides, *Sefer Hamitzvot* ['The Book of Commandments'], negative commandment, 290. See also Criminal Appeal 10023/06 *Toalbo v. State of Israel* (Nevo 9.12.2009) par. 9 (Hendel).

4 For the Jewish standard of causation see, e.g., Maimonides, *Mishneh Torah, Nezikin, Rotzeah ushmirat hanefesh,* 2:1-2: "If anyone killed another with his own hand, as when he struck him down with a sword or a deadly rock, strangled him to death or burned him alive, he must be executed by the court, because at any rate, he murdered a person by himself. On the other hand, if a person hired a murderer to kill somebody, or sent servants to kill him, or tied him up and put him in front of a lion or similar beast and it killed him, and also if an individual attempted suicide, each of these is guilty of shedding blood and bears the crime of murder; he deserves to die by an act of God, but is not executed by the court". On the bifurcated nature of Jewish criminal law see below in detail. For now, see Maimonides, *Mishneh Torah, Nezikin, Rotzeah ushmirat hanefesh,* 2:4-5: "And of these and similar murderers, who are not sentenced to death by a court, might be put to death by a royal decree if a Jewish king desires this for the benefit of society… If the king did not have them executed, if circumstances did not demand such a measure, the court must, at any rate, have them lashed to the point of death, and harshly imprisoned for many years, punishing them severely in order to terrify and frighten other criminals, so that this may not turn into a pitfall and a snare for others to say: 'I will arrange to kill my enemy indirectly as did so-and-so, and I will be acquitted.'".

Taking his cue from Jewish law, Hendel likens his ruling to that given by a Jewish court that finds a perpetrator responsible for the death of another by the standard of "practical causation," but not by the standard of "pure causation." He reasons:

> "Jewish law succeeded in providing an adequate solution, in accordance with practical policy considerations, but without ignoring the guiding light of the 'ideal' law. It is likewise in this case. The exemption from the charge of manslaughter does not indicate an exemption from criminal sanction. The offense of endangering human life in a traffic route is simply more applicable to the case at hand. Determining that one person caused the death of another is one thing, but determining guilt as per a particular criminal offense is another."

Notably, Hendel did not attempt to implement any particular Jewish norm in the case he adjudicated. Rather, he consulted Jewish law's taxonomy of causation for inspiration and analogy. In that sense, he was not interested in the practical punitive measures offered by the Jewish tradition to resolve situations in which the strict standard of "pure causation" is not met, yet the standard of "practical causation" is satisfied, as much as he was fascinated by the multifaceted classification of the very standard of causation and the bifurcated nature of the Jewish criminal justice system at large.[5]

In the present article, which posits a causation-based approach to criminal complicity, I similarly turn to the fountain of Jewish law and, more specifically, to its intricate taxonomy of causation as a source of dialogue and inspiration. I argue that the distinctions emerging from the classical Jewish tradition between different types of accomplices and accessories to crime—distinctions that are formed along the lines of causation, and particularly the classification of "essential" vs. " non-essential" forms of complicity and the doctrine of aiding and abetting, are important sources of reference and dialogue for contemporary discussion of criminal law.

Its distinctive features notwithstanding, Jewish criminal law contains important doctrines, principles, and analytical distinctions

5 For the position that Jewish law should generally be consulted by Israeli courts as a source of inspiration, dialogue and analogy see, e.g., B. Porat, *A Proposal to Amend the Foundations of Law Act, with an Analysis and Critique* (Jerusalem: 2016), 41-6 (and references to previous scholarship). More will be said on this matter below.

which can be constructively abstracted from the particular religious and normative contexts in which they are couched, and serve more broadly as important references for contemporary discussion of criminal justice. In what follows, I hope to demonstrate that the rabbinic causation-based classification of accomplice liability can serve as a model for a long-anticipated reform of the Anglo-American law of criminal complicity.

A Theory of Criminal Complicity

Criminal complicity constitutes a distinct and theoretically problematic area within criminal law.[6] The doctrine of accomplice liability, as it is often understood today (especially in the context of Anglo-American legal systems), enables the State to hold individuals liable for crimes they did not commit, as long as they aided, assisted, abetted, encouraged, or influenced the perpetrator,[7] doing so with the required mental state.[8]

6 The literature on accomplice liability is vast. For a general orientation see, e.g., G.P. Fletcher, *Rethinking Criminal Law* (Oxford: 2000 [1978]), 634-82; S.H. Kadish, "A Theory of Complicity," in *Issues in Contemporary Legal Philosophy: The Influence of H.L.A. Hart,* ed. R. Gabison (Oxford: 1989), 287-303; G. Hallevy, *Complicity in Criminal Law* (Tel Aviv: 2008) (Hebrew); C. Kutz, "The Philosophical Foundations of Complicity Law," in *The Oxford Handbook of Philosophy of Criminal Law,* eds. J. Deigh and D. Dolinko (Oxford: 2011), 147-65. See also M.S. Moore, "Causing, Aiding, and the Superfluity of Accomplice Liability," *University of Pennsylvania Law Review* 156 (2007): 395-452, where he argues for the superfluity of accomplice law; the various justifications proposed for accomplice liability based on other criminal doctrines simply suggest that accomplice liability can and should be reduced to existing doctrines.

7 See, e.g., Model Penal Code § 2.06(3): "A person is an accomplice of another person in the commission of an offense if: (a) with the purpose of promoting or facilitating the commission of the offense, he (i) solicits such other person to commit it; or (ii) aids or agrees or attempts to aid such other person in planning or committing it; or (iii) having a legal duty to prevent the commission of the offense, fails to make proper effort so to do; or (b) his conduct is expressly declared by law to establish his complicity"; and 18 U.S.C. § 2(a) (2012): "Whoever commits an offense against the United States or aids, abets, counsels, commands, induces or procures its commission, is punishable as a principal."

8 The *mens rea* requirement for accomplice liability is widely debated. See, for example, S.H. Kadish, "Reckless Complicity," in *Journal of Criminal Law & Criminology* 87 (1997): 369-94; A. Rogers, "Accomplice Liability for Unintentional Crimes: Remaining Within the Constraints of Intent," *Loyola of Los Angeles Law Review* 31 (1998): 1351-86; R. Weisberg, "Reappraising

Thus, the furnishing of essential or non-essential instrumentalities of a crime, or the provision of significant or insignificant services in the course of the commission of a crime, are generally regarded as a form of complicity. Under the doctrine of accomplice liability, the accomplice is perceived as if he or she were the same as the principal, and is thus held liable for the completed offense.[9]

Scholars have long challenged the doctrine of complicity, as perceived and practiced in many contemporary jurisdictions, as both legally incoherent and morally problematic.[10]

1. First, unlike a single perpetrator of an offense, as to whom the prosecution must establish the presence of all elements of the crime—i.e., the *actus reus* and *mens rea* requirements—an accomplice is essentially "stripped" of his/her individuality and is constructively held liable for the actions of another. There seems to be an underlying presumption at play according to which the principal and accomplice constitute a single entity, jointly fulfilling the *actus reus* requirement, without regard to the individual actions of each.[11] Indeed, it seems intuitively wrong to convict one person for another's actions.[12]

Complicity," *Buffalo Criminal Law Review* 4 (2000): 217-81; B. Weiss, "What Were They Thinking?: The Mental States of the Aider and Abettor and the Causer Under Federal Law," *Fordham Law Review* 70 (2002): 1341-490; and S. Girgis, "The Mens Rea of Accomplice Liability: Supporting Intentions," *Yale Law Journal* 123 (2013): 460-95.

9 For this understanding of accomplice liability see below, in detail.

10 For a broad critique of the Anglo-American doctrine of accomplice liability see, e.g., J. Dressler, "Reassessing the Theoretical Underpinnings of Accomplice Liability: New Solutions to an Old Problem," *Hastings Law Journal* 37/1 (1985): 91-140; J. Dressler, "Reforming Complicity Law: Trivial Assistance as a Lesser Offense?" *Ohio State Journal of Criminal Law* 5 (2008): 427-48; A. Kaiserman, "Against Accomplice Liability," in J. Gardner et al. (eds.), *Oxford Studies in Philosophy of Law: Vol. 4* (Oxford: 2021), 124-55.

11 See Dressler, "Reforming Complicity Law," 433 ("...the accomplice and the principal are treated as if they were one; the law ignores their separate identities. It is for this reason that the principal and accomplice are treated alike in terms of guilt and punishment—after all, as far as the law is concerned, they are one and the same person."); *State v. Curry*, 636 S.E.2d 649, 654 (S.C. App. 2006): "[If] a crime is committed by two or more people who are acting together in committing a crime, the act of one is the act of all."

12 See Kaiserman, "Against Accomplice Liability," 130: "[T]here is, I think,

2. Second, the doctrine of accomplice liability essentially relinquishes the requirement of factual causation (that is, "cause-in-fact" as opposed to "legal causation"). This means that the perpetrator is deemed a "but-for cause" or at least a "sufficient cause" of the offense, a critical feature in the attribution of criminal liability.[13] Indeed, one can be held liable to a criminal offense simply by providing inconsequential and trivial assistance to the principal, even when he or she are neither a "but-for cause" nor a "sufficient cause" of the crime.[14]

---

a more fundamental problem with accomplice liability. Regardless of the details of the case, it is, quite simply, morally wrong to convict someone of a crime they did not commit. Paradigmatically, we praise or blame moral agents for what they, and they alone, have done, and not for what others to which they are somehow related have done; the criminal law should reflect this foundational aspect of common-sense morality"; and see ibid., at n. 27: "That's why the criminal law, unlike the civil law, has no general doctrine of vicarious liability, for example, whereby employers are held liable for the actions of their employees— 'they must each answer for their own acts and stand and fall by their own behaviour.' "

13 For a general discussion of causation in the law see, for example, H.L.A. Hart and T. Honoré, *Causation in the Law*, 2nd ed. (Oxford: 1985); T. Honoré, "Causation in the Law," *Stanford Encyclopedia of Philosophy*, http://plato.stanford.edu/entries/causation-law/; J. Stapleton, "Law, Causation and Common Sense," *Oxford J. Legal Studies* 8 (1988): 111-31; idem, "Legal Cause: Cause-in-Fact and the Scope of Liability for Consequences," *Vanderbilt Law Review*, 54 (2001): 941–1000; idem, "Unpacking Causation," in P. Cane and J. Gardner (eds.), *Relating to Responsibility* (Oxford: 2001), 145-85; idem, "Choosing What We Mean By 'Causation' In The Law," *Missouri Law Review* 73 (2008): 433-480; and R. Goldberg (ed.), *Perspectives on Causation* (Oxford: 2011).

14 For the need to reform complicity law based on the principles of causation, see esp. Dressler, "Reassessing" and Dressler, "Reforming Complicity Law." Cf. S. Kadish, "Complicity, Cause, and Blame: A Study in the Interpretation of Doctrine," *California Law Review* 73 (1985): 323-410, who argues that causation cannot possibly be a prerequisite for accomplice liability since one cannot be the "cause" of something that involves the voluntary intervention of another person. Since the actions of an accomplice are, by definition, accompanied by the principal's voluntary conduct, there is simply no role for causation in complicity law. Voluntary human action "serves as a barrier through which the causal inquiry cannot penetrate" (ibid., 336). Kadish relies here on Hart and Honoré's distinction between voluntary human conduct, on the one hand, and non-human and involuntary human conduct, on the other hand, insofar as the definition of causation is concerned. This limited definition of causation, however, was

3. Third, the doctrine of accomplice liability, as practiced in many jurisdictions, lacks sensitivity to degrees of involvement and participation in the commission of a crime. Rather than providing a graded and nuanced scale of complicity that distinguishes between major and minor accomplices and between various forms of aiding and abetting, complicity law in most Anglo-American jurisdictions remains binary.[15] Although the degree of involvement is considered at the sentencing stage, we must keep in mind that "justice in the criminal law isn't simply a matter of proportionate sentencing; it's also a matter of fair labelling. We should ensure, as far as possible, that 'offences are subdivided and labelled so as to represent fairly the nature and magnitude of the law-breaking.'"[16]

4. Fourth, the doctrine of criminal complicity as it stands is also too restrictive, in the sense that it creates a dependency between the liability of the principal and that of the accomplice. The liability of the accomplice is seen as parasitic and derivative, an assumption which precludes accomplice liability when the principal cannot be convicted for some reason.[17]

To solve these moral and legal difficulties, scholars have offered several theoretical frameworks to account for the doctrine of complicity. Certain scholars have suggested that an accomplice should be held liable on the basis of a loose analogy from the civil doctrine of agency. According to this line of reasoning, the perpetrator is regarded as the accomplice's agent in executing the crime, thus justifying the latter's responsibility. As pointed out, however, this analogy is problematic, as it sidelines important differences between the civil principle of agency and the criminal principle of complicity.[18] A more nuanced (although

---

convincingly questioned by other scholars.

15 Dressler, "Reforming Complicity Law," 433: "[C]omplicity law is binary: a person is or is not an accomplice. Legally speaking, there is no such thing as a 'major' or 'minor' accomplice".

16 Kaiserman, "Against Accomplice Liability," 127-8: "If we take this principle at all seriously, it's hard to justify a system that charges a person who commits a violent, unprovoked, premeditated killing and the person who looks after their dog while they do it with the same crime, regardless of how much judicial discretion we allow in sentencing decisions."

17 See, e.g., Kadish, "Complicity, Cause and Blame," 328; Kaiserman, "Against Accomplice Liability," 128-30.

18 See Dressler, "Reforming Complicity Law," 433-4, quoting F.B. Sayre, "Criminal Responsibility for the Acts of Another," *Harvard Law Review* 43

no less problematic) articulation of this theory suggests that accomplice liability rests on the premise of a "forfeited personal identity," meaning that by aiding and abetting the perpetrator, an accomplice effectively surrendered his "autonomy" in the sense of the right to be judged according to his own actions.[19]

Others have suggested that criminal complicity is essentially a risk-based, not harm-caused, doctrine. The basis for accomplice liability rests not on the responsibility of an accomplice for the actions of another, but on his/her reckless behavior, which creates, in and of itself, an unjustified risk to society that another person would commit an offense.[20] In fact, it is often said that joint criminal activity is even more dangerous, and poses a greater risk to society, than crimes committed by single perpetrators, insofar as gravity and scope are concerned.[21] This explanation, to be sure, lends itself mainly (albeit not exclusively) to instrumentalist theories of criminal punishment (aimed at deterrence and crime-reduction) and is thus somewhat less amenable to retributivist theories of punishment.[22]

(1930), 695: "[B]etween the two fields of law [complicity and civil agency] there seems utter disparity of thought"; Kadish, "Reckless Complicity," 369; Kadish, "Complicity, Cause, and Blame," 354-55; L. Alexander, "Insufficient Concern: A Unified Conception of Criminal Culpability," *California Law Review* 88 (2000), 944-7.

19 See the critical remarks in Dressler, "Reassessing," 111: "Ordinarily a person is held criminally responsible for his own actions. However, when an accomplice chooses to become part of the criminal activity of another, she says in essence, 'your acts are my acts,' and forfeits her personal identity. We euphemistically may impute the actions of the perpetrator to the accomplice by 'agency' doctrine; in reality we demand that she who chooses to aid in a crime forfeit her right to be treated as an individual. Thus, moral distinctions between parties are rendered irrelevant. We pretend the accomplice is no more than an incorporeal shadow."

20 See, e.g., D. Yaeger, "Helping, Doing, and the Grammar of Complicity," *Criminal Justice Ethics* 15 (1996), 25-35; Kutz, "The Philosophical Foundations," 150: "[T]he normative justification for accomplice liability generally is the risk-enhancing character of aiding or encouraging another's criminal efforts"; A.P. Simester, "The Mental Element in Complicity, *Law Quarterly Review* 122 (2006), 600: "...judgments about culpability must be reconciled with the demands of criminalization."

21 See, e.g., Y. Rabin and Y. Vaki, *Dine Onshin*, 3rd ed. (Tel Aviv: 2014), vol. 1, 591.

22 See Kutz, "The Philosophical Foundations," 149-50. One might argue, however, for some form of intent-based or risk-based retributivism. See,

As many intuitively believe that complicity, like criminal law in general, should essentially be based (even if not exclusively) on retributivist theories of punishment and the concept of desert, and since civil notions of vicarious liability and agency seem to be inadequate analogies for criminal complicity, it seems that the moral and legal difficulties inherent in contemporary complicity law can only be resolved by properly amending the existing doctrine to conform to the fundamental demands of causality, desert, and proportionality. Several scholars have called for a reform of Anglo-American accomplice law that will "adequately distinguish in terms of liability and punishment between accomplices who are critical parties to a crime—e.g., ringleaders, people who provide essential services or criminal instrumentalities, or who are otherwise deeply embedded in the criminal enterprise—and accomplices whose involvement is peripheral."[23] It has further been proposed along these lines to adopt a statutory distinction between "causal" and "non-causal" accomplices: "[C]ausal accomplices (persons but for whose assistance the offense would not have occurred) could continue to be convicted of the offense committed by the principal; non-causal accomplices would be convicted of a lesser offense and punished accordingly."[24]

Similar considerations have led certain jurisdictions to adopt a statutory distinction between an accomplice, whose liability is matched to that of the principal, and an accessory who merely aids and abets the principal, whose maximum penalty is set at half of the penalty set out for the principal. Israel is a case in point. In 1994, Israel adopted such a distinction in the context of amendment no. 39 to its Penal Law of 1977. According to Section 32 of the amended provision: "The [maximum] penalty for being an accessory (מסייע) to the commission of an offense is half the penalty set by enactment for committing the main offense."[25]

---

e.g., Yaeger, "Grammar of Complicity," 31-3; A. Ashworth, "Criminal Attempts and the Role of Resulting Harm under the Code and in the Common Law," *Rutgers Law Journal* 19 (1988), 735.

23 Kaiserman, "Against Accomplice Liability"; Dressler, "Reforming Complicity Law"; Dressler, "Reassessing."

24 Dressler, "Reforming Complicity Law," 429-30. As we shall see, however, a "causal" accomplice need not be defined strictly as a "but-for cause" of the completed offense. Suffice it that he meets the standard of "sufficient cause" of the completed offense.

25 Section 32 of Israel's Penal Law, 1977. The Section continues: "[H]owever, if the penalty set is – (1) the death penalty or mandatory life imprisonment, then the penalty shall be twenty years imprisonment; (2) life imprisonment,

The statutory distinction between an accomplice and an accessory facilitated, in turn, a scholarly debate regarding the analytical nature of this distinction. Certain scholars argue that an accomplice should be defined as a full-fledged *participant* in the commission of a crime as opposed to an accessory who merely *enables* the commission of a crime;[26] while others suggest that an accomplice should be defined by his or her possession of *functional control* over the execution of the criminal plan, a factor absent in an accessory who merely aids and abets a crime.[27] Still others suggest isolating the acts of each participant. If, in and of themselves, they amount to criminal attempt, the participant should be defined as an accomplice. If, however, the acts remain in the sphere of preparatory acts that do not amount to criminal attempt, the participant should be classified as an accessory.[28] Finally, certain scholars argue that an accomplice, as opposed to an accessory, should be defined by his or her participation in the *early stages of the criminal planning*.[29] In the absence of such involvement, the acts of a participant only constitute accessory to crime.

The literature offers analytical distinctions to classify accomplices and accessories, that are "academic" in nature, and might have little to

---

then the penalty shall be ten years imprisonment; (3) a minimum penalty, then the penalty shall not be less than half the minimum penalty; (4) any mandatory penalty, then it shall be the maximum penalty and half thereof shall be the minimum penalty." Section 31 of the same law defines an accessory (מסייע) as follows: "If a person does anything – before an offense is committed or during its commission – to make its commission possible, to support or protect it, or to prevent the perpetrator from being taken or the offense or its loot from being discovered, or if he contributes in any other way to the creation of conditions for the commission of the offense, then he is an accessory." Contrary to an accessory, the maximum penalty set out for one who entices (משדל) another to commit an offense ("if a person causes another to commit an offense by means of persuasion, encouragement, demand, cajolery or by means of anything else that constitutes the application of pressure") is equal to that of the principal. See Section 30 of Israel's Penal Law, 1977.

26 A. Enker, "On the Distinction between a Principal Offender and an Accessory," *Mehkare Mishpat* 17 (2002), 339-46.

27 M. Kremnitzer, "The Principal Actor in Criminal Law – A Sketch," *Plilim* 1 (1990), 73-75. Cf. the discussion of this theory in Hallevy, *Complicity*, 294-301.

28 M. Gur-Aryeh, "Complicity and not Causation, Principal and not Accomplice," *Mishpatim* 11 (1981), 522-3.

29 Hallevy, *Complicity*, 317-23.

do with the actual decisions of courts in concrete cases.[30] Nevertheless, they seem to reflect an important assumption about the nature of criminal law in general, and that of accomplice liability in particular. The very attempt to create a classification of various grades of complicity supports a basic intuition that it is morally wrong to group together different kinds of accomplices and treat them as if they were one and the same. Accomplice liability, like criminal law in general, should be founded first and foremost on the principles of retributivism and desert, wherein people should be held liable and morally responsible for their own actions, not for the actions of others.

I believe that the statutory distinction between an accomplice and an accessory should be interpreted along the lines of the "causation approach" to complicity law outlined above. Without denying the "practical" tests suggested in the literature to differentiate an accomplice from an accessory, I posit that, from an analytical perspective, an accomplice should be defined in terms of his causal contribution to the offense. This means that the court should consider whether the accomplice was a "but-for cause," without whose contribution the offense would not have taken place, or a "sufficient cause," one whose contribution was substantial or essential (though perhaps not a necessary cause), of the offense. An accessory, by contrast, should be defined as one whose contribution to the completed offense is trivial or non-essential and does not qualify as actual causation.

In what follows, I argue that a causation-based taxonomy of criminal complicity and the distinction it fosters between essential and non-essential accomplices/accessories are rooted in the classical Jewish tradition. As such, Jewish law can serve as an important source of reference and dialogue for contemporary discussions of accomplice liability. Jewish law not only illuminates the theoretical underpinnings of the statutory distinction set out in Israel's Penal Law, between an accomplice and an accessory, but can also serve, more broadly, as a model for a thorough reform of Anglo-American accomplice law. By making this case, I hope to reinforce the significance and potential contribution of the Jewish tradition to the development of contemporary law, not only in the field of civil law but also in areas such as criminal

30 See M. Gur-Arye, "Complicity – Amendment no. 39 to the Penal Law in the Light of Judicial Decisions," in E. Lederman (ed.), *Directions in Criminal Liability: Inquiries in the Theory of Criminal Law* (Israel Bar Association and Tel Aviv University: 2001), 90-9, who argues that the theoretical distinctions made by scholars and the courts have, as a matter of fact, little weight on the actual decisions of the court.

law, in which the Jewish and Western traditions exhibit fundamentally different assumptions. The distinctive vantage point offered by Jewish criminal law notwithstanding, the Jewish tradition contains important doctrines, principles, and analytical distinctions which can be constructively abstracted from the particular religious and normative contexts in which they are couched, shedding light on contemporary discussions of criminal justice.

A Comparison of the Jewish and Western Traditions

Jewish law generally exempts offenders who act together to complete an offense, be it a criminal offense in the modern sense or a ritual violation punishable by a Jewish court.[31] The exemption of joint offenders can be understood both in terms of scriptural exegetical determinations and in terms of the criminal doctrine of doubt and the principle of factual causation. Either way, the rabbis *did not* provide a blanket exemption for joint offenders, as is often assumed.[32] On the level of doctrine, the rabbis made important distinctions, in the context of joint offenders, between divisible and indivisible acts, concurrent and consecutive acts, and between acts that can be performed by a single offender (but were carried out jointly) and those which necessitate a joint effort (either doctrinally or factually). The early rabbis, moreover, did not present a unanimous front on the matter of accomplice liability, but rather differed on several points. Finally, in the sphere of "pure" criminal offenses—and especially in the context of homicide—the exemption of joint offenders was often understood in a more limited fashion as exemption from punishment by the court, in accordance with the classical-hermeneutic system. Joint offenders were still labelled as such, however, and were punished through a variety of extra-doctrinal channels of the criminal justice system.

As early as the tannaitic period, the rabbis grappled with different

31 Throughout this article, I use the term "criminal" in reference to Jewish law in a broad sense, which also encompasses the sphere of ritual violations (e.g., violations of the laws of the Sabbath) punishable by the court. As we shall see, there are important distinctions made in the Jewish tradition between the application and enforcement of "pure" criminal law (especially regarding cases of homicide) and the application and enforcement of ritual violations of the law. That said, at least on the classical-hermeneutic level, the differences between "pure" criminal offenses and ritual violations are blurred.

32 Cf. S. Albeck, *Yesodot Haavera Bedinei HaTalmud* (Ramat Gan: 1997), 38-42; Hallevy, *Complicity*, 50.

permutations of complicity, but it is not until the Babylonian Talmud that clearer analytical distinctions between "essential" accomplices (defined as either "but-for causes" or "sufficient causes" of the completed offense) and "non-essential" accessories to crime (who merely aid and abet the principal in a trivial manner) emerge.[33] In this context, while certain rabbinic authorities hold an essential contributor to joint criminal activity liable for the completed offense (pending certain factors), the non-essential acts of an accessory (*mesayea*), which merely aid and abet the principal in trivial and inconsequential ways, are legally "insignificant" (*ein bo mamash*) and do not inherently incur liability.[34]

There are, obviously, important differences between the rabbinic taxonomy of essential and non-essential complicity and contemporary attempts to define accomplices and accessories. First, the Talmud *exempts* "non-essential" participants on the level of doctrine,[35] whereas Western law goes as far as *reducing* the liability and punishment of an accessory in relation to a full-fledged accomplice. Second, unlike the prevailing assumption in Western law, according to which accomplice liability is essentially equal to that of the principal, the rabbis, as we shall see, exempt not only non-essential accessory to crime (*mesayea*), but also certain types of accomplices.

Moreover, the disparity between the Jewish and Western traditions runs deeper. Certain scholars have argued that, insofar as criminal law is concerned, the Jewish and Western traditions are so fundamentally

33 For the Babylonian Talmud's heightened tendency towards conceptualization, theorization, and legal abstraction, see L. Moscowitz, *Talmudic Reasoning: From Casuistics to Conceptualization* (Tübingen: 2002); S. Friedman, *Talmudic Studies: Investigating the Sugya, Variant Readings and Aggada* (New York and Jerusalem: 2010), 117-26.

34 The category of *mesayea* is discussed in bShabbat 93a-b and bBeitza 22a. For the definition of *mesayea* see below in detail. For now, see the limited definition offered by Rabbi Shlomo Itzhaki's commentary on bShabbat 93a: "A person who merely aids in an act, but if he were to perform it by himself he would not be able (to complete it); such an act is (legally) insignificant and has no (legal) consequences."

35 For the precise meaning of "exemption" see below. As we shall see, at least in the sphere of "pure" criminal offenses, and particularly in the context of homicide, the exemption of joint offenders means that they are exempt (on a doctrinal level, as expressed through the classical-hermeneutic system) from corporal punishment by the court. However, they are still labeled as offenders and may be punished through a variety of practical channels of criminal justice (such as temporary measures).

different that any attempt to compare them is fraught with difficulty.[36]

1. First, Jewish criminal law, at least in its classical-hermeneutic articulation, is largely impractical and was never designed (be its historical *Sitz im Leben* as it may) to serve as a stand-alone criminal justice system.[37] The procedural and evidential requirements for a condemnatory verdict according to the classical system are so unrealistic and unattainable that they seem to have been primarily designed to acquit the defendant in a criminal trial, especially where capital offenses are involved. Consequently, Jewish criminal law assumed a bifurcated form, in which the classical-hermeneutic system was complemented by practical measures of enforcement, such as the "law of the king" (משפט המלך), "temporary orders" (הוראות שעה) issued by the court, and imprisonment (כיפה). Considering its impracticality, the classical-hermeneutic system is often described, not as a criminal justice system, but as an educational program aimed at the indoctrination and internalization of religious values.[38]

36 See, for example, A. Enker, *Fundamentals of Jewish Criminal Law* (Ramat Gan: 2007), 23-74, who discusses the disparity between the Jewish and Western approaches to criminal justice. The author agrees, however, that in certain areas, such as criminal defenses, a comparison of the two traditions is warranted, as he himself presents in the second part of the book; M. Kremnitzer, "Proposals to Amend the Foundations of Law Act: Harm without Benefit, A Response to Benjamin Porat's Paper on the Place of Jewish Law in Our Legal System," in B. Porat, *A Proposal to Amend the Foundations of Law Act*, 101-3 (regarding the incompatibility of Jewish law and the Israeli legal system, especially insofar as criminal and public law are concerned).

37 I will not address the historical question of when and under what circumstances Jewish criminal law became impractical. I assume, as do many others, that the criminal justice system as described by the classical rabbis is primarily a theoretical and literary construct that serves theological and ideological purposes.

38 See, e.g., bYevamot 90b, bSanhedrin 46a; Maimonides, *Mishneh Torah, Nezikin, Rotzeah ushemirat hanefesh*, 2:1-5; Rabbi Nissim of Gerona, *Derashot HaRan*, chapter 11; Enker, *Fundamentals*, 23-74; A. Kirschenbaum, *Jewish Penology: The Theory and Development of Criminal Punishment Among the Jews Throughout the Ages* (Jerusalem: 2013), 42-82; Y. Brand, "The Law of the King in the Sermon of Rabbi Nissim of Gerona: Philosophy, Halakhah, and Polemics," *Zion* 75/4 (2010), 393-425.

2. Second, Jewish and Western criminal law differ with regard to the main purpose and rationale of criminal punishment. Western law criminalizes and punishes behavior that is perceived as harmful and dangerous to society, to deter and prevent future criminal behavior. Jewish law is religious in nature and, as such, views criminal punishment, *inter alia*, as a form of atonement, which manifests religious and theological values in its implementation and execution.[39] As such, liability in Jewish criminal law hinges on the level of sin involved in the particular offense as well as the degree of perceived defiance of God and of the system's core values.[40]

3. Third, being a religious legal system (in contrast to Western criminal law), Jewish law has the "luxury" to defer punitive measures to God. Indeed, the rabbis delineate a variety of death-worthy offenses, the penalty for which is to be carried out by God and not by the court, through the mechanism of *karet* and *mita bidei Shamayim* (Divine extirpation).[41]

Given the general disparity between the Jewish and Western approaches to criminal law, scholars have argued that group criminality should be viewed through the lens of the fundamentally diverging approaches of the two traditions to criminal justice. According to this view, the Western tradition understands group criminality as presenting a risk

39 See, e.g., Kirschenbaum, *Jewish Penology*, 553-66; On p. 125, Kirschenbaum writes: "punishment theory [in classical Jewish criminal law] is educational-deterrence-based insofar as the public and rehabilitative-atonement-based insofar as the person being punished"; Aharon Shemesh, "An Offer God Can't Refuse: The Punishment of Flagellation in Rabbinic Theology," in *Divine Wrath and Divine Mercy in the World of Antiquity*, eds. Reinhard G. Kratz and Hermann Spieckermann (Tubingen: Mohr Siebeck, 2008), 231-8; Yair Lorberbaum, *Image of God: Halakhah and Aggadah* (Tel Aviv: Schocken, 2004), 335-44.

40 See esp. Enker, *Fundamentals*, 23-74.

41 See G. Blidstein, "Halakha: The Jewish Normative World," in A. Berholtz (ed.), *Journey to the Halakhah* (Tel Aviv: 2003), 33-4. For the nature of *karet* see A. Shemesh, *Punishments and Sins from Scripture to the Rabbis* (Jerusalem: 2003), 57-100. See also D. Weiss, "Divine Concessions in the Tanhuma Midrashim," *Harvard Theological Review* 108 (2015), 80-3; C. Hezser, "Geldbußen, Peitschenhiebe und göttliche Vernichtung: Rabbinische Strafdrohungen in der Mischna," *Zeitschrift für Altorientalische und Biblische Rechtsgeschichte* [Journal for Ancient Near Eastern and Biblical Law] 20 (2014), 212-4.

to society, perhaps even greater than that presented by individual criminal behavior and therefore seeks to prevent and deter such behavior by means of criminalization and punishment of a broad range of complicit behavior. By contrast, Jewish law, in line with its religious features, views the actions of an accomplice or accessory (especially when playing a relatively minor role in the criminal activity) as not subversive enough to warrant punishment by the court. This, either because they are perceived as somewhat less sinful, less defiant of God and the core values of the system, or simply because they do not meet the hermeneutic-interpretive threshold of liability.[42]

Despite these challenges, it seems that there are important doctrines and principles imbedded in Jewish criminal law in general, and in the sphere of complicity law in particular, that can contribute to contemporary discussion. Legal scholars and jurists have turned to Jewish criminal law to illuminate contemporary issues in fruitful and innovative ways, whether as implementation, inspiration, or analogy. They turned to Jewish criminal law for several issues, ranging from the criminalization of marital rape,[43] to lethal self-defense,[44] to conviction on the basis of circumstantial evidence.[45] In what follows, I will consider

42 Enker, *Fundamentals*, 59.

43 See, e.g., Criminal Appeal 91/80 *Moshe Ben Meir Cohen v. State of Israel* IsrLR 35(3) 281 (1981) [ע"פ 91/80 משה בן מאיר כהן נ' מדינת ישראל, פ"ד לה (3) 281].

44 See, e.g., Enker, *Fundamentals*, 311-88; D. Jacobs, "Privileges for the Use of Deadly Force against a Residence-Intruder: A Comparison of the Jewish Law and the United States Common Law," *Temple Law Review* 63 (1990), 31-59; B. Porat, "Lethal Self-Defense against a Rapist and the Challenge of Proportionality: Jewish Law Perspective," *Columbia Journal of Gender and Law* 26 (2013), 123-81; Ch. Schlensinger, "The Rule of a Thief in a Homestead [*'haba bamahteret'*] in Tannaitic Literature: Between Self-Defense and Penal Justice" (Hebrew), *Shnaton Hamishpat HaIvri* 29 (2016-2018): 181-234.

45 Criminal Appeal 6392/13 *State of Israel v. Kriaf* (Nevo 21.1.2015), par. 105-111 (Solberg), par. 5-7 (Hendel): "Indeed, due to the need of the hour and so as to eradicate crime, Jewish law conceded to acknowledging the admissibility of circumstantial evidence even in criminal law. Maimonides refers to criminal judgement that is reached not by clear testimony as a 'temporary order.' ... In the context of circumstantial evidence, the 'ideal' law is extremely significant. It is like a shining star guiding the decisor sailing through the sea of law, when he is forced to stray away from his predetermined course. We should not place this law on the shelves of history nor attempt to bring it closer to the law in practice so as to narrow the gap between them. It is the gap that creates a constitutive tension, which reflects the correct balance... I believe that recognizing the ideal

the rabbinic taxonomy of complicity and its relevance to contemporary discussion of accomplice liability.

Complicity in Rabbinic Law

The doctrine of criminal complicity and the civil doctrine of joint tort liability share a common interest in questions of factual causation in situations involving multiple human causes. Yet, criminal complicity is also very different from joint tort liability. The main difference concerns the essential divisibility of damages between joint tortfeasors as opposed to the indivisibility of criminal punishment among accomplices. Joint tortfeasors, who are typically held jointly and severally liable, would not be required to compensate for more than 100 percent of the damages caused, regardless of how this amount is divided between them. In criminal complicity, by contrast, every accomplice is held liable for the completed offense. It is therefore important to distinguish, at the outset, between rabbinic sources centered on joint liability originating from tortious acts and accomplice liability originating from criminal offenses and ritual infringement of the law, especially since the distinction between civil tort law and criminal law is often blurred in rabbinic sources.[46]

---

will aid in applying the Israeli test of the 'only reasonable explanation' in the concrete case. In my view, these points are worthy and they are capable of enriching the positive law in the wisdom and experience of the Jewish law"; Criminal Appeal 5270/14 *Ulmert v. State of Israel* (Nevo 29.12.2015), par. 61-62 (Hendel); Justice Noam Solberg, "Useful Jewish Law," *Mehkare Mishpat* 33 (2021), 53-4: "I purposely chose not to examine the practical doctrine that developed in Jewish law, which found ways to accept circumstantial evidence and inadmissible testimonies, so that the criminal judicial process would be effective… I wanted to present the principle conception of Jewish law, which even if impractical, surely has declarative and ideological value. Examining this ideological stance can bring some comfort, as I mention there, when we are forced to acquit a person who likely committed the acts for which he was tried. This ideological approach is the primal source of the contemporary demand for the evidentiary threshold for criminal conviction – beyond a reasonable doubt"; Criminal Appeal 2884/12 *Habiba v. State of Israel* (Nevo 18.6.2014), par. 6 (Hendel); Serious Criminal Case 54877-09-11 *State of Israel v. Daniel Maoz* (Nevo 1.7.2013), par. 14-120 (Drori).

46 For joint and several liability in rabbinic tort law see A. Sheinfeld, *Nezikin*, Hok LeYisrael, ed. N. Rakover (Jerusalem: 1991), 47-68; E. Halellah, "Od al ribui me'avlim" ['more on multiple tortfeasors'] (Hebrew), Department of Jewish Law, Ministry of Justice, *parashat* Balak 441 (2014). For joint

The Mishnah (mMakot 1:3) makes an important distinction between the divisibility of monetary payments and the indivisibility of corporal punishment in the case of "conspiring witnesses." Whereas monetary payments are divided among the complicit witnesses, corporal punishment is categorically indivisible. This distinction is, of course, hardly identical to the Western distinction between joint liability of tortfeasors and criminal complicity, but the classificatory reasoning is similar.[47]

> משלשים בממון ואין משלשים במכות. כיצד? העידוהו שהוא חייב לחבירו מאתים זוז, נמצאו זוממים, משלשין ביניהן; העידוהו שהוא חייב מלקות ארבעים, נמצאו זוממין, כל אחד ואחד לוקה ארבעים.[48]
>
> Monetary payments are divided [among the offenders], but lashes [of flogging] are not divided [among the offenders]. How is this so? If they testified against a person that he owes his fellow 200 *zuz* and they were found to be "conspiring witnesses," they divide [the monetary payment] proportionately between them. But if they testified against him that he is liable to forty lashes and they were found to be "conspiring witnesses," each one of them receives forty lashes.

The law of the "conspiring witnesses" ("you shall do to him as he plotted to do to his fellow," Deut 19:19) provides an important window into the rabbinic perception of accomplice liability, as the offense of false testimony necessarily involves at least two co-conspirators. According to the mishnah, monetary payments should be divided among the conspiring witnesses, while flogging (forty lashes) should be imposed on each offender separately and in full measure. This would seem to

---

and several liability in rabbinic contract law see, recently, E. Halellah "Al ribuyi hayavim vehalukat haaharayut beineihem leor hamishpat haIvri" ['On multiple debtors and the division of liability among them in light of Jewish law'] (Hebrew), *Shnaton Hamishpat HaIvri* 31 (2022), 45-102.

47 The monetary payments exacted from "conspiring witnesses" seem to function more as a criminal fine than as civil restitution since the conspiring witnesses are held liable not for what they actually caused, but for what they intended to cause. However, the classification of these payments as fine (*knas*) or restitution (*mamon*) was debated among the rabbis, in the Talmudic and post-Talmudic periods. See bMakot 2b and see *Berur Halakhah* ad loc. ("חיוב עדים זוממים – קנס או ממון," 'the monetary obligation of conspiring witnesses – fine or restitution') for a summary of the ensuing post-Talmudic debate.

48 mMakot 1:3 (MS Kaufmann).

indicate that, at least insofar as corporal punishment is concerned, each accomplice is held liable for the completed offense, not unlike the prevailing assumption in Western law.

It must be stressed, however, that the case of the conspiring witnesses is unique, insofar as the offense of false testimony, by its very definition, can only be completed by manner of complicity.[49] In that sense, the case of the conspiring witnesses somewhat differs from the category of *ze eino yakhol veze eino yakhol* (as defined below) in which each offender is physically incapable of, or otherwise practically prevented from, completing the offense alone (such as lifting a heavy burden on the Sabbath); the offence can be completed only by the combined efforts of two or more individuals. That having been said, in both situations the offense requires (either physically or legally) a combined effort of at least two individuals, where both are held liable for the completed offense. This, as opposed to the exemption of joint offenders according to certain rabbinic authorities in cases of *ze yakhol veze yakhol* (as defined below).[50]

The rabbinic approach to accomplice liability is complicated by other legal and exegetical factors. The Talmud (bBaba Kama 10b; bBaba Kama 26b-27a; bSanhedrin 78a) records a tannaitic dispute concerning the liability of multiple offenders who jointly (either concurrently or consecutively) beat a person to death. The relevant baraitha survived in two different textual versions, which appear to exhibit diverging doctrinal approaches towards criminal complicity. According to one version, the baraitha reads as follows:

49 See Deut 19:15: "A single witness shall not suffice to convict a person of any crime or wrongdoing in connection with any offense that may be committed. Only on the evidence of two or three witnesses shall a charge be sustained".

50 See mShabbat 10:5; tShabbat 9:10 (ed. Lieberman, 37-8); *Sifra, dibura dehova, parasha* 7: 9-10 (ed. Weiss, 21d). As we shall see below, the Talmud (bShabbat 93a) creates a tripartite classification of complicity: 1. Accomplices who are "but-for causes" of the offense: situations in which the acts of each perpetrator alone cannot factually/physically effect the completed offense, but the combination of their joint efforts can (*ze eino yakhol veze eino yakhol*); 2. Accomplices who are "sufficient causes" of the offense: situations in which the acts of each perpetrator alone can effect the completed offense (*ze yakhol veze yakhol*); 3. Situations in which the principal, who can complete the offense alone, is aided by the non-essential acts of an accessory, who could not him- or herself effect the completed offense on their own (*ze yakhol veze eino yakhol*).

דתניא הכוהו עשרה בני אדם בעשר מקלות בין בבת אחת בין בזה אחר זה פטורין ר' יהודה בן בתירא או' אחרון חייב[51] מפני שקרב את מיתתו.[52]

For it was taught [in a baraitha]: If ten people beat him [to death] with ten sticks, whether concurrently or consecutively, they are all exempt [from the death penalty]. R. Yehuda b. Bateira says: [If consecutively] the last one is liable, for he expedited his death.

According to this version, the anonymous opinion in the baraitha holds that multiple offenders who jointly beat a person to death—whether the beatings were delivered concurrently or consecutively—are exempt from the death penalty. R. Yehuda b. Bateira agrees with his interlocutors insofar as multiple offenders who concurrently beat a person to death, but contends that when the beatings are consecutive the last offender is liable, since he expedited the victim's death. In contrast to the prevailing Western approach to criminal complicity (and in contradistinction to the law of the "conspiring witnesses" in mMakot 1:3), the baraitha seems to consider joint offenders exempt from the death penalty. Even R. Yehuda b. Bateira seems to agree with this, but asserts that in a situation of consecutive beatings the last offender should be held liable, since his act constitutes a complete crime, regardless of the prior beatings.

In this case, the rabbinic exemption can be understood in two different ways. First, it is possible to view the exemption of accomplices through the lens of the legal doctrine of doubt and the requirement of factual causation. When there are multiple offenders—acting independently or in concert, concurrently or consecutively—there is inherent *doubt* as to the identity of the defendant who, in fact, *caused* the victim's death. This interpretation is compatible with other procedural and evidential requirements in the classical-hermeneutic rabbinic tradition which reflect a high standard of proof—bordering on absolute certainty—for conviction.[53] Along these lines, Rashi, in his

51 See also *Sifra, Emor*, perek 20:1 (ed. Weiss, 104d), which seems to agree with the position of R. Yehuda b. Bateira in the baraitha.

52 This version is found in all textual witnesses of bSanhendrin 78a, in MS Florence and Vatican 116 of bB.Q 26b, and in MS Hamburg, Munich, and Vatican 116 of bB.Q 10b.

53 The classical-hermeneutic rabbinic tradition assumes a strict "doctrine of doubt" that calls for absolute proof before determining a criminal conviction in capital cases, dismissing circumstantial evidence. See, e.g., mSanhedrin 4:5; bSanhendrin 37b; Maimonides, *Laws of the Sanhedrin*,

commentary on bBaba Kama 10b, writes: "For it is not known by whom he was murdered."

Alternatively, there seems to be an exegetical basis for the lenient approach taken by the baraitha towards criminal complicity. In his commentary on bSanhedrin 78a, Rashi suggests that the verse "Anyone who kills (*'ish ki yake'*) a human being shall be put to death" (Lev 24:17) may indicate that the death penalty applies only to a single murderer but not to multiple offenders.[54] This interpretation construes the exemption of multiple offenders in cases of manslaughter along the lines of the exegetical exemption of joint violations of ritual prohibitions (see below).

Whether the underlying reasoning is legal-doctrinal, exegetical, or a combination of both, we should bear in mind that a dominant rabbinic position exempts the guilty party, in cases of homicide, only from the classical-hermeneutic penalty of death by the court and not from criminal punishment per se. The latter may be applied through a variety of practical measures of criminal punishment, such as the "law of the king" (*mishpat hamelekh*), "temporary order" (*horaat shaa*), and incarceration (*kipa*).

20:1; Maimonides, *Sefer haMitzvot*, negative commandments, 290. For the limitation of this doctrine to capital punishment and the opinion that it does not apply to incarceration see: Rabbi A. Weiss, *Minhat Asher*, Exodus (Jerusalem: 2004), 308-12. For the more lenient approach to circumstantial evidence in the "practical" channels of criminal punishment (as opposed to the classical-hermeneutic system) see, R. Isaac b. Sheshet, *Responsa*, 251; R. Yaakov b. Asher, *Tur Hoshen Mishpat*, 2. See also Criminal Appeal 2884/12 *Habiba v. State of Israel* (Nevo 18.6.2014), par. 6 (Hendel); Criminal Appeal 6392/13 *State of Israel v. Kriaf* (Nevo 21.1.2015), par. 105-111 (Solberg); Serious Criminal Case 54877-09-11 *State of Israel v. Daniel Maoz* (Nevo 1.7.2013), par. 14-120 (Drori); Judge M. Drori, "Proving Murder with Circumstantial Evidence: Thou Shalt Not Kill" (Hebrew), Department of Jewish Law, Ministry of Justice, parashat Vaethanan 422 (2013). Compare also the medieval Islamic doctrine directing judges to "avoid (imposing) fixed criminal sanctions (*hudūd*) in cases of doubt or ambiguity (*idraū l-hudūd bi'l-shubahāt*)," for which see I.A. Rabb, *Doubt in Islamic Law: A History of Legal Maxims, Interpretation, and Islamic Criminal Law* (Cambridge: 2015).

54 This approach is also taken by Maimonides, *Mishneh Torah, Nezikin, Rotzeah ushemirat hanefesh*, 4:6; R. Meir b. Todros Halevy Abulafia (1170-1244) in his commentary *Yad Rama* on tractate Sanhedrin suggests that the verse "you shall give a life for a life" ('ונתת נפש תחת נפש', Exod 21:23) indicates that only one life can be taken for the life of another.

A second version of the baraitha reads as follows:

דתניא הכוהו עשרה בני אדם בעשר מקלות בבת אחת חייבין, בזה אחר זה פטורין. ר' יהודה בן בתירא או' אחרון חייב מפני שקרב את מיתתו.[55]

For it was taught [in a baraitha]: If ten people beat him [to death] with ten sticks, concurrently – they are all liable; consecutively – they are all exempt. R. Yehuda b. Bateira says: [If consecutively] the last one is liable, for he expedited his death.

According to this version, there is no blanket exemption for accomplices. Multiple offenders who act in concert (concurrently beating the victim to death) are all held liable for murder, likely because their acts are indivisible. In the case of consecutive and divisible beatings, however, where it is unclear who caused the victim's death, rabbinic authorities disagree. The anonymous voice of the baraitha exempts all participants from death by the court, while R. Yehuda b. Bateira holds that the last participant should be held liable in any event, since his act expedited the victim's death.

Even according to the first version of the baraitha, which was the version recorded by the vast majority of post-Talmudic authorities, certain commentators suggest that the exemption does not categorically exempt accomplices. According to R. Shlomo b. Abraham b. Aderet (1235-1310), for example, the baraitha exempts joint offenders who concurrently beat a person to death only when they strike the victim with ten different sticks. In this scenario, the acts of the offenders are *divisible*, and the identity of the person who delivered the deadly blow is inconclusive. However, if the offenders strike the victim with one stick, in which case their acts are *indivisible*, they should clearly all be held liable. Maimonides, on the other hand, seems to interpret the baraitha (in its first version) as a broad exemption of criminal complicity:

הכוהו עשרה בני אדם בעשרה מקלות ומת בין שהכוהו בזה אחר זה בין שהכוהו כאחת כולן פטורין ממיתת בית דין שנאמר כל נפש אדם עד שיהיה אחד שהרג כל הנפש והוא הדין לשנים שדחפוהו או שכבשוהו לתוך המים או שהיו רבים יושבים ויצא חץ מביניהן והרג שכולן פטורין.

If ten people struck a person with ten [different] sticks and he died, whether they struck him consecutively or concurrently, they are all exempt from

55 This version is found in MS Escorial and Hamburg of bBaba Kama 26b and in MS Florence of bBaba Kama 10b.

> execution by the court. As it says, "[anyone who kills] any human being [shall be put to death]" (Lev 24:17) - until one person alone kills the whole person of another. The same law applies if two people push him into water or hold him there, or if several people are sitting together and an arrow emerged from their company and killed another - they are all exempt.[56]

Another Talmudic discussion of criminal complicity pertains to joint theft. According to Rava, "Partners who commit theft are both liable" ('*shutafin sheganvu hayavin*'). According to Rashi, this case refers to a single person who commits theft *on behalf* of himself and his co-partner.[57] The Tosafists, however, explain that Rava refers to partners who jointly commit theft in concert (for example, they lift the stolen item together).[58]

Beyond the cases of murder and theft, the *locus classicus* of the Talmudic taxonomy of complicity is connected to joint violation of the Sabbath. In this context, the rabbis discuss acts of multiple offenders that together constitute a violation of the Sabbath laws,[59] as well as joint

56 Maimonides, *Mishneh Torah, Nezikin, Rotzeah ushemirat hanefesh,* 4:6. While Maimonides mentions that the perpetrators struck the victim with *ten sticks,* he does not seem to make the same distinction that the Rashba makes, but simply quotes the Talmudic baraitha. This conclusion, however, is debatable.

57 See Rashi on bBaba Metzia 8a. Rashi's interpretation is supported by bBaba Kama 78b, where the Talmud distinguishes between a case in which a partner commits theft on behalf of himself and when he does it on behalf of himself and his co-partner. To be sure, this is not the typical case of agency (*shlihut*), in which it is commonly held that "there is no *agency* for illegal acts" (*ein shaliah lidvar avera*), since the thief may have acted on behalf of his co-partner insofar as they are partners, but the latter did not actually appoint or instruct him in any way with regard to the specific act of theft.

58 Tosafot on bBaba Metzia 8a. This interpretation is supported by bShabbat 93b, where the case of partners who committed theft is brought to weigh on the issue of joint violation of the Sabbath, in which case the offenders acted concurrently and in concert.

59 See, for example, the case in mShabbat 13:7 and tShabbat 13:6, where one person blocks half of the doorway of a house where an animal is present, and then another person blocks the remainder of the doorway. In this case, only the latter is regarded as the direct cause of the entrapment, and he alone is liable for confining an animal on the Sabbath. tShabbat 12:4, and 12:12 address more complicated scenarios, in which multiple participants contribute to the performance of a prohibited act on the Sabbath by providing different elements necessary for carrying out the offense.

violations carried out in concert. When the participants together violate the Sabbath laws, the rabbis generally tend to exempt the offenders from both capital punishment in case of deliberate offenses, and from the sin-offering in case of inadvertent offenses.[60]

המוציא ככר לרשות הרבים – חייב. הוציאוהו שנים – פטורים. לא יכול אחד להוציאו והוציאוהו שנים – חייבים. ר' שמעון פוטר.[61]

שנים אוחזין במלגז ולוגזין, בכרכר ושובטין, בקולמוס וכותבין, בקנה והוציאוהו לרשות הרבים – שניהם פטורין.[62] בעגול של דבילה והוציאוהו לרשות הרבים, בקורה והוציאוה לרשות הרבים,[63] ר' יהודה או': אם אין אחד יכול להוציאה והוציאוה שנים חייבין. ר' שמעון אומ': אע"פ שאין אחד יכול להוציאה והוציאוהו שנים פטורין, שאין שנים חייבין על מלאכה אחת.[64]

'בעשותה אחת' – העושה כולה לא העושה מקצתה. כיצד? שנים אוחזים במלגז ולוגזין בכרכר ושובטין בקולמוס וכותבין בקנה והוציאוהו לרשות הרבים, יכול יהוא חייבין? תל' לו' 'בעשותה אחת' – העושה כולה לא העושה מקצתה. בעגול שלדבילה והוציאוהו לרשות הרבים, בקורה והוציאוהו לרשות הרבים, ר' יהודה אומר: אם אין אחד יכול להוציאו והוציאוהו שנים חייבין. ר' שמעון אומר: אף על פי שאין אחד יכול להוציאו והוציאוהו שנים פטורין. תל' לו' 'בעשותה' – יחיד שעשה חייב, שנים שלושה שעשו יהוא פטורין.[65]

Whoever takes out a loaf of bread into the public domain is liable. If two people took it out they are exempt. If one person could not take it out [by himself], and two people took it out - they are liable. R. Shimon exempts.

Two people are holding on to a pitchfork and stacking, to a shuttle and pressing, to a pen and writing, to a reed and they took it out to the public domain - they are both exempt. If they are holding on to a wheel of dried figs and they took it out to the public domain, to a beam and they took it

60 See, e.g., mShabbat 1:1, 10:5, 13:6; tShabbat 9:10 (ed. Lieberman, 37-8); bShabbat 3a; bShabbat 92b-93a.

61 mShabbat 10:5 (MS. Kaufmann); cf. mShabbat 1:1; mShabbat 13:6.

62 This is according to manuscripts London, Erfurt and the printed editions; MS Vienna is missing the words: שניהם פטורין. See: S. Lieberman, *Tosefta Kifshuta: A Comprehensive Commentary on the Tosefta* (New York: 1955-1988), Shabbat, 134.

63 The printed editions and Erfurt manuscript add here: שניהם פטורין. I followed the Vienna and London manuscripts in the body of the text. See Lieberman, *Tosefta Kifshuta*, Shabbat, 135.

64 tShab 9:10 (ed. Lieberman, 37-8).

65 *Sifra, dibura dehova, parasha* 7:9-10 (ed. Weiss, 21d).

out to the public domain, R. Yehuda says: If one person could not take it out (by himself), and two people took it out - they are liable. R. Shimon says: Even if one person could not take it out [by himself], and two people took it out - they are exempt, for two people could not be liable for one and the same transgression.

'By doing one' - [This applies to] one who does the whole of the deed and not to one who does only part of it. How so? Two people are holding on to a pitchfork and stacking, to a shuttle and pressing, to a pen and writing, to a reed and they took it out to the public domain. Is it possible that they are liable? For this reason, Scripture says: 'By doing one' - [This applies to] one who does the whole of the deed and not to one who does only part of it. If they are holding on to a wheel of dried figs and they took it out to the public domain, to a beam and they took it out to the public domain, R. Yehuda says: If one person could not take it out [by himself], and two people took it out - they are liable. R. Shimon says: Even if one person could not take it out (by himself), and two people took it out - they are exempt. For this reason, Scripture says: 'By doing (one)' - a single person who does it is liable, but two or three people who do it are exempt.

According to these sources, in cases of joint violation of the Sabbath laws, in which the various acts are essentially *indivisible* and performed *concurrently*, the participants are all exempt. Several commentators assume that this broad exemption, according to which only a single offender who single-handedly completed the offense can be held liable, pertains only to violation of the Sabbath laws, but not to other religious infringements.[66] However, the exegetical inference provided in the *Sifra* for the exemption of joint offenders hinges not on the biblical verses of the Sabbath, but rather on the verses of the *asham* ('guilt') offering (Lev 4:27), a fact which suggests that the exemption

66 According to this position, the exemption in cases of joint violation of the Sabbath laws is connected either with the lack of *melekhet mahshevet* or with the fact that joint violation of the Sabbath laws is necessarily executed in an abnormal fashion, i.e., not in the way that labor was performed in the Tabernacle, all being legal maxims unique to the Sabbath laws that do not apply broadly. This may have been the position of Maimonides in *Mishneh Torah*, Laws of the Sabbath, 1. See also Rabbi Avraham Itzhak Hacohen Kook, *Mishpat Cohen* 125; Rabbi M. Rata, *Kol Mevaser* 1:82; M. Tikuchinski, "Shared Liability: An Examination of the Issue of 'Two Performers'," *Akdamot* 23 (2009), 161-7.

of multiple offenders applies, at least in principle, to other religious violations and is not limited to the laws of the Sabbath.[67] In addition, the exegetical explanation we examined regarding the doctrinal exemption of accomplices to homicide also suggests that the exemption of joint offenders extends beyond the particular laws of the Sabbath.

The tannaitic passages relating to joint violation of the Sabbath distinguish between situations in which the acts of each offender alone could have effected the criminal offense (*ze yakhol veze yakhol*) and situations in which only the combination of the offenders' joint efforts could have effected the violation (*ze eino yakhol veze eino yakhol*).[68] In the first case, each accomplice is a "sufficient cause" of the offense, as the offense would have taken place even without his contribution. In the second case, each accomplice is a "but-for cause" of the offense, since his acts were essential, and the offense could not have taken place without his contribution. While in the first case the tannaitic rabbis unanimously exempt the co-conspirators, the second case was debated: R. Yehuda holds accomplices who are "but-for causes" of the offense liable, while R. Shimon does not.

There is another (complementary) way to understand the tannaitic debate: according to R. Yehuda, in contrast to the first case in which the forbidden labor can be performed by a single perpetrator, in the second case the forbidden labor can only be carried out by joint performance. In the first case, then, complicity constitutes an abnormal manner of performance that diverges (legally and exegetically) from the scriptural definition of prohibited labor, while in the second case complicity is, for all intents and purposes, presumed by the Scriptural definition. R. Shimon, on the other hand, exempts accomplices in both cases, perhaps under the assumption that only offenses committed by a single perpetrator can be deemed a complete offense.

Non-essential Accessories and the Doctrine of Aiding and Abetting

We have seen that the tannaitic discussion of complicity centers on two types of complicity, both of which meet a standard of factual causation: 1. Accomplices who are "sufficient causes" of the offense, such that the acts of each offender would have sufficed to effect the offense (*ze yakhol veze yakhol*). 2. Accomplices who are "but-for causes" of the offense,

67 See the discussion of Tikuchinski, ibid, 168-71.

68 For sake of conceptual clarity, I use here the terminological classification of *yakhol* ("able") and *eino yakhol* ("unable") proposed by the Babylonian Talmud (see below), although the Tannaitic sources do not consistently apply these categories.

such that the acts of each offender alone would not have effected the offense, but the combined efforts of both effected the violation (*ze eino yakhol veze eino yakhol*). Both types of complicity seem to meet a certain standard of factual causation, as their acts are essential for the completion of the offense.

However, the rabbis envisioned a third type of complicity, in which the principal is aided or assisted by the non-essential acts of an accessory. Whereas the tannaitic discussion does not explicitly address the case of a non-essential accessory, the Babylonian Talmud provides a systematic classification of the three types of accomplices, while clearly distinguishing between essential and non-essential forms of complicity:

> אמ' רב יהודה אמ' רב, ואמרי לה אמ' אביי, ואמרי לה במתניתא: זה יכול וזה יכול, ר' מאיר מחייב, ור' יהודה פוטר.[69] [זה אינו יכול וזה אינו יכול], ר' מאיר ור' יהודה מחייבין, ור' שמעון פוטר. זה יכול וזה אינו יכול, דברי הכל חייב.[70]

> Rav Yehuda said on the authority of Rav, and others state, Abaye said, and others again state, it was taught in a baraitha: If each alone is able - R. Meir holds them liable, while R. Yehuda exempts. If each alone is unable - R. Meir and R. Yehuda hold them liable, while R. Shimon exempts. If one is able but the other is not able - all agree that he [=who is able] is liable.

While the Babylonian Talmud accurately paraphrases the positions of R. Yehuda and R. Shimon as known to us from the tannaitic traditions,[71] it introduces a third tannaitic position, attributed to R. Meir, who maintains that all types of accomplices who are causes-in-fact of the offense are liable. More significantly, however, the Babylonian Talmud classifies three types of complicity as opposed to only two types that can be gleaned from the tannaitic traditions.[72] To be sure, the phrase

69 This is according to all manuscripts; the printed editions have: ור' יהודה ור' שמעון פוטרים.

70 bShabbat 92b (MS. Oxford 366).

71 mShabbat 10:5; tShabbat 9:10; *Sifra, dibura dehova, parasha* 7:9-10 (ed. Weiss, 21d).

72 The threefold classification is attributed either to Rav Yehuda (second generation) in the name of Rav (first generation), to Abaye (fourth generation), or to a baraitha. According to the first two possibilities, it is explicitly acknowledged that this distinctive classification of the earlier Tannaitic positions stems from an Amoraic (and not a Tannaitic) origin, but even according to the third possibility it would seem that we might be

ein ehad yakhol used in the Mishnah and Sifra does not mean that the acts of one accomplice were insufficient to effect the prohibited labor, while the acts of the other were sufficient. Rather, it means that the acts of neither are sufficient to effect the prohibited labor (for example, the burden is too heavy for a single individual to carry). The Babylonian Talmud, by contrast, explicitly classifies a third type of complicity, in which the principal is aided or assisted in some way by the non-essential acts of an accessory (*ze yakhol veze eino yakhol*).

Following the threefold classification of complicity, mapped onto earlier tannaitic positions, the Talmud explains that in the third scenario, in which the principal is aided and abetted by the non-essential acts of another, only the principal is liable while the accessory is exempt. This assumption is supported by an innovative Talmudic maxim that is absent from earlier Palestinian rabbinic traditions, according to which the acts of a non-essential accessory to an offense (*mesayea*) are deemed legally insignificant (*ein bo mamash*) and do not warrant liability. The remainder of the Talmudic discussion records attempts by several Babylonian authorities to sustain this legal maxim by providing it with supporting tannaitic references:

אמ' מר: זה יכול וזה אינו יכול – דברי הכל חייב. הי מיניהו מיחייב? אמ' רב חסדא: זה שיכול. דאי זה שאינו יכול, מאי קא עביד? אמ' ליה רב המנונא: משו' דקא מסייע בהדיה. אמ' ליה, מסייע אין בו ממש.

אמ' רב זביד משמיה דרבא: אף אנן נמי תנינא, היה יושב על גבי המטה וארבע מטליות תחת ארבע רגלי המטה – טמאות, מפני שאינה יכולה לעמוד על שלש. ור' שמעון מטהר. היה רכוב על גבי בהמה וארבע מטליות תחת ארבע רגלי הבהמה – טהורות, מפני שיכולה לעמ[ו]ד על שלש. ואמאי, הא קא מסייעי בהדי הדדי? לאו משום דאמרי' מסייע אין בו ממש. אמ' רב יהודה מדסקרתא: לעולם אימ' לך מסייע יש בו ממש, ושאני הכא דעקרא בה לגמרי. והא כיון דזמנין עקר הא ליהוי כזב המתהפך, מי לא תנן: זב שהיה מוטל על חמשה ספסלין או על חמשה פונדאות, לארכן – טמאין, לרחבן – טהורים. ישן,

dealing with a reworked baraitha, as its content diverges significantly from the parallel accounts in the Mishnah, Tosefta, and Sifra. On the matter of Babylonian reworking of Tannaitic sources, see S. Friedman, "Uncovering Literary Dependencies in the Talmudic Corpus," in S. Cohen (ed.), *The Synoptic Problem in Rabbinic Literature* (Providence: 2000), 35-57; idem, "The Baraitot in the Babylonian Talmud and their Parallels in the Tosefta," in D. Boyarin et al. (eds.), *Atara L'Haim, Studies in the Talmud and Medieval Rabbinic Literature in Honor of Professor Haim Zalman Dimitrovsky* (Hebrew) (Jerusalem: 2000), 163-201; idem, "Towards a Characterization of Babylonian *Baraitot*: Ben Tema and Ben Dortai," in Y. Elman et al. (eds.), *Neti'ot Ledavid: Jubilee Volume for David Weiss Halivni* (Hebrew) (Jerusalem: 2007), 195-274.

ספק מתהפך עליו טמאים. [ואמאי, קא מסייע בהדיה? אלא לאו משום דאמרינן מסייע אין בו ממש?][73]

אמ' רב פפא[74] משמיה דרבא: אף אנן נמי תנינא, ר' יוסי אומ': הסוס מטמא בידיו וחמור ברגליו, מפני שמשענת הסוס על ידיו ומשענת החמור על רגליו. ואמאי, והא קא מסייעי בהדי הדדי? לאו משום דאמרינן מסייע אין בו ממש?[75]

אמ' רב אשי: אף אנן נמי תנינא, ר' שמעון אומ':[76] רגלו אחת על הכלי ורגלו אחת על הרצפה, רגלו אחת על האבן ורגלו אחת על הרצפה, רואין כל שאילו ינטל האבן וינטל הכלי יכול לעמוד על רגלו אחת – עבדתו כשרה, ואם לאו – עבודתו פסולה. ואמאי, הא קא מסייעא בהדי הדדי? לאו משום דאמרינן מסייע אין בו ממש?[77]

אמ' רבינא: אף אנן נמי תנינא, קיבל בימין ושמאל מסייעתו – עבדתו כשרה. ואמאי הא קא מסייעי בהדי הדדי? לאו משום דאמרינן מסייע אין בו ממש? ש"מ.[78]

It was taught: If one is able but the other is not, all agree that he is liable. Which one of them is liable? Rav Hisda said: He who is able. For if the one who is unable, what exactly did he do? Rav Hamnuna said to him: Since he aided him! He replied: Aiding is not regarded as a concrete act.

Rav Zevid said on the authority of Rava: We have likewise learned: If he [a *zav*] is sitting on a bed and four cloths are under the feet of the bed, they are unclean, because it cannot stand on three; but R. Shimon declares them clean. If he is riding on an animal and four cloths are under its feet, they are clean, because it can stand on three. But why is it so? Surely each one helps the other? Hence it must be because we maintain that aiding is not regarded as a concrete act. Rav Yehuda of Diskarta said: One might reply that aiding is indeed regarded as a concrete act; but here it is different because it [the animal] removes it [the foot] entirely [from the ground]. But since it alternatively removes one foot and then another, let it be as a *zav* who turns about. Did we not learn, 'If a *zav* is lying on five benches or

73 This entire sentence is omitted in Oxford 366. Vatican 108 omits only: ואמאי קא מסייע בהדיה.

74 This is the version found in Oxford 366; other witnesses have: פפי.

75 Munich, Vatican 108 add: ש"מ\שמ' מי'.

76 This is the version found in Oxford 366; other textual witnesses have: אליעזר.

77 Vatican 108 adds: שמ' מי'.

78 bShabbat 93a-b (MS Oxford 366).

five hollow belts, if along their length, they are unclean; but if along their breadth, they are clean; [But] if he is sleeping, [and] there is a doubt that he may have turned [about upon them], they are unclean'? Hence it must surely be because we say that aiding is not regarded as a concrete act.

Rav Papa said on the authority of Rava: We have likewise learned: R. Yose said: A horse defiles through its forefeet, an ass through its hindfeet, because a horse rests its weight on its forefeet, while an ass rests its weight upon its hindfeet. But why is it so, seeing that they [the feet] aid each other [to bear the animal's weight]? Hence it must surely be because we say that aiding is not regarded as a concrete act.

Rav Ashi said, We have likewise learned: R. Shimon said: If one foot is on the utensil and the other on the pavement, one foot on the stone and the other on the pavement, we consider: wherever if the utensil or the stone be removed, he can stand on the other foot, his service is valid; if not, his service is invalid. Yet why is it so, seeing that they [the feet] aid each other? Hence it must surely be because we say that aiding is not regarded as a concrete act.

Ravina said: We have likewise learned: If he [the cohen] catches [the blood] with his right hand, while his left helps him, his service is valid. But why so, seeing that they [the hands] aid each other? But it must surely be because we say that aiding is not regarded as a concrete act. This indeed proves it.

The Babylonian discussion records several attempts by Babylonian authorities to sustain (or challenge) the legal maxim according to which non-essential aiding and abetting (*mesayea*) is legally insignificant. The maxim appears to have been formulated by Rav Hisda (second generation of Babylonian rabbis, Sura) and then crystalized by Rav Zevid and Rav Papa in the name of Rava (fourth generation of Babylonian rabbis, Mehoza) and finally by Rav Ashi and Ravina (seventh generation of Babylonian rabbis, Mata Mehasya).

From a doctrinal perspective, the Talmud creates an unprecedented distinction between essential forms of complicity, in which the accomplice's acts are considered either a "but-for cause" or a "sufficient cause," and non-essential forms of complicity, in which the accomplice assists the principal, but his acts cannot have caused the offense. According to the Talmudic classification, certain tannaitic authorities (namely R. Meir) held that accomplices which meet the standard of factual causation (in any of its forms) should be held liable for the completed offense. By contrast, an accessory whose inconsequential and trivial acts only aided and abetted the principal cannot be held liable.

If we abstract this classification from the ritual context in which it is couched, as do several rabbinic commentators, and read it as a taxonomy of criminal complicity, rabbinic law appears to be highly relevant to contemporary discussions of criminal complicity; and its potential to illuminate the theory and practice of criminal law become apparent. The Talmudic doctrine can not only shed light on the statutory distinction set out in Israel's Penal Law (and a few Continental jurisdictions) between an accomplice and an accessory, but also serve as a model for a comprehensive reform of Anglo-American accomplice law.

Conclusion

In this article I argued that the distinction found in Jewish law between essential and non-essential forms of complicity, and the related doctrine of aiding and abetting that emerged in its wake, can serve as important references and sources of dialogue for contemporary discussions of criminal complicity. The Talmudic doctrine can shed light on the statutory distinction between an accomplice and an accessory as adopted in Israel and several other jurisdictions, and serve, moreover, as a model for a more comprehensive reform of Anglo-American accomplice law.

I posited that the most plausible theoretical explanation for accomplice law, in terms of both legal doctrine and morality, is based on the intricacies of causation. A causation-based approach to complicity necessitates a doctrinal distinction between a causal/consequential accomplice and a non-causal/consequential accessory to an offense who only peripherally aids and abets the principal. I thus turned to the Talmudic taxonomy of causation that underlies the rabbis' classification of "essential" and "non-essential" forms of complicity as a source of guidance, one that prefigures contemporary attempts to fashion a graded scale of complicity along the lines of causation.

By making this case, I hope I have contributed to the recent trend of consulting Jewish law in Israel and beyond, and to the reinforcement of its significance for contemporary legal studies, even in areas such as criminal law, in which a wide theoretical gap seems to divide the Jewish and Western traditions. Its distinctive vantage point and religious nature notwithstanding, Jewish criminal law contains important doctrines, principles, and analytical distinctions that can be constructively abstracted from the particular religious and normative contexts in which they are couched and serve, in turn, as important references and sources of dialogue for contemporary discussions of criminal justice.

Appendix: Complicity in the Zoroastrian Legal Tradition

To complete the picture, this appendix will consider the possibility that the taxonomy of accomplice liability and doctrine of non-essential aiding and abetting (*mesayea*) in the Babylonian Talmud may have been prompted by the Sasanian legal culture that surrounded it. In what follows, I examine the Talmudic taxonomy against the backdrop of a similar classification fostered by Zoroastrian jurists during the Sasanian period.

In the past two decades, many studies have been devoted to the study of Talmudic law in its Sasanian context.[79] In some cases, the Talmud explicitly alludes to Sasanian law and its institutions, using the term *dina deParsaei* (Persian law), or employs a technical legal term – either in its original Iranian form or in direct Hebrew/Aramaic translation – making it easier to trace the connections between Talmudic and Sasanian law. In other cases the Talmud contains no explicit mention of Sasanian law, but a diachronic analysis of the legal development of the rabbinic tradition calls for its contextual analysis in light of Sasanian law. Indeed, there are many examples in which the Talmud reflects a distinctive legal development (vis-à-vis Palestinian rabbinic literature), that can be further illuminated by recourse to local currents in Sasanian law. The Talmudic doctrine of *mesayea* is a case in point.

While the interest in criminal complicity is ubiquitously found in other ancient and modern legal systems, I posit that high-resolution affinities between the Babylonian rabbinic and Zoroastrian traditions, as well as particular concerns common to the Babylonian rabbis and Zoroastrian jurists, reflect a shared intellectual environment that gave rise to similar classificatory systems. Thus, while issues relating to criminal complicity are already addressed in tannaitic literature, the Babylonian Talmud reflects a unique perspective that moves beyond earlier rabbinic discussions, and is compatible with contemporaneous

79 For a recent summary see Y. Kiel, "The Sasanian East and the Babylonian Talmud," in C. Hayes (ed.), *The Literature of the Sages: A Re-visioning*, Compendia Rerum Iudaicarum ad Novum Testamentum (CRINT) (Leiden: 2022), 401-59.

discussions in the Zoroastrian tradition. It is precisely the innovative doctrine of non-essential aiding and abetting conceptualized in the Babylonian Talmud that seems to connect the Talmudic discussion with the Zoroastrian legal culture.

Much like the rabbis, the Zoroastrian sages were concerned not only with "pure" criminal matters in the modern sense, but also with violation of ritual law. The first passage I examine concerns the Zoroastrian offense of digging a grave, which is derived from the Zoroastrian prohibition against burial of dead matter, both of which are regarded as violations of the law warranting punishment (not unlike the rabbinic treatment of violations of the Sabbath laws).[80]

While the burial of a corpse is regarded as a capital offense in the Zoroastrian tradition, the derivative offense of digging a grave and disposing of the dirt with the intention of burial is defined as a lesser offense on the level of *tanābuhl*.[81] In the context of the extended Pahlavi commentary on the *Videvdad* (3.40),[82] the Zoroastrian jurists address a case of complicity, in which one participant digs a hole in the ground and the other sweeps the dirt away:

80 For rationales and details see M. Boyce, "Corpse," *Encyclopedia Iranica*, Vol. VI, Fasc. 3, 279-86; J.R. Russell, "Burial, iii in Zoroastrianism," *Encyclopedia Iranica*, Vol. IV, Fasc. 6, 561-63; G. Herman, "'Bury My Coffin Deep!': Zoroastrian Exhumation in Jewish and Christian Sources," in J. Roth, M. Schmelzer, and Y. Francus (eds.), *Tiferet LeYisrael: Jubilee Volume in Honor of Israel Francus* (New York: 2010), 31-60.

81 On the Zoroastrian grades of offenses, see Šāyist nē Šāyist 1.1-2; "Supplementary texts to Šāyist nē Šāyist" 11:1-2, 16:1-4; Pahlavi Rivāyat of Ādurfarnbay 72; M. Macuch, "On the Treatment of Animals in Zoroastrian Law," in A. van Tongerloo (ed.), *Iranica Selecta: Studies in Honour of Professor Wojciech Skalmowski on the Occasion of His Seventieth Birthday*, Silk Road Studies 8 (Turnhout: 2003) 177-8; J. Jany, "Criminal Justice in Sasanian Persia," *Iranica Antiqua* 42 (2007): 347-61.

82 On the *Videvdad* see, e.g., P.O. Skjærvø, "The *Videvdad*: Its Ritual-Mythical Significance," in V.S. Curtis and S. Stewart (eds.), *The Idea of Iran: The Age of the Parthians* (London: 2007), 105-62. For the Pahlavi translation and commentary see M. Moazami (ed.), *Wrestling with the Demons of the Pahlavi Widēwdād: Transcription, Translation, and Commentary* (Leiden: 2014).

ka sē frēg bē kanēd ud rōbēd tanāpuhr-ēw…

<ka> ēk ōh kanēd ēk ōh rōbēd tanābuhl. ōy ēk kand ēstēd, bē rōbēd, kand rāy nē bawēd.

When he digs three spades and sweeps, it is a *tanābuhl*…

If one digs, and another sweeps, it is a *tanābuhl* sin. He who has dug, without sweeping, there is no [sin] for the digging.

According to this passage there are two factual elements that together constitute the offense of grave-digging (alongside the *mens rea* requirement of intention to burry a corpse): digging a hole in the ground and sweeping the dirt away. If one digs and sweeps a measure of three spades, he is liable for the completed offense. If one merely digs, without sweeping the dirt away, the act is regarded as incomplete and, therefore, he is not liable. Insofar as accomplice liability, the Pahlavi commentators add that when joint offenders act together – one digs a hole and the other sweeps the dirt away – a *tanābuhl* offense accrues to each of them. In other words, according to this passage, and similar to the contemporary doctrine of criminal complicity, accomplices are held liable for the completed offense.

Another discussion of criminal complicity concerns the offense of corpse-bearing, which is regarded as a capital offense in the Zoroastrian tradition. According to *Videvdad* 3.14 and its Pahlavi translation, the completed offense of corpse-bearing is explicitly defined in terms of single bearing ("alone" or "in one body") of dead matter. This detail in the Avestan text was understood by the Pahlavi jurists as a Scriptural exclusion of multiple bearers of dead matter from the death penalty.[83]

ma kas [mardōm][84] *barād ēw-tāg [pad tan-ēw]*[85] *ka rist [kū murd]*

83 This passage is discussed in Y. Kiel, "Shaking Impurity: Exegesis and Innovative Traditions in the Babylonian Talmud and Pahlavi Literature," in Sh. Secunda and U. Gabai (eds.), *Encounters by the Rivers of Babylon* (Tübingen: 2013), 413-34. Here, I provide only the relevant reference to single bearing of a corpse.

84 In the Avestan text there is only one term to denote a "person" (*čiš*). Pahlavi *kas* seems to be a direct translation of the Avestan term, while *mardōm* is probably intended as an interpretive gloss.

85 The expression *pad tan-ēw* is interchangeable with *tanīhā*. The latter is used in the context of corpse-bearing in the *Zand ī fragard ī jud-dēw-dād* (MS TD2, p. 531); *Dēnkard* 5.20. The phrase *pad tan-ēw*, lit. "by one body,"

Let no person [a human being] carry singly [alone (lit. "with one body")] when deceased [that is, dead].[86]

The extended Pahlavi commentary further relates that, while a single bearer of a corpse is liable to a *margarzān* (death-deserving) offense, if two individuals carry dead matter together, they are held liable only for the lesser offense of *tanābuhl*.

ka pad dō mard wazēnd har dō tan pad baršnūm

wastarg pad xšwašmagišn...

ka tan ēdōn rēman kunēd ī-š pad baršnūm abāyēd šustan ā-š tanāpuhr-ēw ō bun.

When they move [the corpse] with two men, both bodies [should wash] with the *baršnūm* and the garment [should be washed] with the six-month-purification...[87]

When one makes the body impure in such a way that it is necessary to wash oneself with the *baršnūm* - there is one *tanābuhl* to his account.[88]

According to the extended Pahlavi commentary, there is a direct correlation between the level of ritual contamination contracted by the bearer of dead matter and the extent of his/her liability. The more severe the impurity contracted, the worse is the offense and its punitive consequences. The highest degree of ritual contamination, which

---

can also be compared with the Talmudic expression: טב למיתב טן דו "It is preferable to remain together (lit. two bodies)" that appears several times throughout the Babylonian Talmud (bYevamot 118b, bKetubot 75a, bKidushin 7a, bKidushin 41a, and bBaba Kama 111a). In the Talmud, the form *tan-dō* (טן דו) appears to be a Persian loanword that connotes "togetherness" or "in matrimony," but literally translates as "two bodies." See M. Sokoloff, *A Dictionary of Jewish Babylonian Aramaic of the Talmudic and Geonic Periods* (Ramat Gan: 2002), 508. I am indebted to Shaul Shaked and Shai Secunda for this discussion.

86 *Pahlavi Videvdad* 3.14.

87 The *baršnūm* is an extensive purification ritual that lasts nine days and nights, to remove most types of severe impurity. *Videvdad* 8-9 provides a detailed description of the *baršnūm* that is performed when a man or woman becomes polluted by dead matter. See M. Boyce, "Barašnom," *Encyclopedia Iranica*, vol. III (London and New York: 1989), 756-7; J. Choksy, *Purity and Pollution in Zoroastrianism: Triumph over Evil* (Austin: 1989).

88 *Pahlavi Videvdad* 3.14 [X-Z].

renders the bearer of dead matter defiled for all eternity (*hamē hamē rawišnīh*) is correlated to a *margarzān* (death-deserving) offense.[89] A somewhat lighter degree of contamination, cleansable through the *baršnūm* ceremony, is correlated with a *tanābuhl* offense. The lightest degree of contamination, which merely requires washing with *gōmēz* (bull's urine) and water, is correlated with the light *xwar* offense.[90]

In terms of complicity, when two individuals jointly bear the weight of a corpse, the offense is reduced from a capital offense (and the accompanying irreversible state of eternal contamination) to a resolvable *tanābuhl* offense, the contamination of which is cleansable through the *baršnūm* ceremony. The logic of this ruling is probably connected not only to the lack of any causal relationship between act and offense, but also to the exegetical divergence from the Scriptural definition of the offense in the *Avesta*, resulting in reduced liability. While a single bearer of dead matter is liable for the statutory capital offense, joint bearers of a corpse acting together are only liable for a lesser, *tanābuhl*, offense.

The Pahlavi jurists exempt joint corpse-bearers from the death penalty. This is, in some respect, reminiscent of the rabbinic exemption of joint violation of the Sabbath laws (and, according to some commentators, also the exemption of accomplices to murder); in both cases, the reason for the exemption is based on a combination of exegetical and legal principles. On the one hand, there is a common perception that, at least in certain cases of joint violation, cases of complicity do not meet the statutory standard of a completed crime. On the other hand, as exegetes of their respective holy texts, both the rabbis and the Pahlavi jurists relied on hermeneutical principles to infer that only a single violator of the law can be held liable for the completed offense. The rabbis rely on the biblical phraseology "by doing [singular]" (*baasota*), or "anyone who kills," while the Zoroastrian jurists rely on the mention of single corpse-bearing, "alone" or "in one body," as found in the *Avesta* and its Pahlavi translation.

The similar legal and hermeneutic frameworks characteristic of the rabbis and Pahlavi jurists led both systems to the conclusion that in cases of joint violation of certain ritual or religious precepts, the perpetrators should be exempt from capital punishment. The Pahlavi jurists render joint corpse-bearers liable for the lesser *tanābuhl* offense, entailing extensive purification requirements and a monetary fine. The

89 *Pahlavi Videvdad* 3.14 [A].

90 *Pahlavi Videvdad* 3.14 [A-C].

rabbis, by contrast, completely exempt joint violators of the Sabbath laws from court-inflicted punishment.

The similarity of the rabbinic and Zoroastrian discussions of complicity does not, in itself, reflect cultural dependency: The rabbinic discussion of complicity is already found in tannaitic literature, which was compiled in Palestine long before the Babylonian rabbis encountered the Zoroastrian legal tradition. However, we will now see that the Pahlavi doctrine of non-essential aiding and abetting is intimately connected to the Talmud's innovative doctrine of *mesayea* (מסייע).

The discussion of non-essential aiding and abetting is found in a Pahlavi work known as *Šāyist nē Šāyist*.[91] Though redacted circa the ninth or tenth centuries, it contains traditions that date back to the Sasanian period. In the context of the legal discussion of joint corpse-bearing, the author of *Šāyist nē Šāyist* (2.69-70) records the following:

> *ud ka nasāy-ēw ī sag nē dīd mard-ēw pad dast ī anīy mard-ēw bē jumbēnēd kē az dast ī mard kē jumbēnēd ān-iz kē dast xwēš nērōg andar harw dō-ān tan rēman u-š tanābuhl-1 xwad 1 ōy ī did rāy ō bun ēd rāy čē-š tan ī xwēš ud ān-iz ī ōy harw dō pad wināh-kārīh rēman kard o ud ka nērōg y ōy kē-š dast xwēš hāmbun-iz andar nēst ēdōn bawēd čiyōn ka-š pad dār-ēw jumbēnīd hē ōy kē-š pad dast dāšt pad rāh ī hamkarzagīh pad pišag šōyišn u-š tanābuhl-ēw ōy rāy kē dast xwēš xwar-ēw xwad rāy ō bun.*
>
> And, if he moves a corpse not seen by a dog[92] with the hand of another

91 *Šāyist nē Šāyist* literally means "That which is appropriate and that which is not appropriate." See J.C. Tavadia, *Šāyast nē Šāyast: A Pahlavi Text on Religious Customs* (Hamburg: 1930), 1-25. Compare the expression "*dharma* and *a-dharma*" in Hindu legal literature. See, for instance, *Mīmāmsā Paribhāsā of Krsna Yajvan: Sanskrit Text with an English Translation and an Elaborate Introduction*, ed. Bh.P. Bhattacharya (Sanskrit Pustak Bhandar: 1998), 23.

92 The dog is regarded as an essential element in the disposal of corpse impurity, as its gaze is believed to chase away the *nasuš* (the corpse-demoness) from the corpse. The *sag-dīd*, a term that means "being seen by a dog" or "a dog's seeing," i.e., the carrion demon, is described by Mahnaz Moazami as follows: "After death, to counteract the influence of the *nasuš*, before it is left exposed outside, a corpse must be exposed to the gaze of a dog or a bird of prey, which are believed to drive away the *nasuš*. The dog is led several times along the same path the corpse is carried. Only afterward is it safe for people, cattle, fire, and the *barsom* to proceed along that path. For the same reason, a dog must also be present at the great purification ritual of the baršnūm." See M. Moazami, "The Dog in Zoroastrian Religion: Vidēvdād Chapter xiii," *Indo-Iran* 49 (2006), 128.

> man, [then] the bodies of both him who [gets strength] from the hand of the man who moves [it] and him in whose hand the strength resides are polluted. And [a sin of] one *tanābuhl* accrues to himself and one to the other, because, by this sinful deed, he made his own body and that of the other both polluted.
>
> And if there is absolutely no strength in him whose hand it is [that touches the corpse directly], [then] it is as if he had moved it with a [piece of] wood. He who held him by the hand, by reason of intimate contact, is to be washed with the *pišag*,[93] and he has one *tanābuhl* [to his account]. For him whose hand it was [that touched the corpse directly] there is one *xwar* for himself [accruing] to his account.

This passage distinguishes between two cases of complicity: one in which both offenders equally use their strength to bear the weight of the corpse, and one in which only one of the offenders uses his strength, while the other merely aids and abets the principal with his hand without using strength. In line with the Pahlavi commentary on the *Videvdad*, the author argues that, in the first case, where both accomplices equally use their strength in bearing the weight of the corpse, they are both liable to a *tanābuhl* offense. In the second case, however, where only one participant uses his strength to bear the corpse, the author states that only the principal is liable for a *tanābuhl*, while the accessory, who aids and abets the principal, is not liable for the offense of corpse-bearing (although he is liable for the lesser *xwar* offense of deliberately touching dead matter).

In the first case, both participants causally contributed to the execution of the offense, although it is not entirely clear whether the acts of each offender alone would have effected the completed offense, as in the rabbinic classification of *ze yakhol veze yakhol*, or whether the completed offense was only made possible by the combined acts of the offenders, as in the rabbinic classification of *ze eino yakhol veze eino yakhol*. Either way, the offenders are causes-in-fact (either "but-for causes" or "sufficient causes") of the completed offense. By contrast, in the second case the participants are not equal contributors to the

---

See also *Videvdad* 8.16; E.B.N. Dhabhar, *The Persian Rivayats of Hormazyar Framarz* (Bombay: 1932), 259-60; *Šāyist nē Šāyist* 2.1-5, in Tavadia, *Šāyast nē Šāyast*, 30-32; J.J. Modi, *The Religious Ceremonies and Customs of the Parsees* (Bombay: 1922), 58.

93 The *pišag* is the stick of nine knots used in the *baršnūm* purification ceremony.

offense, rather, the principal is aided and abetted by the non-essential acts of the accomplice

The Pahlavi classification of essential and non-essential forms of complicity and its discussion of trivial aiding and abetting are quite similar to the Babylonian rabbinic taxonomy of complicity and their discussion of *mesayea*. As the doctrine of *mesayea* does not appear in Palestinian rabbinic sources, it is remarkable that it was conceptualized and developed by the Babylonian rabbis in a manner resembling the Pahlavi discussion of joint corpse-bearing, as preserved in the contemporaneous and adjacent Pahlavi tradition.

The Jewish Law Annual, Vol. XXII

From Germany to Jerusalem, from Community to State: The Separate Paths Taken by Neo-Orthodox Jurists Abraham Chaim Freimann and Isaac Breuer

Asaf Yedidya*

The Balfour Declaration of November 1917, the British conquest of the Land of Israel, and the League of Nations Mandate, all of which raised hopes that the Zionist Basel Program would soon be implemented, initiated discussions among Zionist rabbis and thinkers regarding the role of halakhah in a modern sovereign Jewish state.[1] The return to the Land of Israel, the processes of secularization that were becoming widespread in Jewish society, as well as technological and scientific advances, all raised new halakhic issues that had hitherto not been addressed. The long-awaited sovereign reality dawning on the horizon also gave rise to fundamental differences in the focus of halakhic questions. These now dealt with questions of nation and state, rather than the individual and his community. Halakhah, which was largely shaped during the many long years of exile, could not provide relevant precedents for the new issues that arose. Some of the *halakhot* that dated back to ancient periods of sovereignty directly contradicted the prevailing strictures of international law, and could therefore not be utilized.

The halakhic discussion at the time focused primarily on issues such as the rights of women,[2] the rights of minorities, and the public domain, including policy questions regarding Shabbat and *kashrut* in public kitchens and food

* Prof. Asaf Yedidya is an associate Professor in the Jewish History Department at Ariel University and Efrata College, Jerusalem.

1 E. Schweid, *Democracy and Halakhah* (Lanham: 1994), 47-90; Z. Gries, "Nationalism and Religion in the Writings of Rav Tzair (Rabbi Chaim Tchernowitz)," in D.J. Lasker (ed.), *Jewish Thought and Jewish Belief* (Hebrew), (Beer Sheva: 2012), 219-25; R. Schatz Uffenheimer, *The Messianic Idea from the Expulsion from Spain* (Hebrew), (Jerusalem: 2005), 239-42.

2 M. Shilo, *Zionist Women's Struggle for Suffrage in Mandatory Palestine 1917-1926* (Hebrew), (Jerusalem: 2013), 116-22, 185-9, 236-54.

outlets, and the halakhic feasibility of a democratic system of governance. The deliberations initiated after the Balfour Declaration was rekindled in the 1940s in anticipation of the establishment of a sovereign Jewish state. Some expressed opinions regarding the disparity between traditional halakhah and the demands of international law, suggesting methods of innovating halakhah to bring it in line with the modern sovereign reality.[3] Prominent among them were the opinions of two Orthodox German Jewish jurists, both well-versed in modern jurisprudence and the sovereign challenge facing halakhah, who nevertheless followed separate and opposing paths that represented the polar extremes of how Orthodoxy contended with this issue. Abraham Chaim Freimann and Isaac Breuer were both of distinguished lineage: Freimann was the great-grandson of Rabbi Jacob Ettlinger (1798-1871), and Breuer was the grandson of Rabbi Samson Raphael Hirsch (1808-1888). They each formulated outlines of a Jewish political system according to halakhah; however, as they represented different schools of German Jewish Orthodoxy, their approaches differed accordingly. This article traces the development of their legal doctrines concerning halakhah and the challenge of sovereignty by comparing them and focusing on the connection between their methods and the German Jewish streams of Orthodoxy whence they originated.

Abraham Chaim Freimann

Abraham Chaim Freimann was born in Holeszów, Czechoslovakia, in 1899. His family moved to Posen and then to Berlin, where his father, Jacob Freimann, was appointed Av Beit Din (a head of the rabbinical court) and a member of the board of trustees of the Orthodox rabbinical seminary founded by Rabbi Esriel Hildesheimer. Freimann studied law at the universities of Frankfurt and Marburg, specializing in Jewish jurisprudence, and then served as a district judge in Königsberg. As he wrote to Gershom Scholem in the winter of 1927: "I enjoy working in the courts of law. Here I am truly a free man, like my name, not subservient to anyone – which is very important to me."[4] In the same letter, he writes of his desire to immigrate to the Land of Israel and of the difficulties of finding work in his field, which led him to the following rumination: "I have despaired of the return to Zion, and yet my heart tells me that my place is there, therefore I will try."[5] When

3 A. Yedidya, "No Longer Halakha for Messianic Times: The Balfour Declaration and the Pioneering Debate on Halakha and the Challenge of Sovereignty," *History–Thought–Reality* 8 (2021), 55-86.

4 A letter from A.C. Freimann to Gershom Scholem, Adar I 5687, The Jewish National Library Archives, Gershom Scholem Collection, ARC. 4* 1599.

5 Ibid.

the Nazis gained ascendancy in 1933 he was dismissed from his position and immigrated to Eretz Israel. In 1943 he was appointed lecturer in Jewish law at the Hebrew University in Jerusalem, and in 1948 he was killed on his way to work when a Hadassah convoy came under attack.

A Democratic Aspect of the Halakhah

While still in Germany Freimann began researching the families of the *Rosh* (Rabbi Asher ben Yehiel, 1250-1327) and Maimonides, and published works on the *rishonim*. His studies were based on the principle of public acceptance of authority, which is actually a democratic aspect of the halakhah. In the second part of his study of the *Rosh* and his descendants, published in 1920, he wrote:

> The unity of the Jewish people is based on the unity of its Torah, that is, the existence of a book of law that is recognized by the entire nation. Once the greatest scholars were in agreement, the Mishnah was recognized as a parliamentary binding book of law. The authority of the Babylonian Talmud is based on its absolute acceptance by the entire Jewish community. The halakhic writings of the Geonim and their rulings came forth from the Babylonian *yeshivot*, which were, in their time, the supreme Jewish authority.[6]

This principle was lauded by Rabbi Abraham Isaac Kook (1835-1935), the rabbi of Jaffa, and later chief rabbi of Jerusalem and the land of Israel, who maintained that the source of halakhic authority was not decreed by our Sages but rather by the nation's acceptance of halakhah as a binding set of rules.[7] This principle was expressed throughout Freimann's life in his main field of research – Jewish law.

6 A.C. Freimann, "Die Ascheriden" ['The Descendants of Asheri'], *Jahrbuch der Juedisch- Literarischen Gesellschaft*, 13 (1920), 198-9.

7 Rabbi Abraham Isaac Kook, *Eder Hayakar* ['The Precious Flock'] (Hebrew), (Jerusalem: 1985), 39. The concept "the nation's acceptance," as a binding concept, existed already in Maimonides' introduction to his *Mishneh Torah*: "But whatever is already mentioned in the Babylonian Talmud is binding on all Israel. And every city and country is bound to observe all the customs observed by the Sages of the Gemara, promulgate their decrees, and uphold their institutions, on the ground that all these customs, decrees and institutions mentioned in the Talmud received the assent of all Israel." And in Rabbeinu Asher's Responsa (43, 8): "One Sage was in our country and his name was Gershom. He instituted good ordinances about divorce in the Geonic Period. And his ordinances and decrees are constant and steady like they were given from Sinai, because they (the collective) received them and transmitted them to the next generations."

The Anthology of Israel's Communities' Legal Sources

Shortly after arriving in Israel, Freimann composed a memorandum of guidelines for the study of Jewish law. His purpose was to create 'a guide to the legal reality of our times,' with the emphasis on the post-Talmudic period,[8] that would include all the laws, customs, and regulations that had been generated in Jewish communities up to the present time.[9] This was, in fact, an applied science project that aimed to facilitate the adaptation of halakhic rulings to modern sovereign reality.

The general idea behind this project was like Benjamin Menashe Levin's *Otzar HaGeonim* project. By collecting commentaries of the *geonim* on all tractates of the Babylonian Talmud, Levin envisioned a kind of spiritual ingathering of exiles, that would ultimately lead to the restoration of the one and only center of Torah authority in the Land of Israel.[10]

Freimann, in a later study, also regarded "the dispersal of the sources of Israel's laws as the dispersal of the nation itself, and therefore gathering them together would be a kind of ingathering of exiles." He maintained that "it is the duty of the scholar of Israel's laws to bring forth from this scattered, dispersed material the legal creative expression of various eras, its roots and its absorption – not only in the sense of the study of antiquity, but as a guide to the legal existence of our time, paving the way for the future of the law in our land."[11] He viewed rabbinic literature and the communities' literature from the Middle Ages and the beginning of the new era as a living, evolving legal method, one that was largely dismembered when legal autonomy was abolished in the nineteenth century. Freimann believed that the way to ensure its continuity lay in bringing together the vast amount of legal material that had accumulated up to the present time. His unique

8 This method was similar to Simchah Assaf's method. On this, see: A. Radzyner, "'Hamisphat haIvri' bein 'leumi' le'dati': Hadilema shel hatnua hadatit-leumit" ['"Jewish Law" between "National" and "Religious": The Dilemma of the Religious-National Movement'] (Hebrew), *Mehkarei Mishpat* 26 (2010), 136-42.

9 E.E. Urbach, "A. C. Freimann HY"D," *Yavneh* 3 (1949), 232.

10 A. Yedidya, "Benjamin Menashe Levin and Orthodox *Wissenschaft des Judentums*," *Cathedra* 130 (2008), 143-4.

11 A.H. Freimann, *Seder Kidushin Venisuin Aharei Hatimat HaTalmud: Mehkar Histori-Dogmati Bedinei Yisrael* ['Law of Betrothal and Marriage after the Completion of the Talmud: A Historical-Dogmatic Study in Jewish Law'] (Hebrew), (Jerusalem: 1945), 6.

initiative intended to collect the exiled legal sources for the purpose of applying halakhic rulings against the background of rulings that had crystallized in the new era, and within the framework of the main precedents of halakhic rulings given worldwide.[12]

One such example can be seen in his discourse regarding the halakhic obligation to provide sustenance for a child born out of wedlock. According to the *Shulhan Arukh* (Even Haezer, 71, 4), a man cannot be obligated to provide child support if the mother claims that he is the father, without his acknowledging paternity. This halakhic approach, which was recognized as the official halakhic position at the time, earned loud condemnation from women's groups. The background for this ruling was the increased number of children being born to unwed mothers as compared to previous years.

Through dozens of literary sources, responsa, and Jewish rulings, Freimann demonstrated that, in fact, in many cases men were obligated to pay child support for a child whose single mother claimed him as the father, although he did not admit paternity. From this he concluded that:

> Legal history teaches that the legal lack of protection for a single mother and her child are not an insurmountable decree, because our independent courts in the Diaspora knew how to institute the necessary boundaries and limitations "to prevent the proliferation of shtukim [those whose father's identity is unknown] in Israel, who would be a burden on the community."
>
> However, it is claimed that most single women in this condition today are not in need of legal assistance and the counsel of a *Sinai* [Knowledgeable] who is versed in law, but rather the medical assistance of one who is "*Oker Harot*" [terminates pregnancy]. But this does not absolve us, the community of jurists, from seeking to rectify a flawed legal situation, one that provides an opening for those who condemn the laws of Israel.[13]

By gathering halakhic traditions from various *kibbutzim*, Freimann demonstrated that it was possible to find halakhic practices that dealt with social issues, whereas prevalent halakhic solutions no longer sufficed for modern times.

12 Ibid.

13 Idem, "Mezonot Shel Yeled Shenolad Shelo Benissuin Al-pi Dinei Yisrael" ['Maintenance of a Child Born out of Wedlock, According to Jewish Law'] (Hebrew), *Hapraklit* 2 (1945), 173.

In addition, like the trends that had prevailed in the field of Judaic studies since its inception and continued in the Orthodox schools of *Wissenschaft des Judentums*,[14] Freimann, too, lent his voice to the apologetics against accusers, both within and without.

Rulings of the Sages

Freimann implemented his scholarly concept in his book *Law of Betrothal and Marriage after the Completion of the Talmud* (1945). In the introduction to the book, he emphasized the importance of the Sages' rulings as the primary basis for the innovation of halakhah in past generations. Many of the Sages' rulings such as the decree of Rabbeinu Gershom Meor haGola, which aimed to solve social problems, were enacted during the period of exile by local Jewish courts.[15] Twenty years earlier, Rabbi Kook expressed his willingness to institute the necessary general rulings in the framework of the Chief Rabbinate, "so long as most of the rabbinical authorities are in agreement and are thereafter accepted by the public, they will have the power of a *din Torah* (matter of litigation)."[16] The Chief Rabbinate of the Land of Israel was established in 1921, with Rabbi Kook elected as its Ashkenazi Chief Rabbi. However, the only ruling that it introduced was the establishment of the Court of Appeal, which was the condition set by the British regime for recognizing the institution of the Chief Rabbinate.[17]

Approximately one year before the publication of his book, Freimann published an article entitled "New rulings of the Chief Rabbinate of Eretz Israel on Family Law." That same year, the Chief Rabbinical Council (henceforth, the 'CRC') enacted three rulings: to require a father to pay

14 A. Yedidya, "The Nazi Attacks on the Talmud and the Apologetic Responses of the Jews in Germany and Austria in the 1930s," *Search and Research* 25 (2016), 45-54.

15 For a historical and legal review of the Sages' regulations, see: M. Elon, *Jewish Law: History, Source, Principles: Hamishpat HaIvri*, trans. B. Auerbach and M.J. Sykes (Philadelphia: 1994), 643-65, 780-879.

16 Rabbi Abraham Isaac HaCohen Kook addresses the Conference of the Chief Rabbinate in the Land of Israel. In: A. Morgenstern, *Harabanut Harashit LeEretz Yisrael: Yisuda Ve'irguna* [The Chief Rabbinate of Israel: Foundations and Organization] (Hebrew), (Jerusalem: 1973), 180.

17 A. Radzyner, "Rabbi Ouziel, the Tel-Aviv-Jaffa Rabbinate and the Rabbinical Court of Appeal: A Play in Four Acts," *Mehkarei Mishpat* 21 (2004), 132-7.

child support for his children up to the age of fifteen; to obligate a *yabam* (the brother of a deceased childless husband) who refuses to release his sister-in-law (thus permitting her to marry another) to pay for her support until he lawfully sets her free; and to increase the minimum amount in the *ketuba* (Jewish marriage contract) from ten to fifty *lirot*.[18] In his article, Freimann discusses the new rulings and praises the CRC for their implementation, which has advanced the creation of a unified Torah based legal system for the general Jewish public in the Land of Israel:

> The new rulings of the Chief Rabbinical Council signify a turning point in the formation of a unified legal creation for all the tribes of Israel who dwell in their land, the Holy Land. Therefore, this new constitution is destined to hold an important place in the development of our rules and laws.[19]

He hoped that the CRC, which in effect constituted the supreme religious body in Israel, would institute the requisite new rulings in light of the swiftly approaching new political situation. In practice, the CRC did little to institute new rulings. In basic areas such as daughters' right to inherit, the CRC could not even come to an agreement. Freimann's hopes for religious rulings in this area never came to fruition.

One aim of his book was to examine this institution and draw practical conclusions for its use:

> This attempt to deal with the development of betrothals and weddings from their early Talmudic beginnings until the present day, did not stem from a desire to teach itself but rather from a desire to teach the entire method of research. This central topic in the laws of matrimony is designed to serve as the touchstone for basic questions in the legal history of our people: what are the forces that create the laws of Israel? How much legal authority do they have as regards amendment and renewal, change and annulment? And why were they enacted?
>
> I have chosen this topic not only for its great **practical** importance, but

18 A.C. Freimann, "Hatakanot Hahadashot shel Harabanut Harashit leEretz Yisrael Bedinei Ishut" ['The New Enactments of the Chief Rabbinate of Israel on Family Law'] (Hebrew), *Sinai* 14 (1944), 254.

19 Ibid., 263.

> also for its **dogmatic** importance in defining the areas of legal authority for enacting legitimate amendments in Israel's constitutional law, the traditional Written Torah, precisely in the most sensitive and delicate area of all our legal system, the laws of matrimony.[20]

In his book, Freimann amassed some 140 rulings on marriage, culled from various times and diverse communities "that teach us about changes and innovations that the leaders of the generations saw fit to insert into the existing legal status." These changes and innovations indicate the sensitivity of these leaders to the needs of the hour and their flexibility in the face of contemporary circumstances. The main purpose of the book was to create a scholarly infrastructure for the renewal and arrangement of *kidushin* (matrimonial laws) in the Land of Israel, since, in the course of time, "various *kibutzim* [a cluster of communities] have moved away from one another in their customs and rulings, even as regards the laws of betrothal and marriage, upon which the unity of the nation depends."[21] It was his intention to ensure that only one certified central rabbinical institution would impose its authority on all the communities in Israel through its new rulings. He suggested to base the new rulings on those the Sephardic communities, as they have an ongoing tradition of involvement with these laws:

> These instructions and ordinances are known to have particular importance, since most Sephardic communities and Oriental Jews have always enjoyed wide legal autonomy as regards the laws [of matrimony]. Their courts have dealt unceasingly with judicial personal matters, and therefore their rulings are outstanding in their continuity of tradition and the stability of their teachings. They form the solid foundation of every sound legal deliberation.[22]

20 Freimann, *Seder*, 5.

21 Ibid.

22 Ibid., 6. On continuity and changes in the Jewish communities in the Islamic countries, see: Z. Zohar, *The Luminous Face of the East: Studies in the Legal and Religious Thought of Sephardic Rabbis of the Middle East* (Hebrew), (Tel Aviv: 2001), 77-195, 183-298; Y. Tobi, "The Organization of the Jewish Communities in the East in the 19-20th Centuries" (Hebrew), in I. Bartal (ed.), *Kehal Yisrael: Jewish Self-Rule Through the Ages*, Vol. 3 (Jerusalem: 2004), 191-209.

Freimann arranged the regulations he had compiled in chronological order, according to four periods: 1. From the time of the *geonim* to the Expulsion from Spain; 2. From the Expulsion from Spain to the Khmelnitsky pogroms of 1648; 3. From the Khmelnitsky pogroms to the loss of legal autonomy; and 4. The period of the loss of legal autonomy, in geographical order: Babylon-Israel, Western Europe (France-England-Ashkenaz), Italy, Provence, Spain, North Africa, Egypt, Ottoman Empire, Poland and Lithuania, the Portuguese Communities, India-Yemen, Austro-Hungary, Russia, and America.

Among the various regulations, he placed the most emphasis on those governing the marriage ceremony (*kidushin*) so that future mishaps would be prevented, permitting marriages to be annulled if they were carried out in violation of the regulation. The two most prominent causes of expropriation of marriage were abduction and clandestine marriage without registration in the municipality or the Ministry of the Interior, in places where State law required such registration. By offering expropriation as a legitimate public amendment, he sought to solve problems that existed in the developing Jewish community in Israel.

At the end of his book, Freimann contends with an extremely serious problem related to the laws of matrimony, one that saw a sharp increase in his lifetime – the problem of *agunot* (lit: 'anchored.' The reference is to women bound in marriage to a husband who refuses to grant a divorce or is missing and not proven dead).[23] This problem greatly expanded following the mass immigration from the Russian Empire to Israel in the 1890s. The situation was later exacerbated by the two world wars:

> Our judicial independence and the power of enforcement of our courts have been abrogated in most of the Diaspora. The introduction of civil marriage and divorce in western countries and the increased flow of Jewish immigration to countries overseas has raised an extremely painful and perilous problem in marital life: that of the malicious 'anchoring' of the daughters of Israel to husbands who evade them and are estranged from

23 On this problem, see: A. HaCohen, *The Tears of the Oppressed: An Examination of the Agunah Problem: Background and Halachic Sources* (New York: 2004); M.J. Broyde, *Marriage, Divorce and the Abandoned Wife in the Jewish Law* (New York: 2000); D.J. Bleich, "Survey of Recent Halakhic Periodical Literature: A 19th Century 'Agunah' Problem and a 20th Century Application," *Tradition* 38/2 (2004), 15-48.

> them, to a degree that has been unprecedented since the time we became a nation.[24]

In a long appendix, Freimann reviews the proposals put forward in recent years as a solution to this problem, all based on legal principles: the expropriation of the wedding ceremony by the local *beth din;* authorization to draw up a *get* (religious divorce) during the wedding ceremony that can be implemented in the event that a woman becomes an *aguna;* and the transition to marital life with no *kidushin* according to the laws that govern a concubine. Freimann rejects them all:

> Most of these suggestions have widely missed their mark: in their efforts to improve the lot of *agunot* they jeopardize the very foundations of matrimony and family upon which every Jewish home rests. "Conditional matrimony" harms the basic principles of public order and social morality. For this reason the legal systems of enlightened nations do not allow conditions to be imposed upon a marriage. Are we about to institute conditional matrimony as the norm for matrimonial relations in Israel? How stringent are the reforms when it comes to severing marital relationships? How many millions of Catholics are in marriages whose bonds will never be loosed? Yet do we intend to make divorce attendant upon every marriage, folded and tucked away in a box from the time the couple stands under the wedding canopy? As to the last suggestion - reverting to the status of concubine - this means abrogating marriage, divorce, levirate marriage [the marriage of a man to his late brother's childless widow], and *halitza* [removal of shoe under levirate law], loosening the reins, leading to chaos, and ultimately destroying our national existence. This is not the way.[25]

In his opinion, the solution to this thorny problem can only lie in a general ruling by the Rabbinic Supreme Court in Israel, whose authority has not been challenged since the destruction of European Jewry. Any ruling based on the authority of this central court of law has the power to annul *kidushin*:

> The remedy must come from the weak spot. The evil source of malicious "anchoring" of *agunot* stems from the abolition of our judicial

24 Freimann, ibid., 385.

25 Freimann, ibid., 396-7.

> independence and authority, from the collapse of our inner discipline, and from the fact that a large segment of our people has rebelled against Israeli jurisdiction. It is not in our power to restore the crown of legal autonomy to our Diaspora courts of law, but the establishment of a supreme religious institute in *Eretz Yisrael*, the place of national vitality, has reinstated a religious center with authoritative jurisdiction for the entire Jewish world. Ever since the destruction of the centers of Jewish learning in the countries of Europe, nothing has been left to us but the Torah of this land. The eyes of all Israel are turned towards this supreme religious institution as the last stronghold for safekeeping religion and tradition, all that remains of the ruins of the Diaspora. Again, we cannot expect any authoritative, legitimate action in the sphere of religion and law from any other source. We cannot apologize, saying that perhaps there is an equally great and important court of law in our generation. This status is accorded to the courts of the Chief Rabbinate of *Eretz Yisrael*. Its power and strength, along with its jurisdiction, are unprecedented in any other Jewish court of our generation. This important court of law has great power to judge and instruct, to annul marriages, and to enact rulings.[26]

Despite Freimann's intellectual daring, his grasp of the essence of the problem, and his awareness of the acute need for a solution, he was also extremely aware of the sensitivity of the issue and maintained that the solution could not depend on each individual rabbi or community, but must be stem from a central mechanism. In this, too, he did not pin much hope on the Chief Rabbinate.

On the one hand, Freimann's enterprise had innovative and practical halakhic importance. He sought to bring together all the regulations and halakhic rulings from the period of exile and apply them as halakhic precedents for contemporary questions, even contrary to the rulings of the *Shulhan Arukh*. On the other hand, he was careful in his conclusions and did not propose to hastily use the precedents he found to resolve any given problem. Instead, he offered the precedents as a source of inspiration for a new regulation, to be amended by the authoritative rabbinical body with the widest consensus of the Jewish community in the Land of Israel – the Chief Rabbinate of Israel.

26 Ibid., 397. On Rabbi Uziel's approach to the authority of High Rabbinical Court, see: Radzyner, "Rabbi Ouziel", 161-4.

Communal Enactments

Towards the end of 1945, the year when his book appeared, Freimann wrote his programmatic article "The Laws of Israel in *Eretz Yisrael,*" published in *Luah Haaretz*. He was aware that it was a time of transition from British Mandate rule to an independent Jewish government, and wished to express his views about the legal system most suitable for the Jewish state. He began with a historical overview of the legal situation in Israel during the time of the destruction of the Second Temple, maintaining that:

> When the state was lost to us, some aspects of public law were annulled, such as the laws of the *Sanhedrin* and capital offences. But the entire body of private law and some branches of public law remained in force even after the destruction and during the entire period of the Diaspora, until the legal autonomy of most Jewish communities in the Diaspora was done away with during the time of the Emancipation.[27]

When legal autonomy came to an end, most of the legal aspects of halakhah became *hilkheta lemshiha* (halakhah that will be enacted in messianic times), such as those dealing with ritual purity and impurity after the destruction of the Temple. The exceptions were Jewish communities in the lands of Islam, where legal autonomy in matrimonial and family law was maintained. This limited autonomy was also passed down to the Yishuv in *Eretz Yisrael* during the time of the British Mandate, when the status and the authority of the Chief Rabbinate was established.

Nevertheless, Freimann was distressed by the fact that specifically at a time of national revival, most of the Jewish public in the land of Israel had no desire to reinstate national Jewish law in every walk of life, preferring the legal proceedings of the Mandate over rabbinical courts and Jewish magistrates. In this context, he quoted a Jewish magistrate from in 1917:

> What a historical paradox: When we lost our country, we strove with all our might to hold onto our national laws and rulings. We used them to build a Chinese wall, a boundary – and in this way we managed to endure for two thousand years, to the amazement of all the nations. But now, when the

27 A.C. Freimann, "Dinei Yisrael BeEretz Yisrael" ['Jewish Law in the Land of Israel'] (Hebrew), *Luah Haaretz* (1946), 110.

> dream of the nation's revival in our country is being realized, this is the first thing we have managed to do. We have abandoned the national laws and regulations that were glorious for their richness and profundity, their lofty ideals of justice and righteousness, and instead we have lovingly welcomed foreign law, one that is now foreign even to those who created it…[28]

Freimann then discussed the most suitable legal system for the future state. For practical reasons, he rejected the slogans of the two polar extremes then prevalent in public discourse: Torah law as endorsed by the religious sector, and the separation of State and religion as proposed by the secular liberals. He argued that Jewish law was not yet applicable to the present time, and adapting it to current circumstances would require legal-historic research: "It is incumbent upon the science of practical Jewish law to first ascertain the practical legal status of all the branches of law among the various Jewish *kibbutzim* until their legal independence was annulled."[29] This is similar to the direction he himself followed in his research on the laws of betrothal and marriage after the Talmudic period. Freimann hoped that this research would construct "a bridge over the empty void that came into being once our law fell into disuse. That which is lacking must be restored, in the same way that our laws would have developed had they remained involved in the changing and evolving life of the nation."[30]

The next stage in processing the legal material for a new constitution requires interpretations that accord with contemporary reality, as well as the institution of new regulations in cases where the judicial interpretation does not lead to the desired outcome. This stage cannot be accomplished through the yeshiva mode of study, which is a-historical and he no pretenses of application. This type of learning "floats in a noble world of abstract study, 'making peace in the highest realms' between various theories and methods of the *tannaim* and the *amoraim*, the *rishonim* and the *aharonim*, without aiming for a practical outcome."[31] The most suitable method for this stage would be a historical-societal review of the legal material, which would result in purposeful interpretation capable of resolving the legal problems that had arisen in recent years:

28 Ibid., 118.
29 Ibid., 120.
30 Ibid., 121.
31 Ibid., 122.

> In the same way that in the past social and economic changes found expression in new legal creations such as the *prozbul, heter iska, herem deRabbeinu Gershom,* and inheritance rights for women and daughters through community and state legislation - in contrast to the established halakhah - so the historical-societal school of legal study will pave new roads to solve problems of our times, such as work legislation, women's emancipation, the concept of cooperation and collective economy, and so on.[32]

Freimann raised the question of who should be involved in rulings and legislation in the future State. Immediately following the Balfour Declaration, its religious-Zionist participants assumed that most of the Jewish people wanted a Torah-based legal system and recognized the authority of their religious leaders. Now, however, the majority of the Jewish Yishuv in *Eretz Yisrael* evidently did not recognize halakhah as a binding authority, preferring to design their sovereign existence according to the rules of representative democracy. Freimann did not even raise the possibility that the rabbis would exclusively lead the process of new legislature. He claimed that most of the public ordinances that were discontinued during the Exile were terminated by the power of public authority, the authority of democracy:

> The public are partners in all their affairs and every condition that they impose is firm and abiding. The public is entitled to arrange all its internal affairs, as regards regime and appointments, authority and taxes, and all other general matters, according to the majority opinion, on condition that it does not contradict what is written in the Torah.[33]

32 Ibid., 121-2.

33 Ibid., 122. On *Takanot haKahal*, see: B. Lipkin, "Shitot Harishonim BeTakanot Hakahal" ['The Approach of the *Rishonim* to Communal Enactments'] (Hebrew), *HaTora Vehamedina* 2 (1950) 41-54; L. Finkelstein, *Jewish Self Government in the Middle Ages* (New York: 1964); E. Kanarfogel, "Unanimity, majority, and communal government in Ashkenaz during the high Middle Ages: A Reassessment," *Proceedings - American Academy for Jewish Research* 58 (1992) 79-106; M. Elon, *Jewish Law*, 678-779; idem, "Authority and Power in the Jewish Community: A Chapter in Jewish Public Law," *Shenaton Hamishpat HaIvri*, 3-4 (1976-7), 7-34; Y.S. Kaplan, "The Public Welfare," *Dinei Israel* 17 (1993-4), 27-91; idem, "The Status and Authority of Communal Leaders in the Middle Ages," *Dinei Israel* 18 (1995-6), 255-319.

In practice, the communities included the local *batei din* (Jewish courts) who were to agree with the communities' rulings. In the past, the entire community was Torah observant, but in the present reality of the Yishuv it would not be possible to leave legislative authority entirely in the hands of the religious public. He also brings the example of the Chief Rabbinate's ruling (1944) on family matters that unconditionally included the community councils and local committees regardless of their members' identity.[34]

At the end of the article he calls upon rabbinical and *dayanim* seminaries in Israel to imbue their students with legal knowledge, ending with a moving plea to all factions of the public:

> It would serve the two sections of the Yishuv well, both the ultra-conservatives and the ultra-progressives, if they would use the transition period to delve into the entire scope of our legal problems. This group will become convinced that it is impossible 'to impose' Israel's laws upon the Yishuv without thorough preparation, and there is no need to recoil from far-reaching revisions whose only purpose is to preserve and uphold, not to destroy and eradicate, as did the 'reform' revisions in their time. And this group will appreciate the great value of our national legislature as a cultural asset, no less important than the Hebrew language and Hebrew education, which is not disputed in the Yishuv that is building its land and its state.
>
> Would that as the Yishuv is destined to renew its political life, the words of our Divine lawgiver will come to pass: "What great nation has laws and rules as perfect as all this teaching?"[35]

Freimann continued to deal with the legislative power of halakhah in a number of articles, following the Anglo-American Committee of Inquiry that convened in 1946. Secular elements in this committee expressed their opposition to the imposition of Torah law in the State of Israel since, they claimed, it is anti-democratic. In an article entitled *Samkhut Hahakika BeYisrael* ('Legislative Power in Israel'), Freimann used Talmudic sources and responsa and based his assertion on a previous article. He maintained that alongside the legislative power of the *beth din*, the public has wide and binding legislative powers in

34 On the 1944 enactments see: Freimann, *Hatakanot*, 254-63; I.E. Herzog, *Huka LeYisrael Al-Pi HaTorah* ['A Torah-based constitution for Israel'] (Hebrew), Vol. 3 (Jerusalem: 1989), 109-58.

35 Freimann, *Dinei Yisrael*, 125.

its capacity as a partner with contractual freedom, on condition that it does not legislate in contradiction to what is written in the Torah:

> By virtue of the freedom of association practiced in our laws, all conditions pertaining to money are valid. In matters not relating to money it is permitted to set conditions and draw up contracts, provided that the parties do not stipulate against what is written in the Torah, for if anything is stipulated against what is written in the Torah, its terms are invalid. By virtue of the principle of freedom of association that governs the legal system of Israel, the public is also entitled to arrange matters according to its wishes and as it sees fit. Individuals such as city residents are regarded as partners in all public matters. Just as the other partners are entitled to stipulate in their partnership contract any condition they wish, so too city residents are entitled to stipulate any conditions they wish for their city's needs: Townspeople are authorized to stipulate regarding prices, measures, and the pay of laborers, and to enforce their decree. Townspeople are authorized to pronounce, "Anyone seen [dealing with] the authorities [*malkhut*] shall pay thus and so." And they are authorized to enforce their decree. (tBaba Metzia, 11, 23). This halakhah determines the absolute autonomy of the city residents, the organized local public, to stipulate conditions among themselves by virtue of a mutual agreement to impose them on the public as a whole. This is the original form of a social charter.[36]

Freimann maintained that in the Middle Ages, this halakhah formed the basis of legislation for Jewish communities whose rulings were recognized as Torah law.[37] As we have seen from his early studies, Freimann claimed that this democratic principle had formed the basis of halakhah ever since the acceptance of *naase venishma* (we will do and we will hear) at Mt. Sinai, and continued with the covenant forged in the days of Nehemia, the nation's acceptance of the Talmud, and finally the acceptance of the *Shulhan Arukh* as a binding halakhic codex. In effect, it is this principle that today endows the

36 A.H. Freimann, "Darkei Hahakika BeYisrael" ['The Methodology of Jewish Legislation'] (Hebrew), *Yavneh* 1 (1946), 43.

37 Besides Freimann, Rabbi Chaim Hirschenson also evaluated the importance of *Takanot Hakahal* to the democratic character of halakhah, although he did not centralize them. Hirschenson, *Malki Bakodesh,* vol. 3, 68-76.

elected representative Jewish Parliament with legislative authority, on condition that it does not stipulate against what is written in the Torah.

Freimann claimed that communal enactments belonged in the domain of the public law that was preserved after the destruction of the Temple, and not in private law, contra Asher Gulak and later scholars such as Menachem Elon and Shalom Albeck.[38] He explained that our Sages needed to rely on *halakhot* from private law in the matter of partnerships and contracts in order to establish the authority of their regulations according to the principle of the social contract. The source of public authority lies in the social contract which, conceptually, parallels the principle of contractual partnership in private law. According to this concept, the public can impose its authority on individuals who oppose a specific regulation. In other words, the social contract establishes the principle of public partnership in all public affairs. It has the power to appoint a legislative body to enact laws and regulations for the public benefit without the consent of each member of the public, and it is exempt from the various restrictions imposed' on contractual engagements in private law, such as the need for a deed of acquisition, the impossibility of bestowing something not yet in existence, and so on. His synthetic interpretation of diverse sources from rabbinical literature on communal enactments, and his disregard of the methods adopted by *rishonim* who objected to the coercion of the majority over the minority who opposed the regulation, reflect his applied method, one that sometimes blurred the contradictions between various sources who had difficulty reaching an unequivocal halakhic decision.[39] Freimann continued to study the

38 Elon, *Jewish Law*, 681-85; A. Gulak, *Yesodei Hamishpat HaIvri* ['The Foundations of Jewish Law'] (Hebrew), (Jerusalem: 1923), vol. 2, 50-2; S. Albeck, *The Law of Property and Contract in the Talmud* (Hebrew), (Tel Aviv: 1976), 504-16. Elon maintained that communal enactments were only interpreted by our Sages as public law from the tenth century. Elon, *Authority and Power*, 11-2. Freimann also disregards the fact that several *rishonim* disputed the two terms that appear in tannaitic literature regarding communal enactments: '*kofin*,' suited to public law, and '*rasha'in*,' suited to private law. Kaplan, "The Public Welfare," *Dinei Israel* 17 (1993-4), 41-7.

39 Freimann did not foresee the discrepancy between the limited authority of the public (which functioned with limited autonomy within the larger state) and the wider authority of a sovereign state. But, in referring to the Social Contract principle, he assisted in establishing the legal principle that is valid in both cases. On this, see: B. Porat, "Five Jewish Terms of Israeli

issue of legislative authority on secondary issues stemming from the central question.

In a follow-up article entitled "Public Majority and Minority: Public and State *Halakhot* in Israel," Freimann discusses the majority required by halakhah to enact new public rulings.[40] He begins by saying that, with regard to most of the stated opinions in the courts of law,

> as a general rule, the saying 'the ruling follows the majority' applies not only to the Supreme Court and all decisions in Jewish law, but to all public and state laws. Rabbi Shimon ben Gamliel and Rabbi Elazar bar Zadok say that one only sees to the needs of the public on condition that most of the public is accepting, and one does not issue public edicts unless most of the public can abide by them.[41]

Any decision taken by most of the public is also binding upon the minority who oppose it, including coercive measures to enforce regulations taken by the majority.

Freimann goes on to discuss the type of majority required for public decisions: either the majority of people, where everyone has a vote; the majority of taxpayers, those with the most property; or, the wisest of the intellectuals in society. Jewish communities throughout the ages referred to these three kinds of majority. From this he infers that the type of majority required also depends on a consensus of 'most individuals in the community,' since "ultimately everything depends on the basic charter and the public constitution."[42] Based on the responsa of Rabbi Shlomo ben Aderet, who wrote that when it comes to communal enactments, he also concluded that "women are like men, for nobody would rule on their property without their consent." Thus, women have the right to take part in public decisions "when it comes to public matters the rule for women is the same as that for men. This

---

Democracy," in idem (ed.), *Reflections on Jewish Democracy* (Hebrew), (Jerusalem: 2009), 19-20.

40 On different aspects of majority and minority in communal decisions in the Middle Ages, see: J.S. Kaplan, "Majority and Minority in the Decisions of the Jewish Community in the Middle Ages," *Shenaton Hamishpat HaIvri* 20 (1996-7), 213-80.

41 A.H. Freimann, "Rov Umiut Batzibur" ['Majority and Minority in the Community'], (Hebrew), *Yavneh* 2 (1948), 1.

42 Ibid., 5.

is the answer for those who would deny Jewish women their public rights."[43]

He further deduces that it is necessary to hold a debate, on the topic under discussion, in the presence of all those who have a right to vote, similar to the discussion held by a panel of judges in court. The voting majority cannot exclude the others from the discussion to obtain a binding ruling, even if they hold the majority opinion:

> The rule of 'most out of all' upholds the legal right of the minority to take part in all public debates and express their argument in the plenum, at the entire public debate. Perhaps they will succeed in persuading the majority to change their minds. It is forbidden to silence the opposition by holding a discussion in their absence.[44]

He bases this deduction on the criticism leveled by *HaRalbah* (Rabbi Levi ibn Habib) against *Mahari* Berab (Rabbi Jacob Berab), when the Sages of Safed disputed the controversial renewal of ordination in 1538.[45] Their consent was not binding, even though they constituted the majority of Jewish Sages, because they did not consult with the Jerusalem Sages in the form of a court hearing before their decision. This deduction also anchored the rights of the minority to attend the deliberations of the legislature. He therefore concluded that:

> The law provides the Jewish public with a wide measure of autonomy to organize their own lives and to elect the form of organization and regime they prefer - but only on one basic condition: that they do not harm the principles of Torah and justice, for any stipulation on what is written in the Torah is void, whether specified by an individual or by the public.[46]

Freimann's method effectually secured the halakhic legitimacy of parliamentary legislation, on condition that that it would not contradict Torah law in any way. He also secured rabbinical authority to impose

43 Ibid., 4. On this debate, see: Shilo, *Zionist Women's Struggle*, 183-9, 236-54.

44 Freimann, "Rov Umiut Batzibur," 5.

45 J. Katz, "The Controversy on the Semikha (Ordination) between Rabbi Jacob Bei-Rav and the Ralbah," *Zion* 16/3-4 (1951), 28-45; M. Benayahu, "The Revival of Ordination in Safed," in S.W. Baron and others (eds.), *Yitzhak F. Baer Jubilee Volume* (Hebrew), (Jerusalem: 1960), 248-69; S.Z. Havlin, "The Ralbah," *Jeschurun* 11 (2002), 884-900; 14 (2004), 997-1011.

46 Freimann, "Rov Umiut Batzibur," 6.

creative legal interpretations and amend the necessary regulations for the times, in contrast to case law. In essence, Freimann mapped out ways of adapting halakhah to modern sovereign reality. His blueprint was based on three complementary foundations: First, the adoption of suitable halakhic practices from the halakhic-legal corpus of the Jewish communities in the post-Talmudic period, particularly those where legal autonomy had not been abolished during the Emancipation. This would require a project that would gather these halakhic traditions and their accessibility. Second, new regulations would be required to adapt halakhah to reality, similar to those instituted in previous generations from the time of the Mishnah and the Talmud to those introduced by the rabbinical courts of prominent Jewish communities in later centuries. In this context, he claimed that the CRC could serve as a suitable platform. Third, *takanot hakahal* (lit., 'community regulations') are an ancient and legitimate halakhic institution that can form the basis for the halakhic authority of a democratic Jewish Parliament, on condition that it does not legislate contrary to Torah law. The historic experience of this institution also teaches the essential procedures required for the proper functioning of such a legislature. Freimann's recognition of the halakhic authority of a non-rabbinical democratic House of Representatives was in line with his general concept of the democratic aspect of halakhah, as expressed in the principle of national acceptance that he emphasized from his earliest studies on.

On the eve of the founding of the State of Israel, and in its early years, other rabbis, including Shmuel Kalman Mirsky, Shimon Federbusch, and Ben-Zion Chai Uziel, expressed similar views, according to which the source of authority for new religious legislation is to be found in the public consent. Rabbi Uziel also relied on communal enactments to bestow halakhic legitimacy on the Knesset laws, by virtue of which rabbinical courts operate.[47]

47 A. Yedidya, *Halakha and the Challenge of Israeli Sovereignty* (Lanham: 2019), 133-9; Y. Mirsky, "The New Heavens in the New World: The Religious Hebraism of Samuel K. Mirsky," in A. Ferziger (ed.), *The Paths of Daniel: Studies in Judaism and Jewish Culture in Honor of Rabbi Professor Daniel Sperber* (Ramat-Gan: 2017), 101*-128*; M. Hellinger, "Religion and State in Sepharadi Religious-Zionist Thought: R. Meir Hai Ouziel and R. Hayyim David Halevi," in A. Ravitzky (ed.), *Religion and State in Twentieth-Century Jewish Thought* (Jerusalem: 2005), 233-9.

Isaac Breuer

Isaac Breuer (1883-1946), who was also a German Orthodox scholar and jurist, represented a completely different approach.[48] Born in Pápa, Hungary, in 1890 he immigrated to Frankfurt am Main with his family, where his father was appointed rabbi of the Orthodox community. Between the years 1890-1898 he studied at the Orthodox school of the community, which was established by his grandfather, Rabbi Samson Raphael Hirsch. Between 1898 and 1904 he studied at his father's yeshiva in Frankfurt am Main, and from 1904 to 1909 he attended Strasburg University, Marburg University, and Berlin University, and co-founded the *Bund Juedischer Akademiker*. In 1912, he was one of the founders of *Agudat Yisrael*. Unlike many other members of *Agudat Yisrael*, Breuer supported a unique Orthodox version of Jewish nationalism, hailing the First World War as a "Messianic" War, and the Balfour Declaration as the "harbinger of the Messiah."[49]

According to Breuer, Jewish nationalism emerged after the Divine revelation at Mount Sinai, based on the Torah as national law. Its principle is a historic mission to establish a Torah State — the fulfilment of the vision of law and justice — that would eventually restore Divine sovereignty to the world. National emancipation (auto-emancipation), which was made possible after the Balfour Declaration and the British Mandate, is a further stage in the fulfilment of the mission of the Torah nation. This requires living according to Torah law, specifically in the Land of Israel, as an autonomous people, destined to establish a Torah State that will integrate law and justice and reveal God's true sovereignty to all. However, he believed that Zionism deviates from the essence of the Jewish people and their goal because it sees the nation as an ordinary historical nation, ignoring both it being the nation of the Torah as well as its meta-historical nature. Religious Zionism, by joining Zionism, legitimizes this deviation, similar to

48 See: I. Breuer, *Mein Weg* (Jerusalem/Zurich: 1988); J.S. Levinger (ed.), *Concepts of Judaism: Isaac Breuer* (Jerusalem: 1974); M. Morgenstern, *From Frankfurt to Jerusalem: Isaac Breuer and the History of the Secession Dispute in Modern Jewish Orthodoxy* (Leiden: 2002); A.L. Mittleman, *Between Kant and Kabbalah: An Introduction to Isaac Breuer's Philosophy of Judaism* (New York: 1990); A.D. Biemann, "Isaac Breuer: Zionist against his will?," *Modern Judaism* 20 (2000), 129–46; A. Gebel, "Yitzhak Breuer and the Question of Sovereignty in the Land of Israel," *Iyunim* 31 (2019), 215-43.

49 I. Breuer, *Messiasspuren* (Frankfurt am Main: 1918); idem, *Mein Weg*, 106-9.

communal Orthodoxy in Germany, which did not withdraw from the old community.

During the war Breuer served as a military censor of the German army, and after the war worked as a lawyer in Frankfurt am Main. In 1925, he travelled to the land of Israel and tried to convince the Mandate's authorities to give equal legal status to the Ultra-Orthodox community in Jerusalem. He left Germany in 1936, three years after the Nazi rise to power, and settled in Jerusalem, where he was appointed director of the *Agudat Yisrael* Yishuv Fund ('*Keren Hayishuv*'). However, after five years of differences of opinion with his colleagues, he resigned and resumed practicing law.

Breuer was a staunch supporter of the *haredi* settlement in the Land of Israel, and was the *de facto* spiritual head of *Poalei Agudat Israel*, whom he regarded as his students. In 1944 he published *Moria*, his first book in Hebrew, wherein he presented a historiosophical view of Jewish history, determining the nation's role at the time. Breuer died in Jerusalem in 1946. Five years later, his comprehensive work *Nahaliel* on *taamei hamitzvot* (the reasons for the *mitzvot*) was published, in which he outlined the basis of Jewish theocracy according to which his vision of a Torah State would materialize.

Anti-historicism

As far back as 1910, Breuer took up the challenge posed by the modern system of jurisprudence based on equality before the law regardless of religion, nationality or gender. He was drawn to this challenge following the case of a Jewish couple who appeared before a German court, seeking a divorce. The woman filed for divorce on the grounds of adultery. The court decided that whereas according to Jewish law only the husband has the right to divorce his wife on the grounds of adultery, this blatant discrimination against the wife offends every sense of justice, rendering the *halakhah* inappropriate for a German judge. According to German law, declared the judge, the couple must divorce. This prompted Breuer to deal with other essential differences between the laws of Israel and modern jurisprudence regarding the concept of the inequality of slavery and discrimination against non-Jews.

In an article titled "The Philosophical Foundations of Jewish and of Modern Law," published in the same year as the divorce case, Breuer noted that many Jews were dissatisfied with the inequality prevalent in Jewish law:

> Thus, we see Jewish law surrounded by powerful partitions of an individual-sexual, social and national nature, and at the same time we see that everywhere in modern law these partitions are being overcome to an increasing extent. [... T]he loftiest quality on which modern law prides itself, its eternal title to glory, consists in the removal of these partitions, a task of legislative development spanning more than a thousand years. Jewish law appears to stand in irreconcilable contradiction to this whole process of legislative development and seems able to maintain its position only alongside legal systems which have long since been covered by the dust of past eras.[50]

Breuer's suggestions for resolving this contradiction did not in any way resemble those proposed by Freimann, on similar issues. Breuer did not seek to change halakhah through an inner mechanism to make it compatible with modern-day reality and the sense of justice and integrity, which he greatly respected, that prevailed in the Western world. Instead, he philosophically analyzed two legal systems and their attitude towards morality. The modern legal system is based on the concept of humaneness, to which Judaism subscribes, but Judaism is nevertheless committed to a higher ideal. The universal and rational idea of humaneness demands absolute equality in legal rights and does not tolerate discrimination or favoritism. In contrast, Israel's legal system of is based on the transcendent moral concept of the obligations imposed on diverse groups according to their innate characteristics: the Jewish nation, males, priests, slaves, and so on, endowing them with unequal rights. Yet this inequality has never arisen from a position of strength, nor does it allow for arbitrariness or abuse, as was the case with the laws of nations in the pre-modern world:[51]

> The disparity of the delegation of duties is a principle that rules Jewish law. We do not only see it effective in the relationship of man and wife, of master

50 I. Breuer, "The Philosophical Foundations of Jewish and of Modern Law," in J.S. Levinger (ed.), *Concepts of Judaism: Isaac Breuer* (Jerusalem: 1974), 61.

51 On this distinction, see: A. Israel-Vleeschhouwer, "Bikoret haredit al ribonut, individualizem, umusag zekhuyot haadam: Hagut leumit uvein-leumit datit shel harav dr. Yitzhak Breuer" ['A Jewish Ultra-Orthodox Critique of Nationalism Individualism and Rights-Based Regimes: The Alternative Model and Thought of Yitzhak Breuer'] (Hebrew), *Hamishpat: Law Review* 15/2 (2010), 636-41.

> and slave, of Israel and the nations, we see it also effective in the way the Jewish people are divided into three: priests, Levites and laymen, un the prominence it is not the power that is delegated, the personal interest that is given balance, but it is rather the moral law which, in the multiplicity of the spheres of tasks, is to arrive at an ever more complete representation in mutual furtherance and completion.[52]

Breuer opposed the historicist approach of Jewish scholars. He did not claim that inequality stemmed from accepting frameworks of the ancient world, such as polygamy and slavery, and using them in a moral and legal manner, as far as possible. Negative frameworks disappeared from the Western world in the course of time and Judaism was obligated to abandon them because of their inherent lack of morality. A case in point is rulings such as Rabbeinu Gershom's *herem* [decree] that abolished polygamy and the husband's right to divorce his wife against her will. In fact, Breuer was following in the footsteps of his grandfather, Rabbi Samson Raphael Hirsch, who was opposed to the historicist methods of *Wissenschaft des Judentums*, even in the moderate Orthodox version, and viewed Torah laws and commandments as natural laws with no historical development.[53]

Hirsch was the main Orthodox spokesman against *Wissenschaft des Judentums*. He claimed that *Wissenschaft des Judentums* is a "system for the theoretical extenuation of an actual apostasy," that everything it had wrought was "more or less like throwing sand or stones at Judaism as it moves through life," and that this science had, at least in retrospect, lent an air of scientific respectability to the vulgar ambitions of reform.[54] Hirsch's concept of *Wissenschaft des Judentums* proceeded from the assumption that the written and oral law were as much Divine creation as is nature, and that therefore the inquiry into the laws of the Torah and their relationships must be subject to the same method of inquiry as the laws of nature. Thus, for example, just as the Law of Gravity has

52 Breuer, "Philosophical Foundations," 75-6.

53 On continuity and change in Breuer's ideology as compared to S. R. Hirsch's ideology, see: B. Brown, "Breuer, Hirsch and Jewish Nationalism: Change and Continuity – Principle versus Supra-Principle," *Journal of Jewish Studies* 64 (2013), 383-402.

54 S.R. Hirsch, "Wie gewinnen wir das Leben für unsere Wissenschaft?," *Jeschurun* Vol. 8 (1861), 88. (Translation in: M. Breuer, *Modernity within Tradition – The Social History of Orthodox Jewry in Imperial Germany* (New York: 1992), 178).

no history, so too the laws of the Torah. According to him, this subject of research was ahistorical.[55]

Breuer followed Hirsch's path. He, too, rejected applying the historicist method of halakhah in any form.[56] He expressed this rejection in his autobiography:

> In some ways we could say that the study of such law is extremely hazardous for Jewish interests if we ignore biblical criticism. It is certainly more dangerous that the study of philosophy. The main subject of modern philosophy in no way resembles that of Judaism. But the main subject of Roman philosophy, like that of all other nations, is how individuals and nations live side by side. This is also the subject of the Torah in the form of Divine law, as well as that of the Talmud. [...] Law, like language, is subject to the general rules of national growth. We have Roman law, German law, Anglo-Saxon law, Romanian law, and so on, so why not also "Jewish" law? Are not the factual data of all laws basically the same? Why should we not include "Jewish law" in the science of comparative law? Why do we not regard "Jewish law" as the product of the "Jewish" people, in the same way that the laws of all nations are self-made? Indeed, whoever thinks so is completely ejected from the national-Jewish circle. He is lost to Jewish national Torah study. [...] It is only with aversion that I was able to read writings composed by Jewish jurists on the subject of "Jewish law" and I read hardly any of them to the end. To my eyes they dealt with anatomy, the anatomy of a human body whose soul has departed. Our law is the law of the Living God. The more I involve myself in the law of other nations, the more I am made aware of the wide chasm between their law and Divine law.[57]

Freimann, on the other hand, was raised in the school of Hildesheimer that dealt in the study of *Wissenschaft des Judentums* and regarded it as a legitimate and necessary tool for a more precise and deeper understanding of the Torah. Nevertheless, this school of thought had its own concept of the nature and limitations of this field of study. They sought to create an Orthodox alternative to the *Wissenschaft des*

55 Breuer, ibid., 179.

56 On Breuer's opposition to historicism, see: D.N. Myers, *Resisting History: Historicism and Its Discontents in German-Jewish Thought* (Princeton: 2003), 130-56.

57 Breuer, *Mein Weg*, 66-8.

Judentums. Orthodox scholars competed with the basic values and methods of research that challenged traditional concepts of the past, such as objectivity and historicism, and developed research strategies that allowed them to hold on to both their objectives at the same time, scientific research methods and traditional values.[58]

In the second half of the 1930s, Freimann was a member of the Organization of Jewish Studies (*Aluma*) established in Jerusalem in 1935 by the Orthodox scholar Benjamin Menashe Levin. This organization was intended to be the basis of Orthodox *Wissenschaft des Judentums*, founded upon the religious premises outlined by Orthodox scholars throughout the years, within the context of the national renaissance.[59]

In a critical essay written in 1947, Freimann even expressed his strong opposition to Wellhausen's documentary hypothesis. Like Allbright, he called it "an anti-Semitic libel invented by the spiritual fathers of the Nazis who claimed that the priests of Israel smuggled books of later origin into the Books of Moses."[60]

This difference between the two schools of thought also created a different type of apologia. The question of the attitude towards non-Jews in rabbinical literature was a central theme in Jewish apologetic writings in Germany during the nineteenth century. Talmudic texts that defamed gentiles and advocated a double legal and moral standard for Jews in their dealings with other Jews, as compared to their dealings with non-Jews, were cast in the face of those Jews who, at the time, were struggling for emancipation.

The liberals, generally, maintained that the Talmud and all the vast body of halakhic literature created in its wake had become entirely irrelevant.[61] They advocated for complete religious tolerance and egalitarian relations with non-Jews. They even removed the blessing "Who has not made me a gentile" from the prayer book. The Orthodox, being obligated to the Talmud, responded apologetically. The Hildesheimer school made efforts to find halakhic precedents with neutral or even egalitarian attitudes to non-Jews. Abraham Berliner proposed replacing the well-known negative version of the blessing

58 A. Yedidya, "Orthodox Reactions to *Wissenschaft des Judentums*," *Modern Judaism* 30 (2010), 69-94.

59 Yedidya, "Benjamin Menashe Levin," 150.

60 A.H. Freimann, "Critique of E. M. Epstein, Marriage Laws in the Bible and the Talmud" (Hebrew), *Kiryat Sefer* 23 (1947), 109.

61 M.A. Meyer, *Response to Modernity* (Oxford: 1988), 91.

"Who has not made me a gentile" with the less-known positive formulation "Who has made me an Israelite."[62] David Zvi Hoffmann pointed on the unusual and relatively unknown stand taken by Rabbi Menachem Meiri, who lived and worked in Provence in the second half of the thirteenth century.[63] According to him, Christians and Muslims were "nations fenced in by religion" rather than idolaters, and therefore they should not to be discriminated against in the Talmud as regards the strictures between man and his fellow-man. They are "like Israel in all these things... with no prejudice whatsoever."[64]

In 1919 Freimann published an article entitled *Foreign Law in Israel,* wherein he depicted the attitude of Jews towards the non-Jewish residents of a Jewish State. By using biblical and halakhic sources he drew a unified picture of a halakhic policy that extended equality to non-Jews, while ignoring *halakhot* such as those relating to interest and fraud, where the law is not the same for Jews as for non-Jews. He pointed to the fact that Judaism is not a proselytizing religion and in fact presents difficulties for would-be converts; to the prohibition against harming or damaging the property of anyone, including non-Jews, and any form of oppression; to equal social rights and the obligation to respect the aged, including the aged gentiles. He referred to the fact that even in ancient times the Land of Israel attracted non-Jews due to this policy of equality, claiming that minority rights set in the law were abolished following the destruction of the Jewish State and that Jewish law was no longer used as the State law.[65]

The apologetic stance taken by Rabbi Samson Raphael Hirsch and his followers was more limited and ahistorical.[66] As a rule they stuck to accepted texts and *halakhot,* interpreting them in a non-chauvinistic

62 A. Berliner, *Randbemerkungen zum tagelichen Gebetbuch* (Berlin: 1909), 14-6.

63 D.Z. Hoffmann, *Der Schulchan-Aruch und die Rabbinen über das erhältnis der juden zu Adersgläubigen* (Berlin: 1885), 4-7.

64 J. Katz, *Exclusiveness and Tolerance: Studies in Jewish-Gentile Relations in Medieval and Modern Times* (Oxford: 1961), 115-8; D. Novak, *The Image of the Non-Jew in Judaism* (Portland: 2011), 195-9; M. Halbertal, "'Ones Possessed of Religion': Religious Tolerance in the Teachings of the Me'iri," *Edah* 1/1 (2000).

65 A. Freimann, "Die Behandlung der Volksfremden bei den Juden," *Mitteilungsblatt des Juedischen Volksrats* 8 (1919), 102-3.

66 Hirsch's apologetics focused on promoting a moral attitude toward non-Jews by selectively quoting supporting texts, and presenting the principal position of loyal Jewish behavior in the Exile, according to the '*midrash* of the three oaths.'

manner. For example, in his commentary on the prayer book, Hirsch did not change the blessings "... who has not made us heathens" or "... who has not made us women." However, he provided a non-chauvinistic commentary on these blessings:

> This is not a prayer of thanks that God did not make us heathens, slaves, or women. Rather, it calls upon us to contemplate the task which God has imposed upon us by making us free Jewish men, and to pledge ourselves to do justice to this mission. These three aspects of our own status impose upon us duties much more comprehensive than those required of the rest of mankind.[67]

As we have seen, Breuer himself followed a similar path. In this article he rated the blessings "Blessed be God, who has not made me a Gentile, ...not made me a slave, ...not made me a woman"[68] as central motifs of Jewish law:

> In these sentences from the daily liturgy we find expressed, with surprising clarity, the completely unique character of Jewish law and its partitions. In these sentences we find these partitions related to God himself, the eternal relevance for all persons subject to Jewish law. *To eradicate these sentences from the liturgy would be tantamount to rendering invalid the complete structure of Jewish law.* It is precisely because the contents of these sentences are perhaps "unpalatable" for many that they bear the greatest importance in our day. To eradicate them, yet to consider the partitions expressed in them as binding, constitutes an act of dishonorable cowardice.[69]

Meta Law

Breuer's objection to historicism in the research of the oral law was consistent with his view about the essential difference between the Torah and the law of the nations.[70] This difference is reflected in his

67 S.R. Hirsch, *The Hirsch Siddur: The Order of Prayers for the whole Year* (Jerusalem: 1978), 13.

68 Breuer, "Philosophical Foundations," 61.

69 Ibid., 61-2.

70 M. Seidler, "Isaac Breuer's Concept of Law," *Jewish Law Association Studies* 8 (2000), 167-71.

attitude towards making significant changes in reality. In an article titled "The Great Turning," published in 1944, he clarified his view:

> Revolution is a political concept common among the other nations of the world. Among them law is the fruit of reality, and if it is in harmony with reality, then it is a just law. When the existing order changes, the law has to be changed; if we do not change it, then a contradiction arises between law and the existing order. Should this contradiction become intensified, and if there are no men of wisdom who understand the times and are able to rectify matters before it is too late, then a revolution breaks out and effects a change in the law by force, strength, and power. As the law of the people of Israel, the Torah is eternal. A revolution against the Torah is violence and revolt, and remains forever violence and revolt, which thousands of years cannot cure and turn into law and justice. It was for this reason that the author of the *Hatam Sofer*, of blessed memory, said: "According to the Torah, whatever is novel is forbidden. [...] except that which is new in the Torah itself.[71]

As an example of a legitimate revolution, Breuer brought the case of his grandfather, Rabbi Samson Raphael Hirsch, who brought the new order "under the sway of the eternal Torah."

In 1938, following the hearings of the (1937) Peel Commission on the establishment of a Jewish State in part of the Land of Israel, Breuer wrote a constitutional program for this State that was consistent with his view.[72] Both the Oral Law and the Bible were dictated to the people heteronomously, and are not a product of the people's spirit or historical development. The first three sections of the proposal are:

1. The Torah is the law of the Jewish people.
2. If the Israeli public gains autonomy, the Torah will be incumbent upon the public as the law of the Jewish people, within boundaries specified according to the Torah.
3. The binding force of the Torah, as the law of the Jewish people, does not depend upon its acceptance or non-acceptance by the people.[73]

71 I. Breuer, "The Great Turning," in J.S. Levinger (ed.), *Concepts of Judaism: Isaac Breuer* (Jerusalem: 1974), 310-1.

72 Elon, *Jewish Law*, 1613.

73 I. Breuer, "Tokhnit Lahuka Bamedina HaYehudit" ['A Constitutional Program for the Jewish State'] (Hebrew), *Yavneh* 3 (1949), 33-40.

Breuer even extracted a clause from the regulations of his congregation in Frankfurt-am-Main, that read: "Every Jew must be circumcised according to the law of the Torah." In contrast to Freimann, Breuer completely rejected every democratic aspect of halakhah. His proposal contained hardly any attempts to contend with the modern and sovereign challenges facing halakhah, not even by creating new systems capable of doing so. According to his proposal, the Chief Rabbinate would not have the authority to introduce new rulings according to the new needs as dictated by time and status. Its most far-reaching purpose would be "to immediately begin processing workers' laws according to the Torah," out of a concern for social justice and peace. Like Freimann, he pointed to the need for a modern codex of work laws; however, Breuer did not mention the need for 'women's emancipation.' Some eight years later, in his autobiography, Breuer even maintained that the agreed-upon representatives of the Torah must be "precisely versed in these manifestations of economic life and draw them close to the laws and judgments of the Torah, in order to prove the eternal relevance of these laws and judgments," because "the manifestations of modern economic life are entirely different from the time of Abaye and Rava, Rabbi Yosef Karo, and Rabbi Shabtai Hacohen."[74] In other words, adapting the Torah to the political constitution can only be done through a process of applying the principles of existing *halakhot* to modern systems that were formerly not in existence, by "clearly formulating the concepts, with reference to the reality of our times, by defining them from a meta-lawful point of view compared to other nations, and wherever possible, developing them in practice."[75] Beyond that nothing should be changed, nor should we consider the concepts of justice and integrity of international law.

Arye Edrei claimed that "Breuer well understood that the Torah state would require extensive halakhic activity," including "halakhic creativity" and the creation of a "new halakhah." Ultimately, his position was closer to that of the Mizrahi rabbis, although he preferred to downplay this.[76] As I have noted, the halakhic activity advocated by Breuer is not at all similar to the proposals of Freimann and the Zionist rabbis who were required to address the issue. It was no accident that

74 Breuer, *Mein Weg*, 254.

75 Ibid, 117.

76 A. Edrei, "Rav tarbutiyut begirsa haredit mukdemet: Yitzhak Breuer memedinat haTorah lekehilat haTorah" ['Multi-Culturalism in Early Ultra-Orthodox Doctrine: Yitshak Breuer – From the Torah State to the Torah Community'] (Hebrew), *Dinei Israel* 32 (2018), 189, 200-9.

he used the term 'translation,' rather than 'inspiration,' 'innovation,' or 'the writing of new chapters.'

Amichai Radzyner and Shuki Friedmann maintain that, from the outset, Breuer couched his constitutional proposal in extreme terms from which it would be possible to withdraw, thus helping to preserve the communal interests of the Haredi public. His proposal should therefore be regarded chiefly as a plan for a 'defensive' constitution, rather than a 'formulated' constitution.[77] In my opinion, Breuer fully believed in his proposal, although he was aware that the majority of the Yishuv were unlikely to accept it, as he wrote to Jacob Rosenheim in a memorandum. He believed in presenting the ideal vision while fighting for the fulfillment of its basic aspects for the existence of the Orthodox community. He wrote to Rosenheim that a State that rejects this constitution is not halakhically legitimate.[78] Unlike most of his colleagues in Agudat Israel, he was, even at an early stage, enterprising and visionary in all that pertained to the Yishuv in Israel and its future statehood. His writings from then until the end of World War II are imbued with this belief, and with his intention to realize his uncompromising vision of a 'Torah State.'[79]

Indeed, after coming to Israel, Breuer concluded that the religious reality in the Yishuv would not change in the foreseeable future. *Agudat Yisrael* had missed the opportunity, provided by the Balfour Declaration, to become the dominant force in Israel and affect the character of the new State. Now that the balance of power had shifted within the Yishuv, the vision of a Torah State would not come to fruition any time soon.[80] As far as Breuer was concerned, withdrawal from the State was not an option, nor did the situation resemble that of Germany seventy years earlier. Withdrawing from the Jewish State is not the same as separating from the Jewish community in Germany:

77 Sh. Friedman and A. Radzyner, *The Religious Community and the Constitution: What Can History Teach Us?* (Hebrew), (Jerusalem: 2006), 29-30.

78 Quoted in I. Levin (ed.), *Material for the Preparation of a Constitution for the Jewish State on a Religious Basis* (Hebrew), (New York: 1948), 5.

79 I. Breuer, *Weltwende* (Jerusalem: 1979). This book contains two long articles, written in 1938 and 1942.

80 Y. Fund, *Separation or Participation: Agudat Israel Confronting Zionism and the State of Israel* (Hebrew), (Jerusalem: 1999), 39-41.

> Faced with the imminent prospect of the formation of a Jewish State, we must beware to not indulge in the luxury of restrained theorizing in discussing the ideology and constitution of a Jewish State. Instead, based on concrete reality, we must seek to clarify these points: what should be the structure of the Jewish state; what can be accomplished; what must be accomplished; and what may be left to future efforts. There can be no doubt that the Jewish State will fall short of our Torah-ideals. While it is possible to counteract an assimilationist community with the creation of a second, independent community, we must realize that we cannot oppose an equally defective state by the formation of a second, independent, and "ideal" state.[81]

Supporters of Agudat Israel were left with the task of influencing the State, when it came into being, to accept the Agudah's vision, so that every Jew could live there according to his or her faith, without secular coercion, and that the Torah-observant community would have broad communal autonomy. Such autonomy would allow compromise with the secular majority, legitimizing a State that does not accord with the Torah vision.[82] This issue formed the basis of the status quo agreement reached with Agudat Israel and the leadership of the national institutions on the eve of the establishment of the State.[83]

However, in his last book *Nahaliel*, written in the final year of his life as the platform for the ideal Torah State to which we should aspire and educate, Breuer described the characteristics of his visionary State, its institutions and law, and how it essentially differed from the modern State:

> A sovereign state whose laws come to it from outside, apart from it, from Mount Sinai, from the Creator: how difficult it is to explain the characteristics of such a state to the nations of the world! How difficult it is to explain it to the straying people of our nation! They cannot understand something unique in history, and therefore they are always seeking other historic phenomena similar to that of Judaism. Exert yourself and you shall

81 I. Breuer, "Jewish State and Torah-Front," in J. Breuer (ed.), *Fundamentals of Judaism* (New York: 1969), 264.

82 Edrei, "Multi-Culturalism," 209-22.

83 On this, see M. Friedman, "The structural foundation for religio-political accommodation in Israel: Fallacy and reality," in S.I. Troen and N. Lucas (eds.), *Israel - The First Decade of Independence* (Albany: 1995), 51-81.

> find - priesthood, the clerical regime, the Catholic church.[84] Once you have found this bed, make haste to take the visionary state, chop it up, castrate it, and destroy it, until its dimensions perfectly match those of the bed you have made. But know that that which you lay upon the bed is nothing but - a bruised corpse.[85]

Once again, he elucidated that the scientific method of legal and religious study is completely irrelevant; it is essential to understand the laws of Israel. He appreciates the legal knowledge he acquired in German universities, and esteems and respects the conceptual clarity and functionality of Roman law, and the sense of justice of modern law. Nevertheless,

> It is crucial that according to the Jewish Torah law is metaphysical, whereas according to the nations the law is a matter of physics, of statehood, of state priests or secular institutions, of political benefit, and even - in normal times - of individual morality.[86]

In Breuer's visionary Torah state, not only is there no place for reforms or new halakhic rulings devised to adapt the halakhah to modern reality; even old rulings that circumvented Torah prohibitions would be annulled. In this way, the original halakhic status, which is a faithful expression of God's will, would be restored. The *prozbul* and *heter iska* would be invalidated and the economy of the Torah State would return to its earliest principles, where labor is productive and money is futile, since it has only contractual substance and no concreteness:

> What are we? Where is our state, the Torah state which alone can regulate our national economy according to the laws of Torah, according to the laws of the futility of money, until there is no need to shirk those laws that show us the glory and elegance of the Torah? What remains of its glory and elegance? A *shtar iska* [bill of transaction]! Alas we have sinned. We have no Torah state nor do we have a Torah economy! May the Almighty have mercy on us and once again take us out of Egypt to give us the land of Canaan, to be our God. [...] There is no mighty fanfare in a *prozbul*. It is a weak voice. May the Almighty grant us His commandments and His blessing.[87]

84 Historical examples of religious regimes.

85 I. Breuer, *Nahaliel* (Hebrew), (Jerusalem: 1951), 311.

86 Ibid., 314.

87 Ibid., 328-30.

Breuer's outlook was more radical than that of Rabbi Abraham Yeshayahu Karelitz (the *Hazon Ish*, 1878-1953), the religious leader of the Lithuanian *Haredim* in the Land of Israel. Karelitz was also adamantly opposed to the institution of new rulings in his time, but he did not restrict himslef to the rulings of previous generations. His objections stemmed mainly from his attitude towards his own generation, which he regarded as spiritually orphaned, and lacking the authority to institute new rulings. The *Hazon Ish* expressed his opposition to two matters in which the rabbis advocated new rulings: the establishment of a fast day to mark the Holocaust, and a ruling regarding inheritance which bestowed the same rights on daughters as on sons.[88] In his words: "How dare we, a generation that would do well to remain silent, think of such a thing, to set things down for generations to come."[89] He went on to say: "For we are an orphaned generation, we are not worthy to institute rulings, which only Torah greatness can aspire to [...] How dare we be so stiff-necked as to say that we are wise, that we have the power to forfeit money and lay down rulings for future generations?"[90]

Similarly, regarding social frameworks such as slavery, that have departed from the world and are universally condemned, there is room in Breuer's Torah State to resurrect Israel's ancient laws:

> The Torah has entrusted the slave relationship between one man and another in the hands of the Jewish people, out of a belief that the Jewish people, who are taught and sanctified by its commandments, will not exploit this relationship, that is liable to destroy the image of all humanity unless the Creator always stands between the master and his slave.[91]

88 B. Brown, *The Hazon Ish: Halakhist, Believer and Leader of the Haredi Revolution* (Jerusalem: 2011), 668-77; idem, "'Let Us Not Be Presumptuous': The Hazon Ish's Opposition to Commemoration of the Holocaust," in D. Porat (ed.), *When Disaster Comes from Afar: Leading Personalities in the Land of Israel Confront Nazism and the Holocaust, 1933-1948* (Jerusalem: 2009), 210-34.

89 A.Y. Karelitz, *Kovetz Igrot* ['A collection of letters'] (Hebrew), (Jerusalem: 1955), 113.

90 Ibid., 112.

91 Breuer, *Nahaliel*, 353. See also Hirsch's idealization of the institution of the Hebrew slave in "the Torah State." S.R. Hirsch, *The Pentateuch - with Translation and Commentary* (New York: 1962), Lev 25:41.

Discrimination against minorities also remains in place, as in ancient times. Their status is that of a *ger toshav* (a non-Jew living in the land of Israel who accepts the Noahide laws) and they cannot be appointed to positions of authority, "and there is no such thing as 'tolerance' or 'intolerance,' or excessive nationalism, or the deification of race. None of these concepts are appropriate for this state, which is in its entirety holy unto God."[92]

Unlike Freimann, who sought to collate all the rulings of the communities up to recent times in order to derive halakhah pertaining to all modern aspects of society, economics, and politics, Breuer based his halakhic dispensation of everything relating to modern society and economy primarily on Maimonides' *Mishneh Torah*. He based his final book, *Nahaliel*, regarding his view of a utopian State, on this halakhic source as well. The Freimann's proposed anthology also constitutes a part of the offensive *Wissenschaft des Judentums* and historicization of halakhah, and therefore has no place in Breuer's method.

Conclusion

Freimann and Breuer dealt with the same issues, but they did not react to one another's opinions. Freimann's ideas were publicized on several academic and Torah-research platforms, whereas Breuer published his theories as political and Torah-philosophy proposals.

In effect, Freimann and Breuer presented two diametrically opposed ways in which Orthodox thinkers grappled with the question of halakhah and the challenge of sovereignty. Freimann sought to apply Torah law to the State, and to this end he utilized methods derived from critical study. He prepared the ground for the changes and adjustments required so that the halakhah would properly suit a sovereign, modern reality, one in which the majority of citizens do not recognize its authority, preferring to establish State laws of their own. He wanted to reinstate the institution of regulations in the framework of the Chief Rabbinate, in order to adapt halakhah to the new reality, paving the way for a representative parliamentary institution as a legitimate legislative institution in all matters that do not contradict Torah law. This, by recognizing the democratic aspects of halakhah and the authority of the public to participate in the legislation process.

Breuer, on the other hand, held fast to an inflexible utopian halakhic outlook that fiercely opposed any historicization or democratization

92 Breuer, *Nahaliel*, 375.

of halakhah. For him, the early Orthodox instinct to reject reform of any kind was elevated to an even higher metaphysical level than it was for his grandfather, Rabbi Samson Raphael Hirsch. Any possibility of renewing the halakhah was tightly sealed.

Whereas Freimann regarded the Jewish community as the source of democratic halakhic legislating authority, Breuer saw it as a platform for upholding the Torah. Further, he maintained that the community would forfeit its right to exist if its members do not conduct themselves in accordance with halakhah.

Realizing that the balance of power in the Yishuv made it impossible for the *Haredim* to impose their halakhic worldview on the secular community, he focused on enabling religious Jews to live in a Jewish State according to the halakhah, free of secular coercion, by means of broad community autonomy.[93]

According to Alexander Kaye, Freimann represents a pluralistic attitude to law, and maintains the idea that Jewish sovereignty may include a plurality of legal regimes and a plurality of legitimate sources of legal authority. This position had the advantage of preserving the distinction between current halakhah and the State, thereby avoiding the imposition of current halakhah on people who did not recognize its authority; and preventing the imposition of radical modifications on halakhah to accommodate the requirements of modern law. Breuer represents the legal philosophy of legal centralism, which maintained that all legal authority in the State must derive from a single source of authority – the current halakhah.[94]

This distinction reinforces Chaim Saiman's critique of Kaye, who claimed that the idea of a halakhic state, based on legal centralism, was not invented in the 1940s, primarily by R. Isaac Herzog, and influenced by the Irish Catholic and democratic republic and post-colonial legal theories. This approach has deep historical roots both in

93 In his last article, Freimann also claimed that defending minorities' rights, regarding their system of religious courts that supervise family laws and personal status, requires rabbinical courts to exist with an authority parallel to those of the minorities in the State. Otherwise, "it would be absurd if the Jewish State supports Moslem and Christian religious courts but cancels the Jewish ones - something which is analogous to Jewish religious persecution in the Jewish State." A.C. Freimann, "Batei Hadin Harabaniim Bamedina HaYehudit" ['The Rabbinical Courts in the Jewish State'] (Hebrew), *Yavneh* 3 (1949), 124-5.

94 A. Kaye, *The Invention of Jewish Theocracy: The Struggle for Legal Authority in Modern Israel* (Oxford: 2020).

the Bible and the literature of the Sages.[95]

Despite the fact that Freimann and Breuer shared a vision of statehood based on Torah law, the policies they envisaged were poles apart. Ranged between these two were many Orthodox thinkers with varying opinions regarding the degree of optimal halakhic flexibility for our time, the correlation between the ideal and the reality when it came to integrating halakhah into the laws of the State, and what was required to change this correlation.

Both Freimann and Breuer died before the establishment of the State of Israel and did not have time to complete what they had begun, regarding the vision of adapting halakhah to the new political reality or even taking part in formulating procedures and legislation concerning religion and State relations in Israel.

95 Ch. Saiman, "The Status of the Halachic State," *Tradition* 53/4 (2021), 128.

BOOK REVIEWS

Yuval Sinai and Benjamin Shmueli, *Maimonides and Contemporary Tort Theory*, Cambridge: Cambridge University Press, 2020, 427 pp.

David B. Schorr*

Maimonides is generally acclaimed as the most illustrious Jewish philosopher and legal codifier. Sinai and Shmueli's (S&S's) ambitious book now argues that the great sage also deserves a place at the table of tort theorists. Analyzing not only the legal rules of the Book of Torts (*Nezikin*) in Maimonides' *Mishne Torah* (his *Code*), but also his more theoretical treatment of liability in *The Guide of the Perplexed*, the authors argue that Maimonides presents a coherent and comprehensive theory of tort liability, largely based on considerations familiar to students of contemporary tort scholarship. The arguments are presented clearly, logically, and comprehensively, with the necessary terms of art from the fields of Jewish law and tort theory alike, lucidly explained.

Though focused on a historical figure, the book has little to say about tort law from a historical point of view – a point to which we will return later. Instead, it takes an admittedly anachronistic approach to Maimonides' theory, putting him in dialogue with recent tort scholarship rather than with the legal thinkers or practice of his own era. The theory doing most of the work in the book is Guido Calabresi's economic-efficiency-centered one; and Calabresi, obviously impressed by S&S's work, contributed a closing chapter to their volume.

After laying some of the general groundwork for their study in the first chapter, the authors turn in Chapter 2 to an analysis of the *Code*'s approach to tort liability. They argue that the leading theoretical explanations for Maimonides' approach in the extant scholarship – fault-based liability and strict liability based on ownership – fail to satisfactorily explain his rulings. Instead, they identify the element of control as the underlying basis for liability in the Book of Torts. Chapter 3 then outlines what the authors see as three insights necessary to

* David Schorr is a Senior Lecturer at the Buchmann Faculty of Law, Tel Aviv University. Thanks to Maya Gonen for research assistance.

understanding Maimonides' approach to tort law: the proximity of this area of law to, and overlap with, what is today classified as criminal law; the importance of distinctions between different broad types of tort cases, such as property damage and bodily harm; and the multiplicity of competing goals motivating this area of law, goals given expression, to varying degrees, depending on the type of case.

The following two chapters then delve more deeply into the goals of Maimonidean tort law, making use of the *Guide*, where the medieval scholar explicitly laid out his theories of tort liability. Chapter 4 looks at the deontological and religious elements of Maimonides' approach, with comparisons to modern tort theorists, especially Ernest Weinrib. The authors take care here to point out the elements of Maimonides' version of the law aimed at the correction and moral uplift of the tortfeasor, goals largely absent from modern, secular tort law. Chapter 5 turns to consequentialist goals of liability, such as deterrence, comparing Maimonides to economic theorists Calabresi and Richard Posner. S&S argue here that Maimonidean liability turned on what they label the "Effective Ability to Control Test," a relative of Calabresi's cheapest cost avoider.

Chapters 6 through 8 return to the *Code*'s tort law, delving into the particulars of various rulings that seem to diverge from the general theories outlined in the *Guide*. The authors claim that Maimonides is best understood as a tort pluralist, committed to multiple and competing goals which are expressed to various degrees in different categories of typical tort scenarios. The ninth and final chapter contains Calabresi's thoughts on, and response to, some of the central arguments of the book.

While S&S's book, as noted earlier, is best classified as tort theory and not legal history, it nonetheless touches on a number of issues relevant to the history of tort law that might prove fruitful avenues for further research, some of which I would like to briefly raise here.

On the one hand, the present work confirms some of what we know about the history of torts. For instance, the lack of clear distinction between civil and criminal law in Maimonides' tort law is quite similar to what we know from other pre-modern legal systems: the Roman law of delict, *wergild* in Germanic law, actions for trespass in the English court of King's Bench, or *diya* in Islamic law.[1] By demonstrating the

1 See, e.g., C. Cascione, "Roman Delicts and Criminal Law: Theory and Practice," in T. McGinn (ed.), *Obligations in Roman Law: Past, Present, and Future* (Ann Arbor: 2013), 267; *Wergild, Compensation and Penance: The Monetary Logic of Early Medieval Conflict Resolution*, eds. L. Bothe, S. Esders, and H. Nijdam (Leiden: 2021); D.J. Seipp, "The Distinction

influence of criminal-law thinking in Jewish tort law and holding it up as a theoretical alternative in today's legal context, the authors essentially invite us to recognize the extent to which criminal thinking continues to influence modern tort law in various ways.

On the other hand, the book raises questions about standard accounts of the historical development of tort law. While the element of fault, for example, is generally thought to have achieved prominence in the nineteenth century, S&S demonstrate its centrality to Maimonides' tort theory. It seems that integrating the history of Jewish tort law with that of neighboring legal systems might lead to new insights into the history of tort law in general. One way to do this is by paying attention to the social and political context of Maimonidean tort law.

Morton Horwitz's historical analysis of American tort law has been highly influential on the study of legal history.[2] Horwitz's specific claim was that the nineteenth-century conditioning of liability on fault was a subsidy to the period's capitalists, at the expense of the working class as well as the landed gentry. But his broader contribution was highlighting distributive issues in the history of tort law, and in legal history more generally. S&S's book does not consider distributive issues, and it presents a rather static picture of tort law in Maimonides' writings, not a dynamic one of change over time. Yet, one might consider (as I hope scholars of Jewish law will) not only how Maimonides' rulings diverged from those of the Talmud or from other halakhic writings, but also what the distributive implications of these divergences were. Whom did they benefit, and at whose expense?

The tension between crop-growing farmers and neighboring animal husbandmen is one of the classic conflicts of tort law, discussed by many modern tort scholars, including Ronald Coase and Robert Ellickson.[3] When Maimonides allowed a landowner to slaughter an ox that entered his field multiple times, the ruling implicated not only the instrumentalist and moralist considerations considered by S&S,

---

between Crime and Tort in the Early Common Law," *Boston University Law Review* 76 (1996), 59; A.B. bin Mohamad, "Islamic Tort Law," in M. Bussani and A.J. Sebok (eds.), *Comparative Tort Law: Global Perspectives*, 2nd ed. (Cheltenham: 2021), 469. See generally M. Dyson, "Tort and Crime," in ibid.

2 See M.J. Horowitz, *The Transformation of Americal Law, 1780-1860* (Cambridge: 1977), 97–101.

3 R.H. Coase, "The Problem of Social Cost," *Journal of Law and Economics* 56 (1960), 837. R.C. Ellickson, *Order Without Law: How Neighbours Settle Disputes* (Cambridge: 1991).

but also a distributive decision – protecting the interests of landowners over those of the animal owners. Though animals certainly provided agricultural labor, it seems likely that in the urban societies of the medieval Mediterranean world owners of fields and owners of animals did not completely overlap, but rather constituted two different classes, where Maimonides' ruling favors the interests of one group over those of the other. A similar point might be made about the case of a ladder that collapses due to a rotten rung, in which Maimonides absolved the falling ladder-user of liability for damage caused to others by the fall. Were ladder-users a group, perhaps artisans, distinct from the type of person who was typically the victim of these ladder accidents, perhaps house owners? Examining the issue through the prism of class, distribution, and politics might illuminate the motives behind Maimonides' rulings as well as those of his opponents.

Beyond the world of Jewish law, it would be enlightening to compare Maimonidean tort law to the Islamic law of his time. This kind of comparative legal history would both highlight the distributive implications of Maimonides' rulings and also suggest possible sources of influence, perhaps arising not only from interaction with Muslim neighbors but also from the Jewish litigants in the Islamic world, who would have had access to an alternative judicial forum with its own substantive tort law. Put another way, in the legal-pluralist environment of medieval Egypt, the distributive implications of Islamic tort law may have limited the range of options open to Jewish law, or encouraged it to move in certain directions.

Moving beyond the distributive and comparative dimensions, it is worth noting that S&S's book focuses on tort theory and doctrine – so-called "law in the books" – but has little to say about "law in action" – how Jewish tort law worked in practice during Maimonides' time. Law in the books is important, as this book shows, but historians (as well as legal realists) want to know how the law works and has worked in practice. Though the book does consider not only to the doctrinal *Code* and the theoretical *Guide* but also to responsa penned by Maimonides relating to real-life cases, even this type of legal literature is limited in its ability to reveal "law in action." If the Book of Torts is the medieval Jewish counterpart to the modern tort treatise, the responsa literature is the counterpart of modern law reports, a source that reproduces appellate court decisions that are precedential and interesting but generally unrepresentative. The sources left to us by Maimonides reveal little about how tort law worked in practice in medieval Jewish communities. While S&S work hard to explain Maimonides' positions on various tort issues as expressions of a systematic theory, I am skeptical that many Jews actually acted in accordance with the official rules, mainly due to the many shortcomings of those rules.

Did communal ordinances, customs, norms from the surrounding non-Jewish societies, or other legal sources form a tort law in practice that was substantially different from those reflected in the classic writings of Maimonides and others? We have quite a bit of information on the history of areas such as contract, commercial, and family law, but tort cases tend to leave fewer traces in the archive. Perhaps the new studies of scholars such as Jay Berkowitz on the records of rabbinic judges and courts will help us understand Jewish tort law as it worked in practice.[4]

I would like to raise one final point, regarding the connection between past and present in legal history. Though historians often criticize as anachronistic the use of the law's past to understand the present,[5] such a critique would be misplaced here. S&S' use of modern concepts helps makes sense of Maimonides' extensive rulings on tort law; without such conceptual tools, it would be difficult to give a coherent account of them. The present book exemplifies, to my mind, what might be thought of as constructive anachronism: The use of present concepts, such as "cheapest cost avoider," gives a name to considerations that were apparently present in Maimonides' thinking, even if he did not think of them in these explicit terms.

Moreover, the dialogue between Maimonidean tort law and that of today allows for insights into modern tort law. The authors do not deny the foreignness of Maimonides' law to our perspective, such as when they emphasize the important place that religious considerations had for his tort rulings. But this kind of foreignness can be productive for understanding modern tort law: Are there not traces of religious thinking in modern tort law? Might it be possible, even today, to use religious norms to advance the various goals of tort law? And might we not see some modern tort doctrines as essentially similar to the religious considerations evident in Maimonides' thought?

To sum up, this well-researched and detailed study will prove of interest not only to students of Jewish law, but to tort scholars more generally, and it can provide a starting point for further research in this history of tort law, whether Jewish, comparative, or trans-systemic.

4 J.R. Berkovitz, *Protocols of Justice: The Pinkas of the Metz Rabbinic Court, 1771-1789* (Leiden: 2014).

5 For a recent discussion of the issue, see N. Wheatley, "Law and the Time of Angels: International Law's Method Wars and the Affective Life of Disciplines," *History and Theory* 60 (2021), 311.

Shai Wozner, *Legal Thinking in the Lithuanian Yeshivoth: The Heritage and Works of Rabbi Shimon Shkop* (Hebrew), Jerusalem: Magnes Press, 2016, 340 pp.

Norman Solomon*

Half a century ago, in 1966, I completed my own PhD thesis on what I named "The Analytic School in Rabbinic Jurisprudence" (it was not published in full until 1993). There could be no more satisfying 'jubilee gift' (though not intended as such) than to receive a review copy of Shai Wozner's fine Hebrew thesis on the methodology of one of the pioneers of the school, R. Shimon Shkop.

Wozner repeatedly remarks on the Analytic Movement as if it were, in some sense, a reaction to Haskala; like other reactions, it selectively adopts language and concepts from its opponents. I coined the term 'Counter Haskala' for this phenomenon, by analogy with 'Counter Reformation,' but it has not caught on. Reaction to Haskala extends far beyond the limited sphere of the conceptual analysis of halakha; indeed, the whole trajectory of post-Enlightenment Orthodoxy can only be understood in this context.

The challenge was not merely, or even primarily, intellectual. The social and educational measures for 'improving' the Jews initiated under Czar Nicholas I (1825-55), who amongst other things formally abolished the Kahal in 1843, were supported by *Maskilim*, but were perceived by much of the traditional religious leadership as a threat to their own authority. If Jews became citizens of the states in which they lived, as they had done in England, France, and some German states (and of course America), they would be subject to the jurisdiction of those states, and not to Torah law as administered by the rabbis.

When *Maskilim* cast aspersions on the Talmud and its laws, this was therefore a matter not only for defending the intellectual and moral integrity of the rabbinic tradition, but for sustaining the authority of rabbis. The survival of these rabbis in the traditional role of justices depended on their ability to demonstrate the moral superiority of Torah

* Oxford Centre for Hebrew and Jewish Studies, University of Oxford.

law, above all in matters of civil and criminal jurisdiction and personal status. This is, at least, part of the reason for the focus on *Nezikin* and *Nashim*.

Wozner divided his book into five well-focused chapters. The first is devoted to a biography of Shkop, who was born in Turetz (Minsk, now Belarus) in 1859. Shkop entered the Valozhyn Yeshiva at fourteen, and in the six years he remained there came under the influence of Hayyim Soloveitchik (1853-1918), at the same time fashioning an original method and style which he was able to develop successively at Telšiai (Telz), Maleč (Maltsh), Bryansk and finally Hrodna (Grodno), where he remained until his death in late 1939. A member of *Agudas Yisrael*, he was by no means unsympathetic to Zionism; he maintained cordial relations with Rav Kook, and even made an abortive attempt to establish a yeshiva in Palestine.

What led Shkop, like Soloveitchik, to forge a novel approach to halakha, in contrast to the 'official' Valozhyn method inherited from the Vilna Gaon and staunchly upheld by the Netziv (Naftali Tzvi Yehuda Berlin, head of the Valozhyn Yeshiva)? Novelty, of course, always has it attractions, but why this particular kind of novelty, which Wozner aptly calls a 'paradigm shift' of technical discourse? Where did the ideas and the vocabulary come from? Shkop had certainly not received any formal education outside the Yeshiva – though his wife had – nor is there clear evidence as to whether he knew Russian, or law, or was directly acquainted with Haskala works, or had read medieval Jewish philosophy, from which much of the new vocabulary appears to derive.

Do we have here an instance of '*Hamlet* without the Prince of Denmark'? Sometime between 1993, when my thesis was published, and 1998, when the first edition of my *Historical Dictionary of Judaism* appeared, I came across the halakhic writings of Rabbi Jacob Isaac Reines and wrote, perhaps overstating the case: "The technique of conceptual analysis that characterizes the Analytic Movement was introduced by Jacob Isaac Reines, who already in 1880 and 1881 had published his two-volume *Ḥotem Tokhnit*, [1] in which he set out the conceptual basis of *halakha*, aiming to demonstrate its logical integrity and its relationship with other systems of jurisprudence. For his vocabulary he drew heavily on the Jewish philosophical classics, and specifically on the Hebrew translation of Maimonides' *Treatise on Logic*; in particular, he developed the *ḥakira*, or conceptual distinction, which

1 "The seal of perfection" (cf. Ezek 28:12).

is the hallmark of the Analytic technique."[2]

Two questions arise. Was Shkop (and/or Soloveitchik) aware of Reines' innovations, and if so, why is Reines never cited? There can be little doubt that the answer to the former is in the affirmative. Reines was in Valozhyn from 1855 to 1857, and made his mark there as the 'Karliner ilui (genius)'. Admittedly, when Reines left Valozhyn he had by no means perfected his system (though he had absorbed the philosophical vocabulary of Ibn Tibbon's translation of Maimonides' Milot Hahigayon), Soloveitchik was about four years old and Shkop was not yet born, so there is no question of direct influence. However, in 1880/1, at about the time Soloveitchik was officially appointed to teach at Valozhyn, Reines' published his *Ḥotem Tokhnit*, sketching the new system, and it created quite a stir.[3] Reines and his ideas must surely have been known in the circles in which Shkop and Soloveitchik moved.

So why was he not credited with his innovations, and why has he been frozen out of Yeshiva discourse to the present day? A letter from the Netziv, dated Tuesday the 31st day of the Omer, 5647 (=10 May 1887), indicates that Reines had sent him a copy of his *Urim Gedolim* with an open letter inviting comment. Berlin did not approve. He addresses Reines with the usual rabbinic honorifics, but candidly admits that after spending a few hours with the book he could make no sense of it, nor had he been able to make sense of *Ḥotem Tokhnit* (presumably received some years previously). He categorically rejects the notion that the hugely difficult task of correctly interpreting rabbinic texts could be accomplished by simply clarifying basic concepts, and points out a few 'errors' in Reines' work, caustically remarking that he knew Reines would be unwilling to accept criticism that would lead him to abandon his system.[4] In subsequent years, Reines was further distanced by the Haredi establishment both on account of his educational work (at Lida he founded his own Yeshiva, in which general subjects were taught side-by-side with traditional texts) and because of his involvement

2 This is the slightly modified version in the 3rd edition (2015) of N. Solomon, *A Historical Dictionary of Judaism* 3rd ed. (Lanham MD: 2015), s.v. Analytic Movement.

3 Details in J. Wanefsky, *Isaac Jacob Reines: His Life and Thought* (New York: 1970), 25.

4 Naftali Tzvi Yehuda Berlin, *Responsa Meshiv Davar* 5:44. See Y. Lindell, "A Science Like Any Other? Classical Legal Formalism in the Halakhic Jurisprudence of Rabbis Isaac Jacob Reines and Moses Avigdor Amiel," *Journal of Law and Religion* 28/1 (2012), 179-224.

with Zionism (he founded the Mizrachi movement).[5]

This raises a further question. If the new method of 'conceptual analysis' was not approved at Valozhyn, how did Soloveitchik and Shkop get away with it? First and foremost, neither made extravagant claims, as Reines had done, to 'explain' the system of halakha and *agada* as a whole. Both of them defensively claimed to not be making *hidushim* (innovations), but merely making plain the opinions of the Rishonim (early authorities); Soloveitchik (though not Shkop) eschewed overtly philosophical vocabulary; and both avoided reference to 'external' sources, that is, to sources other than those traditionally acceptable in Yeshiva circles. In short, they established themselves as 'insiders' in a way Reines did not.

In his second chapter, Wozner describes the new style of learning (*shitat halimud hahadasha*), setting it against the background of the Vilna Gaon's method. The Gaon, as understood at Valozhyn, had rejected both 'scholastic' pilpul and the Polish *hilukim* in favour of *asukei shemata aliba dehilkhata* ('reading the topic in such as a way as to reach the [correct] halakhic decision'). Set in this context, the new method of conceptual analysis was indeed a revolution, in which Soloveitchik and Shkop were pioneers. What is less clear is how they differed from each other. Wozner claims that Shkop, particularly when established at Telšiai, focused more on *legal* concepts, particularly in the tractates of the Orders *Nashim* and *Nezikin*, and adopted a method of analysis different from Soloveitchik's. A review of the contents of Shkop's *Shaarei Yosher* scarcely bears out the former claim. The first section, for instance, is devoted to issues of *safek* (doubt), which range over almost every area of halakha; while Soloveitchik's seminal *Hidushei Rabbeinu Haim Halevi al haRambam* ('Rabbi Haim Halevi's innovations on Maimonides') gives full reign to topics in *Nashim* and *Nezikin*. The claim that the two rabbis' methods of analysis differed significantly would be more convincing if backed by examples; there are evident differences of terminology, but it is not clear that these amount to different 'methods' of analysis.

After some comments on legal and analytic reasoning, Wozner homes in on issues raised by legal formalism, that is, by treating law as a self-consistent, coherent system, from which deductions can be made without recourse to extraneous values. Positive law was very much in vogue, for instance, among the German Pandectists of the

5 Marc Shapiro, who devotes a whole chapter of his *Changing the Immutable* (Oxford: 2015) to the marginalizing of Rav Kook by the Haredi community, notes on p. 146 that the Haredi editor removed a complimentary reference to Reines.

early nineteenth century. But similar tendencies can be detected in earlier Jewish sources, not least the Talmud itself, as well as among more recent authorities such as Aryeh Leib Gunzberg (*She'agat Arye*), Akiva Eger and Aryeh Leib Heller (*Ketzos Hahoshen*) whose works were eagerly studied in the Lithuanian Yeshivot. After all, if "the law of the Lord is perfect" (Ps 19:8), there should be no need to look elsewhere for guidance.

Towards the end of the chapter, Wozner observes that Lithuanian *Rashei Yeshiva* ('heads of the Yeshiva') were theoreticians, not practical halakhists; their focus was on the theoretical basis of halakha, on an ideal world rather than the actual one, so they did not address the life of society, which is what halakha is traditionally perceived to be about. This may be true of their writings, which are essentially *shiurim* ('lessons') that they delivered to their students, but it understates their personal achievements: even if they preferred to delegate fine halakhic decisions to others, both Soloveitchik and Shkop were effective and respected leaders who certainly addressed the needs of their communities, and of Jewish society in general, as they understood it. Wozner's parallel between the pursuit of Torah study for its own sake and current theories of 'narrative law,' such as Robert Cover's, which read law systems as narratives of world views, is valuable; but reading Torah in this way is not unique to the Analytic School.

The third chapter, headed *Hashiva ontologit venaturalistika mishpatit* ("Ontological reasoning and legal naturalism"), addresses Shkop's ideas on the relationship between Torah law and human reason. What is the connection, for instance, between Torah law and ownership? Does the Torah *create* ownership, or does it merely recognize it as a prior fact? Shkop inclines to the view that ownership – the connection between a person and a physical object – is some sort of objective fact of nature, recognized by human reason and the 'laws of the nations.' It is not the only 'fact of nature' so recognized; qualities such as *tum'a* (ritual impurity) and *kedusha* (holiness) likewise have ontological status, independently of the application of Torah law.

The objective status of ownership, personal status, and qualities such as holiness and purity places limitations on the operation of Torah law itself. Sometimes this is trivial; for instance, you cannot reuse a paid-up IOU for a subsequent identical transaction, since it has lost its connection with the 'objective' debt it once represented. However, there are sometimes serious ethical consequences. In difficult cases of conversion, divorce, or bastardy, 'naturalism' inhibits otherwise appropriate ethical action on behalf of the victims. The objective fact ('ontology') recognized (not created) by the Torah is that X is a gentile, or that Y is married, or that Z is a bastard, and no process of Torah law can change that.

Wozner wonders whether the ontological statements of the halakhists should be taken at face value, or whether we should understand them as metaphors. He is convinced that at least some of the texts *are* intended literally. Even if not, the use of that kind of language in itself determines a way of thought that produces results of the kind described – "matter rises over the one who shapes it, language rises over thought" (citing K.M. Walton, *Mimesis as Make Believe*).

This leads into Chapter 4, on the concept of *isur* ('prohibition'). Is the fact that, for example, non-kosher food is prohibited, an ontological status rather than a behavioural norm? Shkop maintains that forbidden things are actually harmful, a point of view already adopted by several medieval rabbis; like them, he maintains that the purpose of the prohibitions is to protect one from harm, whether physical or spiritual. The prohibition, that is, stems from the intrinsic nature of the act/substance. God forbade things because they are bad; they are not bad simply because God forbade them (cf. Plato *Euthyphro*). However, things forbidden by the rabbis are not intrinsically bad, or else the Torah would have forbidden them; one is obliged to refrain from them simply because that is what rabbinic law demands.

This leads to strange consequences in torts. Supposing A handles some food belonging to B in such a way as to render it ritually impure, causing a loss of market value (fewer people may now eat it) but without causing any physical defect (*heizek she'eino nikar* – 'invisible damage'). The Talmud (bGittin 52b/53) records a debate as to whether A must compensate B; eventually, the rabbis ruled that A must indeed compensate B, but they acknowledged that strict Torah law did not require this. But surely, if impurity is a 'fact of nature' rather than merely a product of law, causing impurity should be regarded as objective damage, requiring compensation in principle rather than merely by rabbinic edict?

In response, Shkop asks whether, in general, the obligation to pay compensation for damaging someone's goods arises from (a) the physical damage caused, and the consequent obligation to restore the object, or (b) the pecuniary loss arising from the decrease in value of the goods. If (a) is the operative principle, non-physical damage would not require compensation, but if (b) is the operative principle, it would. This, says Shkop, was the original debate, but the final decision was made in accordance with (a).

We then arrive at a further distinction, common to the Analysts, between *isur* and *halot isur* (in English we might say: between the prohibition itself and its application in a specific situation). As understood by Shkop, *isur* is normative – a command that demands obedience from the one addressed; *halot isur* is a property, such as holiness or impurity, inhering in an object (human or material). 'Realism' means this property cannot be reduced to a command.

This difference generates normative complexities. For instance, a minor is not subject to commands. However, the fact that he is not forbidden (for example) to eat non-kosher meat does not mean that the meat is kosher. It still has the property of non-kosherness, and can harm him, which is why it should not be fed to him. Likewise, you should eat non-kosher meat if necessary to save your life, but this does remove its property of non-kosherness, however, the danger stemming from eating it is minor relative to the value of life.

The idea (though not the term) of *halot isur* – that is, of a prohibition alighting, or being placed, on an object – is present in the Talmud, which distinguishes between two kinds of oaths (bNedarim 2a). A person who, e.g., vows to not drink wine, might formulate his oath or vow in either of two forms: he may say "I swear to not drink wine," or he may say "wine is forbidden to me." The former, technically a *shevua* (oath), is classed as an *isur gavra* (a 'prohibition on the person'), while the latter, a *neder* (vow), as an *isur heftza* (a 'prohibition on the object'). Whether there is any connection here with the Roman law distinction between *actio in personam* and *actio in rem* is open to question. Shkop, at any rate, analyses this distinction in terms of *sibat ha'isur* ('cause of the prohibition'): in the case of *neder* a proper *halot isur* is placed on the object – a sort of 'poison', but this is not the case with a *shevu'a*. The 'bottom line' is that we have three different concepts: *halot isur* on the object, *halot isur* on the person, and a behavioural norm.

The final Chapter, 5, is devoted to the distinction between commercial law (*dinei mamonot*) and Torah law in general. It is best introduced by a quote from Shkop himself:

בכל המצוות הוא מה שהזהירה לנו תורה בעשה ול"ת ... ובדיני ממונות אינו כן, דקודם שחל עלינו מצות ה' לשלם או להשיב, צריך שיוקדם עלינו חיוב משפטי

The *mitzvot* in general are what the Torah commands either positively or negatively … but the laws of property (*mamon*) are not like that, for before the divine command to pay or restore can apply to us, there must be [in existence] (on us) a legal obligation." (*Shaarei Yosher* 5:1)

What does Shkop mean by *hiyuv mishpati*, a 'legal obligation' prior to, and independent of, Torah legislation? Is he saying that the halakha, in general, derives from Divine command, while property halakha is instituted by men (Sages) based on human reason? Is he saying, as argued by Avi Sagi,[6] that property halakha is some kind of "Natural Law"? Wozner thinks this is inexact; Shkop is thinking of property halakha as instituted by humans, not as stemming from natural law. But human institution is not Divine command, so it seems that while halakhic decision is primarily based on 'Divine' sources, other sources may occasionally supplement this.

It would hardly be earth-shaking if Shkop was claiming that property law was a rational system knowable independently of Divine revelation – many medieval Jewish thinkers, not least Maimonides, held that most of the Torah's laws might be known through the correct application of human reason. But Wozner thinks this is not the point Shkop is making. Rather, Shkop is making a distinction between definition and obligation; the part played by human reason is simply definition, and definition (*pace* Shkop) does not of itself create obligation. For example, a minor can owe money – this arises from the definition of property – but he is not subject to an obligation to pay. (Jurists might dispute this; they could argue that a minor is under an obligation to pay, but it is not enforceable.) Be that as it may, the remainder of Chapter 5 is devoted to a skilful analysis of the novel way Shkop utilizes his distinction between definition and obligation to deal with long-standing rabbinic problems such as why, given that theft is undoubtedly a Torah prohibition, it is not subject to the general rule that in doubtful cases one should follow the more stringent ruling.

Wozner's book is the first full-length academic study devoted to R. Shimon Shkop. It is clearly and skilfully written, well-focused, and makes a valuable contribution to a difficult area of research that demands not only a mastery of traditional yeshiva-style learning but also the ability to set the material in appropriate historical, social, and juristic contexts. The main text is complemented with a comprehensive bibliography of Shkop's works, both published and unpublished, including *shiurim* written up by disciples, as well as rabbinic and general bibliographies and indexes of names and subjects.

6 A. Sagi, "Hamitzva hadatit vehamaarekhet hamishpatit" ['The religious commandment and the legal system'] (Hebrew), Daat 35 DAAT (1994), 114-99. Sagi presents a broader picture in his "Natural Law and Halakha—A Critical Analysis" (Hebrew), trans. B. Stein, *Jewish Law Annual* 13 (2000), 149-96. Earlier discussions on the position of halakhists in relation to theories of natural and positive law may be found in *Jewish Law Annual* 6-7, (1987 and 1988).

STYLE SHEET

STYLE SHEET

In preparing your manuscript, please conform to the following guidelines. Manuscripts not so prepared will be edited by JLA staff or returned for revision.

1 Please provide a line or two of information about yourself, such as an institutional affiliation, before the first footnote.
2 Manuscripts should be submitted electronically, in WORD 2010 or lower, and should be double-spaced (text and footnotes).
3 The file should not contain any tracked changes, comments, electronically linked cross-references, highlighting, underlining, different font colors, or other markings. 12 pt. font, preferably Times New Roman, should be used throughout, including the notes.
4 All references must conform to the *Jewish Law Annual* house style specified below.
5 All references containing titles originally in Hebrew should provide both the original title of the work in transliteration, and the official title in English if it is given in the book or appears in an English table of contents (often found at the end of the volume). If no English title is given, please suggest a translation, indicating that it is your own.
6 Authorized Version abbreviations for books of the Bible, listed in dictionaries and style guides such as *The Chicago Manual of Style*, should be used. In referring to the Talmud, tractate names should not be abbreviated. m, b, j, or t should be prefixed to the tractate name to indicate whether the Mishnah, the Babylonian Talmud, Jerusalem Talmud or Tosefta is being referred to.

CITATION STYLE

Halakhic literature

Beit Yosef, Tur, HM 362:57
Kli Hemda, Torah portion 'Pinhas'
Maimonides, Code, Laws concerning Robbery and Lost Property 11:1
R. Jacob Castro (Maharikash), *Erekh Lehem*, EH 143
Perisha, HM 201:1 (at the end)
Rashi, bBaba Kama 27a s.v. *lemikah umimkar*
Responsa Beit Shlomo, OH #57

Responsa Igrot Moshe, YD 2:174
Responsa Mabit, #37
Responsa Tzitz Eliezer, 9:28:3
Sefer Hasidim, §723
Sefer Mitzvot Katan, #265 (Rosenberg edition, 2:371)
Shulhan Shlomo, 2:14-16

Books

W.C. Kaiser, *Toward Old Testament Ethics* (Grand Rapids MI: 1978), 99
E. Urbach, *The Sages: Their Concepts and Beliefs,* trans. I. Abrahams (Jerusalem: 1987), 1:343

Journal articles

R. Kleinman, "Early interpretations of the Bible and Talmud as a reflection of medieval legal realia," *16 Jewish Law Annual* (2006), 25-50 Joseph Raz, "Legal principles and the limits of law," 81 Yale L.J., 823, 828-30 (1972)
A. Shaffer, "Cuneiform tablets from Palestine I: the letter from Shechem" (Hebrew), *Beer-Sheva* 3 (1988), 163-69

Articles in edited volumes

B.S. Jackson, "Legalism and spirituality," in E.B. Firmage, B.G. Weiss and J.W. Welch (eds.), *Religion and Laws: Biblical, Judaic and Islamic Perspectives* (Winona Lake IN: 1990), 243-61
D. Sinclair, "Defending the lives of the mortally ill, the embryo, and the non-Jew" (Hebrew), in G. Frishtick (ed.), *Human Rights in Judaism* (Hebrew), (Jerusalem: 1992), 37 n. 19

Cross-references in notes

22 S. *Assaf, The Courts and Their Procedures after the Finalization of the Talmud* (Hebrew), (Jerusalem: 1924), 38-41.
23 D. Sperber, Material Culture in Eretz-Israel during the Talmudic *Period* (Hebrew), vol. 1 (Jerusalem: 1993), vol. 2 (Jerusalem: 2006).
24 See Assaf 1924, n. 22 above, 67.
25 Ibid., 121.
26 Sperber, n. 23 above, 2:126-33.

TRANSLITERATION

Wherever possible, essential Hebrew is to be transliterated into English rather than word-processed in Hebrew characters, as follows:

alef	a	lamed	l
bet	b	mem	m
vet	v	nun	n
gimel	g	samekh	s
dalet	d	ayin	a
hei (pronounced)	h	pei	p
vav	v	fei	f
zayin	z	tzadi	tz
het	h	kuf	k
tet	t	reish	r
yud	y	shin	sh
kaf	k	sin	s
khaf	kh	tav	t

patah; kamatz	a
hirik	i
shva (pronounced)	e
segol	e
shuruk; kubutz	u
holam	o
tzeirei (long)	ei
tzeirei (short)	e

No diacriticals, apostrophes, hyphens, doubling of consonants or capitalization should be used as elements of the transliteration or to indicate prefixes and the definite article. These transliteration guidelines are not intended to apply to papers addressing linguistic or philological issues.

For Product Safety Concerns and Information please contact our EU representative GPSR@taylorandfrancis.com
Taylor & Francis Verlag GmbH, Kaufingerstraße 24, 80331 München, Germany

www.ingramcontent.com/pod-product-compliance
Ingram Content Group UK Ltd.
Pitfield, Milton Keynes, MK11 3LW, UK
UKHW020005200926
475702UK00015B/2482
* 9 7 8 1 0 3 2 6 1 0 8 8 7 *